Advanced Praise for *Reality Denied*

"Col. John Alexander has brought in a fascinating compendium of mysteries that defy conventional norms of rational investigation. John is a Stoic individual with a sharp military mind who has served our country for decades. It is refreshing and intriguing to read his insider's take on enigmas that compel millions of people from all over the world."

— Dr. Raymond Moody, author of *Life After Life*

* * *

"I met John Alexander decades ago. He is smart and truthful to a fault. So when he speaks, I listen. My career has taken me to what others might find hard to believe. Therefore, I know what John Alexander faces in this book. Read this and know I have nothing but respect for this man.
Listen to what he says, and your notion of reality just might expand."

— Richard Bandler, Ph.D., co-developer of NLP
(Neuro-Linguistic Programming)

* * *

"No one can consider him- or herself an informed world citizen without coming to terms with the phenomena described by John Alexander in *Reality Denied*. Alexander brings the skills of a critical scientist and a respected military strategist to a spectacular array of unexplained events. Underlying this captivating survey is the premise of a unitary, interconnected, nonlocal form of consciousness that is infinite in space and time. This extraordinarily courageous book is in the best traditions of science, whose foundation is the provocation of wonder and open-minded inquiry."

— Dr. Larry Dossey, author of *One Mind: How Our Individual Mind Is Part of a Greater Consciousness and Why It Matters*

* * *

"In *Reality Denied* John Alexander details a number of firsthand encounters that range from UFOs, to remote viewing, spiritual healing, NDEs, and after-death experiences that all defy conventional wisdom. He has met with shamans all over the world and seen things that are physically impossible. Yet they happened and he documented them. In this book, he explicitly challenges traditional scientists who dismiss these events without ever looking at the hard data that exists in many instances."

— George Noory, host of *Coast to Coast AM*

* * *

"Retired U.S. Army Colonel John Alexander is a masterful storyteller. His long list of accolades ranges from Special Forces A-team leader to program manager at Los Alamos National Laboratory, to ufologist. With *Reality Denied* Alexander gives readers an action-packed, eyebrow-raising look into a life lived at the cutting edge of unconventional research. From his work with the Reindeer Shamans of Mongolia, to his dealings with the Voodoo masters of Togo, Ghana, and Benin, John Alexander's book is guaranteed to keep you up at night. A rare treat."

— ANNIE JACOBSEN, AUTHOR OF *AREA 51* AND FINALIST FOR THE 2016 PULITZER PRIZE IN HISTORY

* * *

"In *Reality Denied*, Colonel John Alexander, a highly qualified witness and investigator with decades of experience, provides accounts of his firsthand experiences of events and phenomena deemed impossible by the current scientific paradigm. From shamans deep in the jungle, to macro PK, to post-mortem communications and much more, Alexander explores the meaning and the way forward in coming to grips with things that are not supposed to happen, but do. As a fellow traveler who has also experienced some of the same phenomena, I highly recommend this accessible, honest, and provocative book which provides a powerful challenge to those who stubbornly deny compelling data—data which offers all of us a new understanding of consciousness and its relationship to the physical world."

— LESLIE KEAN, AUTHOR OF *SURVIVING DEATH*

* * *

"John Alexander has written an adventurous globe-spanning romp through worlds shunned by the more conventional. Follow the fascinating journey of a relentlessly inquisitive mind unafraid to keep poking at received wisdom and unafraid to experience profound mystery. Prepare to have your world rocked!"

— WILLIAM BENGSTON, PH.D., PRESIDENT OF THE SOCIETY FOR SCIENTIFIC EXPLORATION

* * *

"With no stone unturned, John Alexander, PhD, lays before us a smorgasbord of challenging topics ranging from the merely outrageous to the taboo. What sets this book apart is his personal first-hand involvement, even immersion, in the events and topics covered during his globe-trotting investigations. With a level of discernment that has no equal, Alexander takes us on a riveting journey through exotic territory that lies just beyond the curtain of everyday existence."

— HAROLD E. PUTHOFF, PH.D., DIRECTOR OF THE INSTITUTE FOR ADVANCED STUDIES AT AUSTIN

* * *

"Every now and again a book appears that marks a watershed moment in the evolution of science and society. John Alexander's book presents and integrates a vast array of extraordinary and seemingly anomalous real-life phenomena that collectively require that we expand our understanding of the human mind, the physical world, and the existence of a greater reality. John is a wonderful writer, and the suite of personal stories he recounts more than justifies the buying and reading of this book. Moreover, his analyses, concerns, wise recommendations, and visions for the future are priceless. I have had the privilege to know John professionally and personally for more than two decades, and I can attest to the fact that he is a skilled as well as skeptical observer. John does not misrepresent or fabricate information; he tells it as it is, with precision and clarity peppered by playfulness and grace. John's book provides a historic convergence of inspiring evidence. It is time that science and society awakens to this opportunity for understanding and transformation."

— GARY E. SCHWARTZ, PH.D., PROFESSOR OF PSYCHOLOGY, MEDICINE, NEUROLOGY, PSYCHIATRY, AND SURGERY, AND DIRECTOR OF THE LABORATORY FOR CONSCIOUSNESS AND HEALTH AT THE UNIVERSITY OF ARIZONA AUTHOR OF *THE AFTERLIFE EXPERIMENTS*

* * *

"There is a joke, which we have all heard at one time or another, that the term 'Military Intelligence' is an oxymoron. The example of John Alexander (Colonel, U.S. Army, retired) refutes that suggestion most emphatically. I ended my reading of this book wishing that my colleagues in science departments in the Western World were half as well informed and one tenth as open-minded as Alexander concerning the many unexplored phenomena that are surveyed in this book. Such phenomena should be of interest to psychologists who try to understand our mental processes, to physicists who try to understand the composition and functioning of the world we live in, and to everyone who has wondered whether death is an end or a transition. In the current era of big science, in which the significance of a project is measured by its engineering sophistication, the size of the team, and the size of the budget, it is refreshing to come across individuals such as Alexander who seek out—and seek to understand—mysteries that are unexplained by current science, and which are indeed studiously avoided by the scientific community."

— PETER STURROCK, PH.D., EMERITUS PROFESSOR OF APPLIED PHYSICS, AND EMERITUS DIRECTOR OF THE CENTER FOR SPACE SCIENCE AND ASTROPHYSICS, STANFORD UNIVERSITY

* * *

"When it comes to unusual phenomena, John Alexander has seen it all. In this remarkable book, his readers will learn about his first-hand observations of fire walking, remote viewing, mediumship, psychokinesis, telepathic dolphins, unconventional healing, voodoo, and avoiding death during war combat. They will learn about ayahuasca, dowsing, out-of-body and near-death experiences, UFOs, poltergeists, and the 'Crystal Skull.' They will even be given instructions on how to arrange a 'spoon-bending party.' However, they will also find out that some so-called 'psychics' use sleight-of-hand, and that many uncanny events can be explained by personal expectations, the placebo effect, and other natural processes. Alexander's credentials are solid, his writing is straightforward, and his stories are fascinating. Readers may accept or reject the conclusions he presents in his final chapter, but at least they will have enjoyed the ride and, perhaps, found their understanding of people and the universe confronted, if not transformed."

— STANLEY KRIPPNER, PH.D., PROFESSOR OF PSYCHOLOGY, SAYBROOK UNIVERSITY, AND CO-EDITOR OF *VARIETIES OF ANOMALOUS EXPERIENCE*

* * *

"John Alexander has pursued numerous fascinating inquiries into events that our modern science would deny as impossible because they defy our theoretical models. In fact, it is the pursuit of such anomalies that leads to true progress in our scientific understanding of the universe. *Reality Denied* offers a treasure trove of his personal experiences and analysis of them to offer a far broader view of the nature of reality— and, along the way, offers the reader an astonishing journey towards very broad opening of the mind. Highly recommended!"

— EBEN ALEXANDER MD, NEUROSURGEON AND AUTHOR OF *LIVING IN A MINDFUL UNIVERSE* AND *PROOF OF HEAVEN*

* * *

REALITY
DENIED

Firsthand Experiences with Things
that Can't Happen – But Did

John B. Alexander

ANOMALIST BOOKS
*San Antonio * Charlottesville*

An Original Publication of ANOMALIST BOOKS
Reality Denied: Firsthand Experiences with Things that Can't Happen – But Did
Copyright © 2017 by John B. Alexander
ISBN: 978-1-938398-99-5
Second Edition

Cover concept and whale tail image by Chuck Walker; galaxy images by NASA.

Book design by Seale Studios

For information about the publisher, go to AnomalistBooks.com, or write to: Anomalist Books, 5150 Broadway #108, San Antonio, TX 78209

TABLE OF CONTENTS

FOREWORD

Reality Denied may seem autobiographical, but it is really about you as well. During my travels all over the world, I have met many thousands of people. What I have found constant is that so many of them have shared with me their stories of personal experiences of unexplained or anomalous events. Everybody has them, even those people who deny that such things occur. As a matter of fact, three in four Americans believe in the paranormal; even CBS News reported that most believe in psychic phenomena.

Having known John Alexander for many years, I am aware that we share several common experiences. We were both paratroopers who served in combat in defense of our countries. From an early age, I served in a unique commando unit, and I believe that we both were fascinated by things that defy conventional explanations. We both have seen things that seemingly can't happen, yet they did. We both have come to an understanding that we are part of a greater whole, at one with the universe.

In my public presentations, I demonstrate amazing capabilities that both have inspired people and invoked substantial criticism by skeptics. Several scientific laboratories have rigorously tested my feats and found them to be valid. Unfortunately, many traditional scientists reject those findings, most often without even examining the data. It is the baseless rejection of facts and reality that John rightfully rails against in this book.

Many of the things John, I, and others have seen are not easily explained. Such observations simply point to greater truths and suggest our traditional science is incomplete. For true scientists, that should be exciting as it presents unknown possibilities just waiting to be discovered. Repeatedly John addresses the limitations of our belief systems. It is time to unshackle our minds and question the very foundations of our perceived reality.

"Spoon-bending" has been closely identified as my trademark and garnered global attention. However, the underlying principles are far more important, as they illustrate the boundless love and energy that permeates the universe. This energy is available to everyone. There is a need to be open to the wondrous possibilities available and incorporate them in your everyday life.

As indicated in *Realities Denied*, these phenomena represent extremely complex issues and there will be no simple, all-encompassing answers. Scientific research on these topics has been modest at best, yet certainly sufficient to confirm the physical reality of many of these events. But we must think beyond the physical and accept that there is a spiritual dimension at play as well. It may well be that all the observations are not quantifiable in a material domain; but that does not make them any less real.

For a world seemingly in turmoil, it is important that we learn to embrace the concept of inclusiveness and understand that it is the sense of separation from others that is an illusion. The events witnessed herein offer clues to the interconnectedness of all things. It is eternal consciousness that brings fullness to our lives and provides guidance on a path towards spiritual tranquility with perfect patience, wisdom, and compassion, for that is the essence of all sentient entities. Know that you are both physical and spiritual beings and act accordingly. It is universal love that suffuses all.

For every reader, I wish you plenty of good health, happiness, and peace of mind. Be positive, optimistic, and believe in yourself.

Uri Geller
Tel Aviv
www.urigeller.com

INTRODUCTION
ANYTHING THAT DOES HAPPEN, CAN HAPPEN

This book is based largely on firsthand experiences. These events call into question what are believed to be many of the most cherished and fundamental "laws of science." They are challenged because many of our scientific theories are wrong. Too frequently they are not questioned by traditional scientists because observations and data that do not conform to their tenets are simply ignored. My basic premise is that "anything that does happen, can happen." To pretend these events do not occur is specious. Unfortunately, data that lie outside prescribed norms are assumed to be in error, even if the existence of error is not substantiated.

Before going too far astray, I'll begin by noting that science has been very useful in our daily lives. There is no intent to denigrate what science has brought; I only wish to expand the parameters when the data don't fit. My objective for many years has been to assist in making it possible for the young, best, and brightest scientists to explore areas of phenomena without risking their reputation or livelihood.

One does not have to look far to find examples of just how vicious conventional scientists can be when they find their belief systems challenged. Consider the egregious experience of John Mack, a tenured professor at Harvard, Pulitzer Prize winner, and talented psychiatrist. When he ventured into a serious study of alien abductions, his peers expressed concern. When he published *Abduction*, his first book on the topic, he was sanctioned by the university; something that should not happen when tenured.

Robert Jahn, dean of the School of Engineering at Princeton, began research into psi phenomena and created the Princeton Engineering Anomalies Research (PEAR) laboratory. For that, many of his colleagues considered him a pariah. Despite the fact that Jahn was a renown physicist with a résumé unparalleled by most scientists, his association with studying such phenomena was enough to generate severe criticism—even though the research was impeccable.

My experience has been similar, though the criticism I've been subject to has not been as severe. For speaking out on unorthodox subjects, I have been attacked in traditional scientific publications. In April 1994, *Scientific American* stated that since I supported research in areas of which "most scientists are highly skeptical, his judgement must be questioned." That year, the *Bulletin of Atomic Scientists* stated that I "might make a colorful character in a science fiction novel," but that I "probably shouldn't be spending taxpayer money without adult supervison." In both cases the topic they were concerned about was my work in advocating the development of non-lethal weapons. But still, they used my expressed interest in the study of unexplained phenomena for their ad hominem attacks.

For a lengthy discussion of these issues, I recommend Peter Sturrock's *A Tale of Two Sciences*.[1] In it, Peter, an eminent astrophysicist at Stanford University, details the difference his work received when he reported on microwave energy research and when he published *The UFO Enigma*, a serious study of the UFO phenomena.[2] Though his scientific rigor was the same in both fields, one was acceptable, the other was not.

It is wrong to assume that I am anti-science because I say that many scientists are not broad-minded. First, we must acknowledge that traditional science has done much good. The daily life of most humans has benefited greatly from their efforts. An excellent example would be to compare life expectancy a century ago with what it is today. In that century, we learned to fly, created the aircraft industry, and put men on the Moon and brought them home again. Energy technologies have made leaps in orders of magnitude. Electricity is ubiquitous. Think about the improvement in battery technology in your lifetime, however short that may be. Terrestrial use of solar cells did not exist until three decades ago, and now they bring power to parts of the world that lived in darkness. Technology improved, prices came down, and now these alternative energy systems are transforming societies. Half a century ago information technology was not even a thing, at least for the general public. Now it dominates the daily lives of many people. It revolutionized communication and brought people together in ways not previously imagined. From our clothes to most of the things we use, without giving a thought to it, material sciences have transformed the way we live.

Today modern science has opened fields not imagined a few decades ago and with them have come moral dilemmas. Genetic engineering has brought about possibilities that were unthinkable, from sex and physical trait selection, to elimination of select genes that portend a propensity for certain inherited diseases. Advances also range from modification of crops to make them impervious to diseases and resistant to pests, to cloning with even the potential for creating human life. Nanoscale engineering has emerged, allowing the building of machines that can be built atom by atom. Remote control has taken on a new art form with devices that fly, swim, or crawl. Sensor systems now monitor in domains previously beyond the scope of possibility. Sensors can record in all areas of the electromagnetic spectrum, penetrate solid walls or into the ground, and even accommodate a "lab on a chip" that can detect a wide range of chemical or biological agents.

Not all scientific advances have been for the betterment of mankind. In general, technology is neutral; it is the application by humans that determines the positive or negative aspects. Consider nuclear engineering, which has produced massive amounts of energy but with unequivocal destructive power, and has brought the world to the brink of disaster on several occasions. Or think about the unintended consequences when those power systems went out of control and the conundrum of handling the waste they generate. Similarly, biotechnology can be used to heal or kill. The widespread application of genetic modification has raised great concern when brought into our food supply. Information technology spreads both knowledge and falsehoods indiscriminately.

Naively, it once was thought that science was pure, and we would follow the data wherever that took the researcher, no matter the consequences. If that was ever true, scientists have strayed far from the path of enlightenment. Too frequently today, scientific results are driven by factors such as quo bono (who benefits) and current political correctness.

For many decades, I have been privileged to work with some of the most brilliant scientific minds, while exploring topics such as near-death studies, psychokinesis, remote viewing, interspecies communications, unidentified flying objects, and many other arcane topics. Traveling to all eight continents, my wife, Victoria, and I have met with shamans and observed things that would be deemed physically impossible. My takeaway from all of my observations is that all of these topics are interconnected, and consciousness is the key component.

Readers will also find that in many cases people introduced in earlier chapters reappear in other topic areas. One of the consistencies in my life has been that because of our similar broad interests, fate has often coalesced our pod.

This book has been subdivided in four parts. Admittedly, the grouping is somewhat arbitrary but designed so that readers can move from one topic to another, not necessarily in sequence. Part I involves many personal anecdotes of unusual events. Part II covers topics I worked on while in the military. Part III discusses experiences that specifically have a spiritual dimension. Finally, in Part IV, I attempt to pull things together and talk about the potential pitfalls facing investigators. It also consolidates the challenges that many of these events pose for conventional science.

Repeatedly, this book will venture into the spiritual realm. Not just whether or not spirits and spirit worlds might exist, but to teleological considerations that explore the notion of total interconnectedness, or nonlocal mind, and the implications for those who believe that we live in only a material world. To quote my friend the late Bob Monroe, "We are spiritual beings having a human experience."

PART I

PERSONAL EXPERIENCES

CHAPTER 1
THE NIDS EXPERIENCE

The phone rang unexpectedly on a Sunday morning. A group of scientists was standing in the kitchen of our home in Santa Fe. Most of the weekend we had been discussing Zero Point Energy research and how best to proceed. At that moment, the issue was getting people back to Albuquerque to catch their flights. There was no way I could have known that the seemingly innocuous call would lead to some of my most amazing encounters with inexplicable phenomena. The events that followed would be real but far outside the current scientific understanding.

The caller announced that he was Bob Bigelow. He had heard about me and asked if there were any projects that needed funding. Coincidence? Possibly, but how did it happen that a complete stranger would call asking about funding projects just as some of the leading scientists in the world had completed a discussion of the topic. Actually, I had encountered Bob once before. He had attended the MIT conference on abductions that was hosted by John Mack of Harvard and Dave Pritchard, an extraordinary optical physicist at MIT. I had given the presentation immediately following John Mack's. That was a tough act to follow. The topic of my talk was on the possible relationship between UFO abductions and Near Death Experiences (NDEs).

Having recently retired from Los Alamos National Laboratory, I was looking for new options and suggested to Bob that we get together. A short time later he flew over to Santa Fe, and as a result of that meeting he did fund a project of a friend of mine, Pharis Williams. "Willie," as he was known, had been working on his Dynamic Theory for a long time and wanted to complete it.[3] Bob also expressed interest in establishing an organization to explore UFOs and the continuation of consciousness beyond death. I mentioned the Santa Fe Institute and their innovative approach to research. They were focused on chaos theory and attracted some of the best minds in the world.

Intrigued, Bob indicated he might like to buy the Institute. While their research was superb, and processes for the cross-fertilization of ideas captivating, their leading light and co-founder was Murry Gel-Mann, a theoretical physicist and 1969 Nobel Laureate for his work on elementary particles. His book *The Quark and the Jaguar: Adventures in the Simple and the Complex* had been published recently and had garnered a lot of public attention.[4] Gell-Mann, however, was notoriously independent and a professor emeritus at the California Institute of Technology. Given Bob's proclivities for tight control, that was not going to be a good fit.

A month later I agreed to join in the development of a new organization that he chartered as the National Institute for Discovery Science (NIDS). It was located in Bob's hometown, Las Vegas, and close to his other offices. NIDS was not his first foray into supporting psi research. For a time, Angela Thompson had done work at the Bigelow Foundation, and Dean Radin was funded at the University of Nevada, Las Vegas, for several years.[5] But NIDS was the first free-standing, full-time organization and would primarily focus on his two specific interests.

Having twice formally retired, I was hired part-time, and before long an experienced biochemist named Colm Kelleher was brought on as the deputy administrator to run the operation day-to-day. One of my early tasks was to help create a world-class Science Advisory Board (SAB). Bob knew a few of the obvious choices, like Jacques Vallee, Hal Puthoff, and lunar astronaut Edgar Mitchell. But because I came from the Los Alamos National Laboratory (LANL), I had other contacts in the scientific community, ones who were not widely known to be interested in these phenomena. What emerged was truly an amazing group, one that could stand up to any scrutiny. They included Gian-Carlo Rota of MIT, who is considered the father of combinatorial mathematics, and O'Dean Judd, a physicist who had been the technical director of the Strategic Defense Initiative (SDI, aka Star Wars) and later became the National Intelligence Officer for Research and Development at the National Intelligence Council. Also on the board was Johndale Solem, a brilliant theoretical physicist from LANL who held the Enrico Fermi chair and had published hundreds of peer-reviewed papers in some 50 different fields. It was Johndale who first proposed the use of nuclear weapons for planetary defense against asteroid impact. For that he was vociferously attacked in *The New York Times* as just wanting to defend the nuclear weapons budget.[6] Also an initial member of the NIDS SAB was another lunar astronaut, albeit a more skeptical one, Senator Harrison "Jack" Schmitt.

Joining us later was Al Harrison, a professor of psychology at the University of California, Davis, who studied how contact with extraterrestrials would impact society. There were several other scientists, most of whom had been openly involved in the scientific study of anomalous phenomena. While

4

many fields of science were represented, the common factor was that they all were open minded and willing to examine data that didn't fit preconceived parameters.

The first chairman of the NIDS SAB was Christopher (Kit) Green, MD, Ph.D., a former CIA senior scientist and then a senior executive with General Motors. Later, Kit would head the fMRI research at Wayne State Medical Center, but he was already known for his interest in psi phenomena. With his multidisciplinary background and questioning mind, Kit was the perfect choice to head this group.

For the six years, I was associated with NIDS, I had an opportunity to engage in some of the most fascinating studies I ever imagined. Of course, one stands out beyond all others; the exploits at what became known as Skinwalker Ranch. Bob and I flew to Vernal, Utah, the day he closed the deal with Terry Sherman to buy the ranch.[7] That was the first night I spent alone on the mesa overlooking the grazing land below. But other than an attack of voracious mosquitoes, there was nothing remarkable to report. Later, that was not the case—there were several incidents that would challenge any model of modern science. (For more complete information about this investigation, I highly recommend the book, *Hunt for the Skinwalker* by Colm Kelleher and George Knapp.[8])

The term Skinwalker Ranch was coined by people not associated with the project. Skinwalker comes from the Navajo tradition and refers to an entity that can change form from a man into any animal, such as a wolf, coyote, fox, or even a bird. They are associated with witches and evil, as opposed to the medicine men who engage in blessings and healings. The term skinwalker was appropriate, as there were credible reports of strange creatures being seen at the ranch. It was reported to us that the local Indians were well aware of unusual happenings in the area, events that occurred long before it became a working ranch. By tradition, it was an area to be avoided, especially at night.

Based on these tales, it seemed like the acquisition of the ranch made sense as it offered a nearly unique opportunity to serve as a laboratory where phenomena occurred frequently. It would exceed our wildest expectations, but it must be emphasized that these spectacular events took place over a period of years. It was not as if something unusual happened every night.

The SAB listened to the remarkable, often fantastic stories that Terry Sherman told us. For the record, we found him to be very credible and a solid citizen who was very perplexed by the events that happened to him and his family. The history of the ranch seemed to support his claims. When Terry and his family moved in, they found heavy metal rings embedded in the walls near the front and rear door of the tiny house. The prior owner indicated that he kept vicious dogs chained near the doors to prevent anyone or anything from approaching the house. Later we learned that he had also experienced a number of incidents that caused him to use that primitive, but effective, measure of security.

One of the inexplicable stories that lends credence to the Skinwalker Ranch phenomena happened shortly after the family had first moved in. While on a break from working close to the house, Terry noticed a dog approaching from the west. As the animal walked right up him, Terry realized it was a wolf and not a dog, as he first thought. The wolf was very large, its head coming to the middle of Terry's chest. He thought it strange that a wolf had been domesticated and was friendly to humans. After petting the animal, Terry returned to work.

Within a few minutes, he heard a commotion in his cattle pen, which was located nearby. There, he found the wolf had reached under the bottom railing, grabbed a 600-pound calf by the snout, and was attempting to pull it out. Picking up a heavy wooden post, Terry smacked the wolf in the ribs as hard as he could. That had no effect. From his truck, Terry quickly retrieved his 44-Magnum. At point-blank range, he fired six rounds into the wolf's chest, which should have contained the beast's heart. That action would have killed any natural animal, yet barely fazed this one.

At that juncture, the wolf let go of the calf and began wandering off, but not in any hurry. Next Terry picked up a loaded rifle he used for elk hunting. He fired at the retreating animal and saw chunks of flesh fly off the animal's body. Eventually the wolf disappeared from sight. Terry then went over to the location where he saw the flesh fall on the ground. Lying there were remnants from the animal. Most surprising, Terry noted, was that although they had just been ejected from the moving body, what he picked up smelled as if putrefied. In most cases putrefaction does not occur until several days after death. Whatever Terry shot did not behave like any known animal. Whether it was a skinwalker or not is impossible to say. It is safe to say that six rounds from a 44-magnum at close range, even if the path of the bullets missed vital organs, should have brought the intruder down. It didn't.

It was another event that caused Terry to sell the ranch to Bob. On several occasions, Terry and the rest of the family reported seeing balls of light, sometimes called orbs, dancing a few feet above the ground. Like most ranchers, the Shermans kept dogs that were both pets and work animals. One night Terry saw his dogs jumping up and snapping at the orbs. There appeared to be some interactions, almost teasing, between the dogs and the orbs as they moved off the eastern edge of his property.

Unlike all previous nights, the dogs failed to return to the house. The following day Terry went looking for them. Beyond the fence, he came upon what he believed was the remains of the dogs. On the ground, he found three greasy spots. That was all that remained of the pets. That scared him as he was concerned that his teenage sons might also attempt to engage the orbs. They decided to vacate the ranch before any harm could come to the family.

From a scientific perspective, one of the most interesting events that took place was the mutilation of a calf. The incident was important, as it provided a lot of physical evidence that cannot be explained. It was calving season at the ranch. One bright sunny midmorning, Terry went out to examine the herd and found a newborn standing next to its mother. As is the custom, the calf was given a tag to identify it with the mother. He also weighed the calf and noted that. Crossing the flat, open field, he found a second newborn and proceeded to tag and weigh that one as well. The procedure took about 45 minutes.

As he drove back to where he had found the first calf, a distance of only about 300 meters, he was shocked to find the mother going berserk. There, on the ground was the dead body of the calf he had tagged and weighed just a few minutes earlier. The calf showed signs of extensive mutilation. The ear that had been tagged was sliced off with surgical precision and was missing. The calf was both eviscerated and exsanguinated. The bones were intact, save for a femur that had been removed and was lying a short distance from the rest of the body. What remained of the calf now weighed 20 pounds less than before.

The body was immediately covered, and NIDS' own veterinarian, George Onet, flown to the scene within a few hours. Extensive testing was conducted. The cut for the missing ear was indicative of a very sharp instrument. The same was true of the strange marks found on the femur. SAB members were consulted on this case, but they could provide no rational explanation for what had happened. The missing blood was problematic. Did it seep into the ground? That possibility was eliminated as there was a test conducted in which blood was obtained from a local slaughterhouse and intentionally poured onto the ground at a nearby location. Even weeks later, the spot where the blood was intentionally deposited was clearly identifiable.

Also considered was predation. There are a few mountain lions in the area to the north, but this was not how they kill. Bears, wolves, and other large animals were categorically excluded, as was the possibility of human intervention. This was an open field and within Terry's line of sight at all times. The probability that someone would risk such an attack, including extensive surgery, in broad daylight is so remote as to be eliminated.

As unlikely as it seems, the conclusion of the investigation, with concurrence of the SAB, was that the evisceration and exsanguination had occurred at another location and the body returned to where it was found. That defies all known scientific theories. It points to something that has the capability of interdimensional transport and interaction with our physical world. It may be considered bizarre, but when all of the facts are considered, it becomes the most parsimonious explanation.

There were many hours of observations made by our highly-qualified staff members. Most nights, nothing of note happened. But on several occasions events that are totally inexplicable did occur. Another example that points to an interdimensional interaction took place in August 1997. Two of our trained researchers were located at an observation point on the escarpment that runs along the north side of the ranch. That area provides an overlook from which you can see most of the ranch and is near where I spent my first night. At about 2:30 a.m., just as they prepared to call it a night, they spotted a dim light near the vicinity of the dirt road below them. Shortly, its intensity increased, revealing an expanding circle of yellow light. It seemed to hover about three feet above the ground. When it reached an estimated four feet in diameter and appeared tunnel-like, a dark object appeared. Using the third-generation night vision equipment that NIDS had procured, they saw a humanoid-looking creature emerge from the illuminated tunnel. They estimated that the entity was about six feet in height and probably weighed around 400 pounds. It pulled itself out of the tunnel of light and landed on the road, or so they thought. In a short period of time, the creature headed eastward down the road into the darkness. The tunnel of light then receded into itself and disappeared.

Given the size of the entity they had seen, the researchers prudently waited before descending to the road. As with reports of many Bigfoot or Sasquatch sightings, they noticed a distinct pungent odor in the area, but no other trace of the creature. A daylight search was even more perplexing. The dirt road is dusty and anything moving on it leaves prints. Obviously, any animal the size that they reported should have left footprints behind. None were ever found. This interaction too is prototypical of a Skinwalker, albeit one of unknown/ extradimensional origin.

While that report relies on eyewitness testimony, other incidents provided substantial physical evidence and were equally disconcerting. For the next several years the ranch was instrumented and time-lapse video recordings of the area were made 24/7. In select areas cameras were mounted, taking a photo every one and one-third seconds, or about 45 frames per minute. The cameras were elevated about 20 feet off the ground on substantial poles. They faced west with most of the ranch property in view. The video cameras were situated in such a way that two of them were observing two other cameras. There were wires running down the poles, under the ground, and into a trailer home that contained the recording equipment. The wires were firmly affixed to the poles with a lot of duct tape. As the wires neared the ground, they were protected by PVC tubing that was secured to the poles by plastic U-clamps. Inside the trailer the recordings were made with the date-time stamp always imprinted. This system functioned smoothly for many months without a single interruption.

One day the wires were found pulled loose at the top of pole mounted camera #2. Significant damage had been done. All of the duct tape, about half a roll, had been pulled loose and was gone. Anyone who has worked with duct tape knows how hard it is to remove. In addition, a three-foot-long length of wires was also gone. The protective PVC had been pulled loose from the pole and the U-clamps were missing.

It was fairly easy to determine the exact time of the incident. When reviewing the video feed from camera #2, the pictures stopped abruptly. The next step was to examine the video recording of camera #1, which had a view of camera #2. What it didn't show was startling. Though it had recorded continuously, it did not show any of the disturbance at camera #2. Even stranger still, at the time that camera #2 stopped sending pictures, the cattle were grazing peacefully around the pole. That is very significant, as whenever anyone approached this herd, the cattle tended to scatter and move away. Dogs and predators would elicit the same reaction. We also eliminated the possibility that a person had approached from behind the pole in a manner that camera #1 would not have spotted them. First, the cattle would have scattered. Second, there was no video of a person climbing the pole, and doing all of the other damage that occurred. It would have been impossible to have caused that amount of damage in the one and a third seconds between frames. When the cut ends of the wires were sent for analysis, it was concluded that the instrument used was probably rusty, but not specifically identified.

Again, the SAB was presented with the evidence. Given the totality of the circumstances, there is no credible scientific explanation that can accommodate the data. Worth noting is that one of our staff seemed to be more sensitive to these events. An astrophysicist, Eric Davis, reported that at times he had mental contact with an unknown source. During one incident, he sensed something moving through the tree branches near where the old ranch house had been located. The description best fit the invisible alien in the movie *Predator*. As readers may recall, all you could see was a disturbance in the visual pattern, but no distinct object. Eric, who has published some notable articles in antiproton annihilation propulsion, told us that the entity had told him that, "We are watching you." It is not clear why he experienced interactions when others did not. That is part of the conundrum we found at Skinwalker Ranch.

There were several attempts made to capture data on these phenomena. All of them were evaded, as if some intelligence was determining what would be presented. I had previously given a name to these phenomena; I call it Precognitive Sentient Phenomena (PSP).[9] PSP is not limited to Skinwalker Ranch, but it certainly played out there. The wording is precise. *Precognitive* means that the controlling factor knows before the event takes place exactly how the observers will respond. If there will be research done on solid evidence, it can predict what will be done and interject aspects that defy logic. *Sentient* means that whatever is controlling the interaction is intelligent. Also, that intelligence is firmly in charge of both how the event is observed, and what the response will be. *Phenomena* means that the event generally will be inexplicable.

The subject of the Trickster is well established in paranormal research. Whatever is generating these incidents does so in a manner that does not remain consistent over time. From a scientific perspective, that makes studying any aspect of it almost impossible. In vain we make attempts to isolate characteristics of the phenomena in order to research them effectively. But what happens is that these phenomena constantly morph over time.

Among other attempts at obtaining useful information on the phenomena, biosensors were established, namely dogs. There were many stories about interactions between dogs and the phenomena, and not all had ended as gruesomely as what happened to Terry's pets. Still it is known that dogs can sense things that are well beyond human capability. In order to have control of the situation, pens were constructed in an area in which activity had been reported. Towers were put in above the pens and various toys placed there. On occasion, the items would be moved about, but true to form, nothing was caught on camera.

The Skinwalker Ranch was not the sole focus of NIDS. One investigation I found interesting occurred when Colm and I visited the Lee family who had reported many strange happenings at their home in Black Forest, Colorado. Here again there was a mixture of unusual events coupled with tales that could not possibly have happened. Television programs had featured their home, and with that notoriety came considerable conflict in the neighborhood, to the point that law enforcement was often called. That actually happened on a night we were visiting. That was unfortunate as it was difficult to determine if the events centered on the immediate area, or the family.

The Lees did have some pretty strong video and photographic evidence to support some of the claims. The misty shadows that appeared inside their home were only mildly interesting scientifically, but they were of considerable concern to the family. More interesting to me were the tapes made by their external surveillance cameras, which were triggered by motion detectors. Being in a forested area, it was not uncommon for wild animals to transit the yard and be photographed. But there were other incidents captured on video that were harder to explain. Specifically, there were many instances in which orbs of light clearly would be seen moving about. The scientific issue of interest here is not whether the orbs were some kind of visual illusion, but what was it about the event that was sufficiently physical in form to cause the video cameras to activate?

At times, they have reported unexplained violent incidents in the home apparently caused by unseen, nonhuman entities. As I recall, Steve Lee had scratches appear on his body. In addition, members of television crews filming at the location also reported physical encounters with an invisible force, including having a camera mounted on a tripod tipped over. Family members also reported malodorous incidents on several occasions.

At NIDS I was involved in several UFO studies as well. At least two involved very high-profile cases and personalities. The research into Phillip Corso was a highlight, but it proved to be an extreme challenge. In my book *UFOs: Myths, Conspiracies and Realities,* I devoted an entire chapter to him entitled "The Corso Conundrum." Thanks to George Knapp, we knew about Phil long before his book *The Day After Roswell* came out.[10] George Knapp was to be the co-author but was not able to participate when the contract was finally signed. In any case, George, Hal Puthoff, and I went to Ft. Pierce, Florida, where Corso lived with his son. We then brought him to Las Vegas where we interviewed him for several days. At that time, Jacques Vallee joined us. Most impressive was the absolute consistency of his interviews.

Following those discussions, I went to the Pentagon in Washington, D.C, and the Army War College at Carlisle Barracks, Pennsylvania, and spent a week checking his background. The results were mixed. In general, he was assigned as he had told us. There were some significant problems though, ones that were never explained. Phil told us that General Trudeau had created a position for him and called it the Foreign Technology Division (FTD). It was from this office he claims to have maintained contact with the material from Roswell and provided pieces to civilian industry when it was perceived they could benefit from it. The recipients, Phil stated, did not know the origin of the material and assumed it to be Soviet.

We determined that the FTD was organized at that time when Trudeau, a three-star general, was the U.S. Army Deputy Chief of Staff for Research, Development, and Acquisition. Corso was assigned to that organization and claimed to be the director. The problem was that both the Pentagon phonebook and the Army organizational chart showed that a Colonel T. H. Spengler was the director. When I asked Phil about the discrepancy, he said he did not know Spengler, who was a full colonel while Phil was only a lieutenant colonel. We do know that Phil had a special relationship with Lieutenant General Arthur Trudeau, who had a legendary reputation in the Army. A futuristic thinker and battlefield commander in Korea, Trudeau had led the fight for Pork Chop Hill.

Among things that Phil correctly told us about was Project Horizon, a plan made under Trudeau to fight from the Moon. As I confirmed with Edgar Mitchell, it was the Army, with assistance of German scientists, that was largely responsible for putting us on the Moon. When it came to Phil's technology claims, things fell apart pretty quickly. According to the story he told us, and is repeated in his book, there were several key technologies that came from ET material found at Roswell. These included integrated circuitry, night vision, and fiber optics, among others. The problem was that the evolutionary history of each of those technologies was well-known. At no point was there a big leap indicative of some outside assistance or intervention.

The night vision claim was of particular interest to me as Lou Cameron was a personal friend and the director who literally built the U.S. Army Night Vision Laboratory (NVL), as it was then known. Lou was very open-minded and had attended several spoon-bending parties. Though he was retired, I did contact him and confirmed what I suspected. There were no alien eyeballs involved in the development of night vision technology. Several of the claims in the book are specifically refuted in the established history of NVL.

Other Corso claims were even more egregious, and my mention of them has brought me into conflict with many of his supporters. Paul Hellyer, the former Canadian Minister of National Defence, is one of those and we have metaphorically crossed swords on this topic. At the top of the list is the specious notion that the Cold War was a cover to prepare us to fight ET. Corso's errors ran from miniscule to this whopper, and I sent Phil a seven-page letter (included as an addendum to my UFO book) detailing the ones I found. While I considered Phil a friend, I could never rectify the incongruence in his statements or his rationale for them.

Another famous UFO case that NIDS played a role in investigating was that of Rendlesham Forest, also known as the Bentwaters Air Force Base case. This remains one of the best cases, and even today more information is being revealed about the incident. The biggest mistake, in my view, is to look at the case as a single incident, or one that occurred twice. To be sure there were a couple of nights in which extremely dramatic events happened, but that is only part of the story.

Over the years, I have had the opportunity to interview several of the key participants and find most of them to be very credible. Even though there were more than 60 witnesses with varying degrees of involvement, the case goes far beyond personal accounts. What has been striking from the first reports was the amount of physical evidence that supported the validity of the case. While skeptics have attempted to knock it down, their explanations never fit the data and they tend to discount critical pieces such as the radiation levels that were recorded.

From a NIDS perspective I got involved when we were contacted by a woman who had lived on the base at the time of those first reports. She had been the wife of one of the base staff officers. As a practical matter, they had a radio that was tuned to the Security Police frequencies so that they could be aware of any significant incidents on the base. According to her, the strange incidents continued well after those that have been publicized. While official interest waned, apparently, some of the family members picked up the trail and would follow up when something unusual was reported. She provided me with a film she had taken several weeks after the late December 1980 encounters. She said there had been several additional sightings, but nothing as dramatic as what Colonel Chuck Halt and Jim Penniston have claimed. Unfortunately, there were no reference points in the video frames by which additional analysis might be made. This does, however, point to what I believe is an important issue from a scientific perspective. That is, like events at Skinwalker Ranch, whatever happened at Rendlesham Forest had gone on for a long time and tended to display poly-phenomenal characteristics.

Another case I handled at NIDS demonstrated the capability to do high-quality photo analysis. In 2000, I was contacted by Peter Gersten about a photo that was posted on the CAUS website showing a man in uniform sitting on a horse. At a distance behind him appeared to be a UFO.

Soon I located Jack LeMonde in Santa Monica. Twice wounded fighting with the U.S. Marines in the South Pacific, in 1945 he was recuperating at his home in Burbank, California. The photo of him had been taken on a morning in June of that year near the Pickwick Riding stables. At that time, Burbank was a relatively rural area and equestrian activities were quite common. That is not at all what the topography is like today. The LeMonde family had a great interest in photography and invested in very good equipment. The camera was a German Voightlander equipped with a Carl Zeiss f3.5 lens (possibly f4.5) with a focal length of approximately 10 centimeters. It is the excellent quality of the optics that made this remarkable photo possible.

When the film was developed, they noticed the unusual object above the horse's neck. It was thought to be either an airplane in the distance or a speck of dust that had gotten on the negative. Remember, in 1945 the words "flying saucer" did not exist, and so it was just filed away with other family photos.[11] Fifty years later the family decided to have copies made of their old photos for posterity.

NIDS engaged a person who had been a technical photo analyst for the Air Force and was then in private practice. Working from the print I delivered, he digitized and analyzed it. The original photo was a 2¼ by 3¼ inches contact print. All aspects of the lighting angles and intensity appear to be congruent. Taken to the grain level under a microscope, there is no indication of a supporting structure of any kind. The clarity of the object suggests this is not something that had been thrown into the air. At the shutter speed listed, a thrown object would be slightly blurred. A fair amount of structure could be seen on the object. All indications are that the photograph was initially developed at about the time reported (1945).

While we believed the photo to be authentic, several people suggested to NIDS that the object in the LeMonde photograph was actually a streetlight fixture of some kind. That seemingly simple answer was rejected for several reasons. Each response indicated that the light was suspended on a wire. As stated in the article that I wrote for NIDS, microscopic examination of the photo down to the grain level failed to reveal any suspending or supporting mechanisms. Further, behind the horse's neck, close to the saddle can be seen the curved arches of a sign that is over a drive-in movie theater. That provides a reference for height. The object in question is well in the background behind the marquee. The distance suggests that the object is much larger than a street light and substantially higher. Were it small and in the foreground, the supporting mechanism would be observable. It is not.

In checking on street lighting in Burbank in 1945 it was determined that the lights described by those who "instantly recognized" the object in the photo were not in use in that community. Rather, the existing streetlights were placed atop granitized concrete posts. No such post is visible. Also, the lamp itself was a totally different variety.

Actually, when LeMonde first gave me the picture, he stated that he estimated the height of the object to be between 750-850 feet above the ground. That figure was derived based on the photographic angle, as he originally believed the object was over two miles away. I was not as convinced that the object was that far away or that it was over 700 feet high. However, it was well above normal streetlight heights. (LeMonde later believed the object was probably about a mile away.) It is a solid object and not a streetlight.

This is another example of a case with hard evidence that has been ignored by traditional science. While it represents a small piece in a much bigger puzzle, it points to the need for a better collection and analysis system. The LeMonde photo is also indicative of our lack of recognition of phenomena until some precipitating event captures the public's imagination and we acknowledge what has always been present. For a few years, NIDS provided a platform for such research. More needs to be done.

Chapter 2
"I Think They're Here"

As evening was falling on October 11, 2015, Chris Bledsoe and I stood in a North Carolina field outside my Hertz rental car discussing the events that had allegedly happened to him several years before. That first event had occurred in January of 2007. The story he told me about his interaction with aliens, missing time, and the continuation of anomalous events in his life seemed, at best, fanciful. But an extremely interesting aspect of the encounter was that there were multiple witnesses that could substantiate the event. Actually, Chris had detailed the entire story months before at a friend's home in Pennsylvania. It was an interview that I filmed and had recently reviewed. To be honest, it was one of those intricate tales that was hard to swallow. There were just too many fantastical details, and yet, there was some ring of truth. There was also physical evidence that was hard to deny. That is why Victoria and I agreed to visit the family, explore the site, and investigate the current circumstances. While open to the possibilities of various phenomena, I could hardly have been less prepared for what was to happen a few minutes later.

The Bledsoe family has been in this area of North Carolina for a couple of hundred years. Just north of their home is Bledsoe Road, named after a long-deceased ancestor. While I do not know their history prior to the advent of these strange events, Chris's family now is very close knit. Part of that can be attributed to the nasty attacks they have received from members of the "UFO community."

Before detailing my experience, some background on the case is useful. On Saturday, January 8, 2007, Chris, his son Chris Jr., and three other men decided to go fishing on the nearby Cape Fear River. As dusk approached, the men built a good-sized fire for a bit of warmth. Chris left for what he believed to be a relatively short time and walked up the winding muddy trail to where he had parked his truck. The area is thickly wooded and visibility only a few feet at best near the sides of the road. The ground rises rather quickly the farther away one gets from the riverbank. About a quarter of a mile from their fishing site, the area opens up into farm fields with a small house close by and off to the northwest. Across the farm fields are more trees and eventually a paved road.

Chris reports that as he walked he became aware that he was being stalked by something in the woods. Familiar with the area and the creatures that normally inhabit it, this spooked him. It would stop whenever he stopped as if more human than animal. As he approached the open area, but before he actually reached it, Chris noticed a bright light that he initially took for the sun sinking low to the west. But then he saw two very large orange-colored objects hovering at a slight angle above the plowed area. He estimated they were less than a mile away at that point. He describes these UFOs as quite brilliant balls as if made of "liquid fire." The scene was frightening to him and he started to retreat back down the road to his friends. Suddenly there was a light or opening above him, and he realized escape was impossible. What happened next is not clear in his conscious recollection. Hypnotic regressions have been employed to fill in those memories.

What Chris does clearly remember is noting that it was then completely dark and he was running back to find his friends. To his great surprise the large campfire they had made about 5 pm had burned down to smoldering embers and the men were quite distraught. His truck, which had been parked near the field, had been moved and was now near the riverbank. Even more astonishingly, later he learned that over four hours had passed, though he thought it was a few minutes. At least that is what it seemed like to him. When he had failed to return earlier in the evening, his friends had gone out searching the relatively small area, but were unable to locate him. Most of them had not seen anything out of the ordinary, at least not until then. Now, with both Bledoes present, the group observed eight or nine bright lights maneuver adroitly in the dark sky above them. These unknown objects were described as being brighter than any star or planet normally visible. After a short time, the lights seemed to descend into the woods across the river from them. That was sufficient to have the entire group depart the area—as rapidly as possible. In a flash, coolers, poles, and other fishing gear were thrown into the bed of his Ford truck and the dash out of there was on.

Chris says when he hit the top of the hill the pickup probably cleared the ground in their effort to escape. To their amazement, there in front of them were the two orange UFOs. He estimates they were 150 meters from them, but now one of them was only about five feet off the ground and coming towards them with churning white lights inside the craft. After a short period, the UFOs drifted toward the river at low altitude, then shot off to the north in a flash.

While that encounter may have seemed strange enough, it turned out that the unusual events were just beginning for him and his entire family. Unexplained phenomena have plagued them since that fateful night and continue to the present.

My involvement picks up at the same location, albeit years later. Chris had graciously accompanied us to the area. We parked at the end of the unimproved dirt road not far from the house previously mentioned. With great interest, we crawled under a rickety metal fence that prevented unwanted vehicles from venturing closer to the bottoms land. Cautiously, and with failing light, we walked down the same rain soaked trail to the river trying to avoid the water that had accumulated in old tire tracks. At the bank, Chris pointed out in fair detail where the group had been fishing and the point at which the fire had been built.

As at the time of the original event, it was getting dark. The photos I took of the area lacked clarity because of the deteriorating light. Attempting to avoid the puddles that festered, we walked slowly back to the car. In so doing I carefully looked into the surrounding woods and confirmed that even during daylight visibility was very limited. Anyone or anything could easily hide within close proximity and easily avoid detection.

Chris Bledsoe and author following their UFO sighting.

Clambering both under and over the fence, we walked a short distance to the car. Again, Chris pointed to the location where he had witnessed the orange UFOs hovering on that fateful night. Victoria and Emily Bledsoe, Chris's teenage daughter who had accompanied us, got into the back seat of the Honda and continued talking. Chris and I leaned back against the left front fender and he began reminiscing about details of the initial event, which he describes as an abduction. As we talked, he continued to orient me to our location. I noted that what he described at this time did not vary from the depiction he provided in our interview weeks earlier. This discussion did allow me to fully understand at least the geographic aspects of the first encounter.

Then it happened.

Without warning, Chris unexpectedly stated, "Oh, I think they are here." The area was quite dark and the sky moonless. During our conversation, we had noted various aircraft and had been able to track their movement. Within about 10 to 15 seconds of Chris's pronouncement, suddenly almost directly above us, a bright light burst into view. It immediately sped off to the south and disappeared as quickly as it had arrived. While short in duration, the object was far more luminescent than anything else in the sky at that time and traveled much faster than anything else we watched that night. As a certified commercial pilot, Chris is quite familiar with the objects and meteorology normally seen in the sky. What we saw that evening was unlike any normal object or event.

As UFO sightings go, the description of the object is hardly newsworthy. For me it was simply a bright white light that instantaneously manifested itself and was gone in a brief but definitive blaze. The duration was only one or two seconds and not long enough to change direction. While I yelled to Victoria, the incident was finished long before she could get out of the car. While my description of the UFO is insignificant, the events leading up to it are not. Chris's admonition immediately prior to the observation is extremely significant. Remember, only a few seconds elapsed between his statement and the object's appearance. That temporal relationship was critical for me.

For the skeptics, I should cover what didn't happen. As mentioned, we watched numerous aircraft transit the area. This was not a conventional airplane. It appeared instantaneously in the center of the sky above us. It did not come from the horizon to the overhead position. From that, I can exclude any possibility it was a comet. One skeptic offered that our sighting might have been an Iridium flare. They are predictable and are eliminated in this case. But there is more, much more to the story.

After Chris returned home from the original fishing incident, another event took place that night. The howling from the numerous hunting dogs alerted him to something happening in his spacious back yard. Initially he believed someone must be trying to break into their shed located near the kennels. Checking, he found nothing amiss, but the barking continued. In an attempt to find the intruder, Chris took off running. Soon he was aware that he was not alone and something was chasing him. He ran about 100 meters to the west end of his property. Out of breath, he stopped and turned to acknowledge he had been caught. In fact, he says he thought he was going to die. Standing about five feet behind him was a short alien creature with a big head and spindly arms and legs. Chris said, "OK, you got me." Telepathically the being responded, "You don't understand, we are here to help you." Then, as Chris Jr. began moving toward his location, the alien simply disappeared.

Father and son then returned to the house to ponder what had happened. The son was still traumatized from the earlier exchange, and Chris went into his office bewildered by the events of the evening. Shortly after that Chris raised the shades to his ground floor room. There, standing about 30 meters away in the yard, was another alien. This one, he states, was about seven or eight feet tall and made no direct contact. No further interactions were reported, and Chris left the house for a location that he believed would be safer, or at least one that would not endanger his family.

In January 2007 Chris Bledsoe had been suffering from Crohn's Disease for 12 years. Under the care of his doctor, he managed to control the severe symptoms of this debilitating illness. For those unaware of this malady, Crohn's impacts the gastrointestinal system and affects about 700,000 people in the U.S. Symptoms include abdominal pain, fever, and the urgent need to defecate frequently. As such, it can inhibit the person's social interaction. It is important to note that patients do report periods of remission. However, for those patients, symptoms almost always return with five years.

That information is necessary to understand the significance of this situation. To control his Crohn's symptoms that January, Chris was required to take two pills a day at specified times. That had been his routine for years and entirely necessary for him to function anywhere near normally. At about 10 o'clock the next morning, January 9, 2007, Chris became aware that he had not taken his morning dose of medicine. That was extremely unusual, as normally failure to do so resulted in rapid onset of the symptoms, nausea in particular. When he suffered from severe Crohn's, Chris would be very nauseous up to 25 times a day. When he only experienced the symptoms eight or nine times, he would consider it to be a good day. But this day, no symptoms occurred. Beginning that day, until the time of this writing, Chris has never again had to take another dose of that medicine. It appears that during his encounters he was cured of Crohn's. It has been far longer than the five-year norm, and he has never had a recurrence.

As mentioned earlier, Chris underwent hypnosis to assist in recalling what transpired during his missing time experience. During a regression, he remembered being chased by alien creatures, which frightened him greatly. In vain he had attempted to flee, but he was pursued and eventually caught. However, the aliens informed him their purpose was benevolent. From the conversation during that encounter he learned they were there specifically to help him. Chris attributes the curing of Crohn's disease to their intervention.

During the period of missing time for Chris, his son also had a distressing experience. Like the other men, he too had searched for his father. Unlike them, he encountered some very unusual creatures who chased him deeper into the woods. Among the unique descriptions, Chris Jr. mentioned they were relatively small and mechanical-like and at times moved on four legs. They had come within 10-15 feet of him but apparently did not see him. According to the son's account, these devices had blinking red eyes that alternated closing left and right. He also indicated that the creatures could become invisible whenever they wished. Specifically, he saw them transmute when they heard the truck approaching. Paralyzed, he had avoided capture but remained hidden in the dense forest. The trauma was sufficient to make him extremely reluctant to come out. In fact, it was only after his father had returned that they found him still frozen from fear in his impromptu refuge. Still in shock and quivering, he asked why his father had abandoned him. Unlike his father, Chris Jr. has conscious recollection of the events of that evening—and they were terrifying.

It would be impossible to cover all of the other paranormal events that have happened over the intervening years. One of the most intriguing is the burning tree in his backyard. This is reminiscent of Moses and the burning bush on Mount Sinai except that no voice emerged from it. But more unusual was that this tree burned from the inside out. This tree has a hollow opening near the base that extends several feet up the trunk. When trees are struck by lightning and catch fire, which sometimes leads to forest fires, they usually burn from the outside in. But this was a spontaneous combustion and lightning was not the causal agent.

Having personally examined the tree, even years after the initial blaze one can readily determine the pyrogenetic aspects of the incident. They match Chris's description of sparks coming out of the trunk without any external source. The visual characteristics alone are both interesting and unusual. There are, however, other unique features associated with that tree. Namely, it appears to have healing qualities that emanate from it. As soon as those were discovered, people began sending the family objects of clothing to be placed in immediate proximity to the hollowed area of the tree.

We, too, experienced unusual activity in the immediate vicinity of that tree. Victoria appears to be ultra-sensitive to these unknown forms of energy and some of her experiences are detailed in other chapters. It was dark and early evening as Chris and Victoria approached the tree. I walked behind them so that I could observe their behavior and photograph anything that might occur. They stopped within a few feet of the tree, and I noticed Victoria beginning to exhibit movements that are characteristic when she is becoming influenced by external energies/agencies, or whatever you want to name them. Nothing quite fits. What I saw was that her body began to sway ever so slightly and her feet moved in a peculiar but recognizable fashion. Not quite dancing, but the movements were definitely not her normal walk. Victoria is aware of the energies but states it is impossible for her to control the movements. The closest description I can make for what I observed is the similarity to how Native Americans begin their spiritual dances at a pow wow. However, she usually stops well short of the exuberant dancing that is characteristic of those ceremonies. From my observation of these situations, Victoria seems unaware when some form of transformation in behavior is occurring, and it is not volitional on her part. Victoria does state she can feel the presence of external powers but is unable to stop her movements.

The reported healing process is similar to what I have observed in other places that are revered as sacred and have histories of spontaneous healing. Those include locations such as the Grotto at Lourdes in France or when we entered the Godavari River in Nashik, India, during the 2015 Kumbh Mela ceremonies. While almost unknown in the west, Kumbh Mela, an ancient Hindu ceremony with a confluence of sadhus (holy men), produces the largest congregation of worshipers in the world. When we attended, 40 million people participated in the month-long religious activities, and an estimated four million entered the river on the day we did.

There are numerous anecdotal cases of unexplained healings that have followed Chris since his initial encounter in 2007. He attributes these external agencies with saving his father's life and adding at least a year and a half to his longevity. Stricken with cancer and serious sepsis, Chris's father was hospitalized with what the family was told, and therefore believed, were terminal illnesses. The family gathered at the hospital to face the inevitable. Suddenly, clinicians came in and announced that the new tests revealed that the cancer was no longer present. Chris states that at the time he became aware of a luminous presence above them and believes it was their intervention that extended his father's life. There are also indications that many other people have benefited from the same healing source through their association with Chris.

From a scientific and medical perspective, these claims are difficult to verify. Doctors know that people sometimes go into spontaneous remission without explanation. However, most of those medical professionals are very reluctant to embrace a concept like miracles or intervention by unseen entities. As demonstrated elsewhere in this book, they do happen and defy conventional theories of medicine.

Another common phenomenon experienced was the sighting of floating orbs of light. These luminous objects often have sufficient intensity to be captured by digital recording devices. In Chris's backyard, especially near that tree, these balls frequently show up. They vary in color, size, and intensity. He believes that these objects are related to the source of the phenomena and can act as conduits for spiritual entities.

I am uncertain if it is this location or a relationship to Chris that generates the phenomena. He believes the phenomena follow him. For more than a year following our experiences in his yard, Chris often sent me, and many others, photos that he has taken. One that I found particularly interesting was a video shot at an indoor party. A ball of light suddenly appears on the video, which then moves about the room. Clearly, this was not a photographic artifact or reflection. The short video was taken on a smartphone with no special capabilities. The image was clear and no imagination was needed to see the ball of light circle the young woman and move off. There was no energy source near where the object appeared, nor the spot where it disappeared.

Orbs that are not visible frequently appear on photos taken of Chris. I had such an experience when he accompanied mutual friends and visited Las Vegas. Just to the west of the city is Mt. Charleston, with a peak at nearly 12,000 feet. Some UFO enthusiasts claim that they too have had encounters with alien beings high on the mountainside. Therefore, late one night in November 2015, we drove up to remote areas at about the 9,000-foot level and attempted to make contact. With temperatures near freezing, we conducted activities that some contend attracts visitors. While nothing overt happened on that occasion, I did take a number of flash photos. The majority came out exactly how one would expect; quite unremarkable. However, on one in particular, a number of round objects clearly can be seen. It is hard to say whether or not they are the result of an optical artifact. However, it seems strange that they only appear in that frame and not on those taken seconds before and after.

A number of researchers have visited Chris at his home. The ones I have talked to believe that something mystical really occurs there. One has attempted communication using a device known as a spirit box. Spirit boxes are commercially available devices often used by ghost hunters. They allegedly work by rapidly scanning AM and FM electromagnetic frequencies in search of responses from discarnate entities. While I take no position on the veracity of these devices, Chris believes he has heard audible and intelligible messages from them. One of the more important messages he heard was when asked about Chris's involvement in these paranormal activities, the reported response was, "He will help us." He still does not understand the meaning behind that transmission and is still searching for answers himself.

I would be remiss if I did not mention more about the Bledsoe family. I've described them being tight-knit, in part because of the way they have handled the ad hominem attacks from both skeptics and some members of the UFO community. Having been with them on a number of occasions, visited their home, and talked intently with them, I can say that the information they provide is entirely coherent. Family members fully recognize just how strange the encounters sound, yet provide their honest and sincere accounts. When talking with each of them independently, they are open, warm, and factual. Most importantly, their descriptions of the events are congruent. Each has their own appreciation for these events, as they have all been affected, albeit in different ways. What was clear was what they say, they believe, and there is no indication of collusion or rehearsal designed to deceive others. You could not ask to ever meet a nicer family, each of whom has experienced events that defy common explanation.

CHAPTER 3
SPEAK TO ME

"I think they are a long way away right now," said Jan Northup. She was attempting to mentally communicate with a pod of wild dolphins. It was mid-afternoon on an idyllic July day in 1987, and we were leisurely drifting on a small fishing vessel about 20 miles north of West End, Grand Bahama Island. This area of the Bahamas was known for dolphin interactions, and our group had set out to test the limits of such encounters. There had been other experiments with dolphins in captivity by some members of the group. This was different, as these highly intelligent animals were unfettered; it was up to them as to whether or not to participate. On this day they would, and the results were both remarkable and inexplicable by traditional scientific theory.

Pods vary in size but there are usually less than 20 in the temporary grouping. Based on availability of food supplies, when hunting, they split into smaller units only to reconvene later in the day. On average, each dolphin covers about 200 square miles in a single day. Therefore, where they might be at any given time was unknown to us.

My interest in interspecies communications began several years earlier while attending a course at Ft. Ord, California. As covered in the chapter "Journeys Out of the Body," the nearby Esalen Institute, located in Big Sur, was a Mecca for major New Age thinkers. At Esalen, I had the opportunity to meet a consciousness studies pioneer, the legendary John Lilly. What an amazing experience that was. A medical doctor, Lilly was one of the few researchers at that time to have access to legal lysergic acid diethylamide, better known simply as LSD. The consummate explorer, he believed in personal engagements with his experiments.

He also led the research efforts in communications with large brain mammals and had authored the first definitive book on the topic, *Lilly on Dolphins*.[12] His early experiments indicated that dolphins have a highly-developed communications system. Lilly believed that communications between dolphins and humans, beyond responding to hand signals in order to get a reward, was quite possible. Building on what Lilly discovered, we attempted to take communication to a new level, mind-to-mind.

Through the generosity of Ted Rockwell, we were able to coordinate a week-long trip living aboard ship, the *Dream Too*, in the cerulean blue Bahamian waters. Included in the group were Ted and Mary Rockwell, Scott and Johnnie Jones, Jan Northup who was my wife at the time, and my son, Mark, a very experienced diver. Accompanying Ted and Mary was their vivacious teenage granddaughter, Angie, who with her skimpy swimming suit managed to continuously distract Captain Scott Smith's young crew members. Based on our prior psychic experiences, there was reason to believe that Jan had an innate capability to telepathically interact with dolphins. This trip would test that concept in the open ocean.

The slow-moving, broad-beam boat was about 65 feet in length and designed for accommodating overnight fishing parties. With a cruising speed of 8.5 knots, it took all night to sail from a port near Palm Beach, Florida, to where we had to clear customs in the Grand Bahamas. With relatively smooth waters, crossing the Gulf Stream was pleasant, and we slept most of the way. Once we were officially approved by the customs agents, the captain headed north to an area where dolphin encounters were a common occurrence. In waters rarely over 30 feet deep, we anchored and dropped the inflatable Zodiac off the stern where it remained tethered for the duration of our stay.

We had strict protocols, including no touching of the wild dolphins. Any physical contact would be left to their discretion. Even in 1987 we were aware that some dolphins were susceptible to human diseases and infections and did not want to be responsible for any such transfer.[13] Captain Smith recently told me that on current dives they do allow touching. However, most dolphins do not like it, and he recommends that swimmers gently permit the dolphins to come to them. Most of our encounters involved entering the water with these magnificent animals, but on a few occasions, we attempted to communicate mentally while remaining aboard our floating vessel.

One thing we soon learned was that, while inquisitive, the dolphins would continue on their way unless we engaged them very quickly. Therefore, we kept our masks and fins where we could grab them as we jumped overboard. Once in the water we would don the equipment; that activity was usually enough to attract the dolphins close to us. While we brought scuba gear along, taking the time to put on tanks was out of the question as the dolphins departed if not engaged very quickly.

The response of the dolphins to our physical presence was amazing. Often, they would circle the swimmers while spiraling upwards or downwards. Some would come very close, zipping by at a range of a few inches. Remember, these animals were six-to-eight-feet long and weighed several hundred pounds.[14] Known for their echo-locating capabilities, they would appear out of the deeper waters and, demonstrating exquisite accuracy, glide by us, twist, and dive again. This would continue until they tired of the antics and resumed their daily hunt for fish. While absolutely exhilarating, the best we could determine was that the dolphins were willing to play with us for short periods of time. That told us nothing about whether or not communication was actually occurring.

We all agreed that the following afternoon, when dolphins came close, we would remain in the boat and conduct a controlled experiment. Jan initially sensed that part of the pod was a considerable way off. It was around 4 p.m. when she sensed the dolphins were approaching from the northeast. Thus alerted, we began visually scanning the horizon. Within a few minutes a pod of about six Atlantic spotted dolphins could be seen rolling in from just to the right of the bow. While coming in our general direction, their projected path would take them in front of the bow. When they got close, Jan sent a mental message to change direction and go toward the Zodiac located to the stern. Abruptly, and in unison, the pod made about a 60-degree left turn and headed south toward the inflatable raft. That was interesting, but hardly definitive.

As the dolphins swam under the raft they began to exit the scene and were about 100 meters away when another message was mentally transmitted. Telepathically, Jan requested that they circle back and return to the Zodiac. That required the dolphins to make a 180-degree turn, something that would not be expected if they were simply following their traditional hunting pattern. Sure enough, within a minute the entire pod turned and circled back to the craft. Once there, they mentally were asked to make an additional 180-degree turn. The pod obliged, then continued their temporarily interrupted journey to the southwest.

It was the consensus of our group that the actions taken by the dolphins clearly indicated that they were responding to the telepathic communication sent by Jan Northup. That was based on their completion of the three separate instructions that had been mentally transmitted. Two of the turns made required them to turn completely away from the direction they had been heading. We also took that to mean that this pod had voluntarily chosen to cooperate with the experiment. While inferring motive to the actions of another species is inherently controversial, it seemed reasonable in this case as there was no physical enticement employed to obtain their cooperation.

In addition to our open ocean adventure, we conducted telepathic communications experiments with dolphins held in captivity at a dolphin show on Galveston Island, Texas, near the Gulf of Mexico. Again, working with Jan Northup as the sensitive, Scott Jones designed a series of tests that strongly supported the evidence for interspecies communication employing only mental transmissions. The results were indicative of a precognitive capability as well.

Using a circular holding tank, signs were posted roughly indicating the cardinal directions: north, south, east, and west. Having not seen the facility before the date of the experiment, Scott made some educated guesses about their layout. The cardboard signs with a large single letter indicating direction were positioned facing the inside of the tank. In each case, a single dolphin was in the pool and two observers were located so that they could record the actions of the dolphin. While the observers knew to look for the responses of the dolphins, they were totally blind to the content of the instructions.

Before arriving, Scott wrote out six sets of relatively complex instructions. For example, one might be go to west, circle the pool twice counterclockwise, and end at north. The six sets of instructions were then placed in opaque envelopes and sealed. The envelopes were then shuffled and eventually numbered from one to six. Jan was not privy to any of the written instructions, and Scott did not know which set of instructions was in any given envelope.

To begin the experiment Scott would roll one die. The number that came up would be used to select the envelope. Jan alone would open the envelope, read the set of instructions, and then telepathically transmit them to the dolphin. Amazingly the dolphins correctly executed five of the six sets of instructions, though one had to be modified. Scott had anticipated the tank would be in a completely open area. As it turned out that there was a metal ceiling located a few feet above the tank.

The modification came when the instructions included leaping twice at a certain post. Jan reported that the dolphin sent her a message that such jumping was out of the question due to the unanticipated physical constraints. In fact, she told me that the dolphin instructed her to "look up." Recognizing the problem, they mentally agreed that a bobbing motion at the specified site would suffice.

The precognitive aspect came with the final envelope. Before Jan could open the envelope, the dolphin began a routine. Upon completion, it was determined that the actions taken by the dolphin matched those in the sealed envelope.

Dolphins were not the only species with which I encountered some form of controlled interaction. In 2015 Victoria and I traveled to the Kingdom of Tonga, which is about the size of Texas, although only about two percent of the island nation is dry land. That is about one third the size of tiny Luxembourg. These isolated islands are east of Fiji and about 1,100 miles northeast of New Zealand. Flying from Nadi, Fiji, we spent the night near the capital, Nuku'alofa. The following morning, we boarded a Chinese made twin-engine passenger plane for another two-hour flight over open ocean to the northern island group of Va'vau. It was there that we would encounter the largest of all mammals, humpback whales, in their natural aquatic habitat.

This amazing adventure focused on diving with the whales, mostly in open water hundreds of feet deep. This area of the South Pacific is a natural calving area for the humpback whales that migrate north each year during the harsh Antarctic winter. And Tonga is one of the few areas in the world where humans can actually get in the water and swim with them, an experience that is ineffable. For perspective, adult humpback whales average 40 to 60 feet in length and weigh as much as 44 tons. Obviously, any small miscalculation, on either the part of the swimmer or the whale, could have catastrophic consequences for the human.

Swimmers within a few feet of Humpback whales. At times, we were even closer, just inches away. They seemed to know exactly where we were. Kingdom of Tonga, August 2014.

We were privileged to have our expedition led by Darren Jew, a professional photographer and one of a handful of Canon Masters. He has amassed an extraordinary collection of underwater photos featuring these magnificent creatures and expertly guided us into position for shots that are unbelievable.[15] Assisting us on the dives was a spirited young British woman, Sonia Bungaroo Valdez, who has now unfortunately chosen to seek refuge on dry land in London. With her help, Victoria, a non-swimmer, was able to step off into seemingly bottomless water with adequate floatation gear and see the whales in action.

We entered the water six of the seven days we were there. The people of the kingdom are very religious. Therefore, on Sunday, by Tongan law, no sporting activities are allowed. Caution is also taken to avoid any operations that might be deemed as harassing the whales, especially the calves. Diving protocols were strictly adhered to, and only a limited number of swimmers were allowed in the water at any given time. Most of the time we located the whales in blue water, meaning it was very deep. Much as in the whaling movies, each day we would scan the ocean in search of the telltale waterspout as the whales came up to breathe. Once spotted, we would dash toward the area and try to determine if the pod was moving or stationary.

In general, we found the whales traveling in threes: a mother, her calf, and the male escort. When possible, we would drop into the water ahead of the whales and film them as they came towards us. It was clear they were aware of our presence as they would either turn a few degrees to the side, or dive deeper under us. At times, we found them just hanging out, but at depths well beyond free diving capability, some 90-100 feet down. Hovering directly above them, we floated, observed their actions, and listened to their songs as they communicated. The calves needed to breathe more frequently than the adults. It was fascinating to watch them approach the surface, then maneuver around us to a clear location. The calf would blow and breathe, then dive back to its mother's side.

During the week, we used several different vessels. One incident stands out while we were using Monkey Man, a 10-meter rigid inflatable craft with twin outboard engines. We had been diving periodically most of the day and were headed back to the docks at Neiafu, the second largest city in the kingdom. As we entered the outer islands from the open ocean, we were suddenly surrounded by a pod of seven humpback whales, each one longer than our craft.

The action was quite frantic as the whales cavorted in close proximity to us. I decided to stay on board and photograph the unfolding events. Using both my Sony Handicam and the Nikon still camera, I followed the action as best I could. Several other divers entered the water and were quickly absorbed in the fray. It was absolutely amazing to experience. As the whales swam about, frequently diving directly under our rubber boat, it was clear they knew exactly where we were. In fact, at times their flippers came within five or six inches of the inflated canvas gunnels.

It seemed obvious that they had decided to interact with us, or at minimum allow us to participate with what appeared to be an exuberant party. Being larger than our craft, they could easily have flipped us over, yet they seemed to take great care with their actions. Diving and rolling next to our swimmers, they avoided physical contact that could have caused serious injuries. Our guide, Darren Jew, exclaimed that this was highly unusual behavior—he had never seen such interactions.

It should be acknowledged that guides from some whale watching cruises have noted that young whales often seem to be interested in their clientele. At times, they get close enough to allow the passengers to reach out and touch them. However, there are only a few areas in the world where swimmers are allowed to enter the water with them. Also, things don't always go well. In March of 2015, off Cabo San Lucas, Mexico, a grey whale breached and landed on a boat killing a Canadian woman.[16] In Tonga we had observed numerous breaches, but none in close proximity.

We have designed experiments for testing the intent of the whales, and to attempt to determine if true telepathic communication can be demonstrated. Unfortunately, we have not been able to locate a sponsor willing to support that research.

Whales and dolphins are large-brained aquatic mammals. In September 2016, I engaged in diving with Great White Sharks off Isle de Guadalupe, Mexico. While I attempted to influence their actions, I found no evidence that they responded. Curious at times, they would swim close to the cage I wisely chose to employ. The only thing they actively engaged was bait. Two weeks later a Great White Shark did get into a similar cage in the same area.[17] Caught on tape, the video went viral. Miraculously, the person in the cage was unharmed.

There does seem to be a special bond between humans and dolphins, which has been reported throughout history. Numerous rescues have been recorded, as have tales of dolphins protecting humans from shark attack. One such response happened off Northern New Zealand in 2004 in which a pod of dolphins prevented a Great White Shark from devouring a group of swimmers.[18]

We know that human-whale interactions have been devastating for the whales, with some species driven close to extinction. It is my personal observation that it is a good thing they don't appear to hold a grudge.

CHAPTER 4
HEALING AND HEALERS

"Your wife's heart may still be beating, but she's not really there. It's too late to save her." Those words were spoken to Anita Moorjani's husband as she lay in a hospital bed in a room down the hall.[19] Moorjani, like so many others, was given a death sentence based on the traditional, materialistic medical model of the world. It is one that fails to take into account the role that human consciousness can play in the healing process. Moorjani actually survived. So have millions of others, healed by both physical and consciousness interventions. For millennia those afflicted with disease have turned to prayer and alternative measures for healing. Sometimes those measures worked. Strongly tied to a patient's belief system, such alternative methods often complement traditional medical practices, but should not be a replacement for them.

There is no doubt that modern medicine has produced wonders. Advances are announced almost every week. Modern medicine has increased life expectancy globally over the past century. Health care systems are another matter, and here the U.S. is falling behind the rest of the developed world.[20] As a combat veteran, I have watched as our ability to save the lives of wounded soldiers has increased dramatically. Just as advances have been made in saving lives, so too have there been phenomenal efforts in the treatment of those survivors, especially with regard to prosthetics and burn injuries. While little good can come from war, improvements in the treatment of traumatic injuries is one area that has yielded benefits. Those advances are then transferred to assist in traumatic injuries in the civilian sector as well.

Health care is one of the thorniest issues plaguing America today. That will not change in the foreseeable future as it has become the ultimate political football. The technological medical marvels come with ever increasing costs. Debate abounds about who should be afforded health care, and what limitations should apply and to which patients. The list of problems goes on ad infinitum.

Expectation for medical care in other parts of the world varies greatly. That is especially true when compared with those in the U.S. or in the rest of the technologically developed world. In America, there is one medical doctor for every 434 people.[21] It is important to note that physicians are not evenly dispersed throughout the country. That is not the highest ratio, and Cuba, a country that has heavily emphasized medicine, has about six doctors for every 1000 citizens. Conversely, in much of developing Africa, there is less than one health care practitioner (not necessarily a doctor) for every 1000 people.

But this is not a book about the problems of health care or about the American health care fiasco in particular. It is about psi phenomena and my firsthand observations. One has but to scratch the surface to find a relationship between psychic abilities and healing. It is part and parcel of the experience. Over the years, I have been privileged to meet many healers who employed unconventional methodologies. Some, like my mentor Elisabeth Kübler-Ross, MD, held medical degrees. Others who practiced alternative methods held no degrees at all. Certainly, most of the shamans we have met had no academic certification, yet they often produced amazing results.

Of necessity people in the undeveloped and developing world have looked to alternative practices for health care solutions. Although deemed primitive by most Americans, it turns out there was a lot to learn from traditional healers. Unfortunately, Big Pharma too frequently has exploited indigenous peoples and their innate knowledge of pharmacology. Biopiracy, as it has become known, began when anthropologists studying remote tribes found them using local plants and herbs to heal their patients. Samples of these herbs and plants would then be transported to American laboratories, so that chemists could determine the active ingredients, put them into a pill, and obtain a patent. The pharmaceutical company then made a lot of money, while the tribes people have marginally benefited.[22]

Alternative healing methods come in a near infinite variety. There are physical interventions such as laying on of hands, diets, use of crystals and other minerals, as well as vitamins and special concoctions. A patient's psychological predisposition is known to be an important element of healing. There are consciousness applications such as visualization of desired outcomes. That may be accomplished by either the patient or a healer. In addition, intercessional prayer is sometime effective. Finally, psychic surgery may be employed, either by a human healer or discarnate one.

While some of the alternatives methodologies will seem incredulous to some readers, that is where the issue of varying belief systems is important to understand. It is also recognized that charlatans do exist who prey on the most vulnerable people. At times, sorting charlatans from well-intentioned alternative healers can be problematic. I have encountered both. Here are some of the alternative healing methodologies to which I have been exposed.

The Bengston Healing Energy Method

It's all about cycling, a mental process in which the healer mentally rotates through a series of self-chosen images having nothing to do with the subject or patient. Scientifically, that makes no sense. The results, however, are undeniable. Bill Bengston is among the very interesting healers with whom I have trained. The Bengston Healing Energy Method is one of the most researched of alternative healing processes.[23] That is not to say it is understood, let alone accepted by the conventional medical or scientific communities. It should be. Bill, a professor at St. Joseph's College in New York, has provided decades of detailed experimentation on energy healing. As the current president of the Society for Scientific Exploration, he often treats the audience to explicit pictures of mice in various states of affliction with cancerous tumors which are eventually healed.

The process Bill employs is purely a mental one, though sometimes assisted with hands-on healing energy, or the application of other materials. That includes the use of spiritually charged cotton that somehow seems to alter the healing process. None of his procedures involve additional pharmaceuticals, though for legal purposes, he strongly advises people to seek or continue competent traditional medical treatments, even if they also go the alternative route.

Extensive research has demonstrated the effectiveness of Bill's method. It has been tested numerous times, healing mice with mammary cancer and methylcholanthrene-induced sarcoma. Often these test animals have lived longer than expected under normal circumstances and none of the mice treated have later developed cancer. The animal testing is very significant when compared with human results, which are often qualitative rather than quantitative. Simply put, the mice don't know they are subjects of an experiment. As far as we know, they do not have the cognitive ability to form intent to please the researcher. Nor do we think they have the capability to intentionally alter their condition. Unlike humans, the mice are simply recipients of the healing with no conscious interaction with the healer. That eliminates the contentious claims of the results being attributed to a placebo effect.

One of the more unusual means to compliment Bill's healing work is the use of psychically charged cotton. Once obtained, the charged cotton is applied directly to the affected area of the body to either relieve pain or facilitate healing. The instructions suggest that the used cotton be disposed of just as one would do for any contaminated medical product.

There are numerous anecdotes about the effectiveness of using the charged cotton. One comes from my brother who had to undergo surgery in a very sensitive area. After receiving the cotton, he placed it near the affected area. Within a short period of time he reported that the pain and sensitivity had decreased significantly. Another example was a friend who was afflicted with severe cancer of the throat. While he ultimately succumbed to the disease, he used the charged cotton for several months and was convinced that it did make the experience far less painful.

Larry Dossey, M.D.

"Why, I was a medical student at Parkland Memorial Hospital that day," Larry responded.[24] At our first dinner together, Victoria had asked her perennial question, "Where were you when Kennedy was shot?" Somewhat stunned at his answer, Victoria said, "I bet you have been questioned about that many times."

"No," Larry answered, "no one has ever asked me about it." Living across town in Santa Fe, New Mexico, and having many interests and friends in common, we became friends with Larry and his wife, Barbara. Regarding Victoria's question, Larry admitted that his job that day was to hold the phone for a news correspondent who had successfully managed to call his network in New York City and was afraid to break the connection. An observer of the cacophonous confusion at the hospital, and contrary to conspiracy theorists, Larry was sure there had been no prior warning to LBJ, or anyone else in the immediate hierarchy, about the assassination of JFK.

A few years later Larry would become a battalion surgeon assigned to the 173rd Airborne Brigade in Vietnam. Combat was another common experience that we shared. But it was his work in alternative medicine that brought us together in the high desert. Barbara is a nurse who shared many of our common interests and often speaks to nurses in the medical community. Doctors are aware that nurses have more personal contact with patients. Thus, nurses often hear about details that doctor's abbreviated interactions miss, including near-death experiences, pre-death visitations or visions, and similar phenomena.

In his 1989 book, *Recovering the Soul*, Larry coined the term "nonlocal mind," referring to a consciousness that transcends the brain. Nonlocal mind, he wrote, "is a spatially and temporally infinite aspect of our consciousness." It is analogous, he suggests, to what has been described as the soul; a concept often rejected by traditional scientists. There is an inherent conflict between a materialistic worldview and a concept of a consciousness-based, infinite interconnectedness, and the implications could not be more profound. He expanded on the concept in his most recent book *One Mind*.[25]

Larry was also instrumental in researching the power of prayer as an integral part of the healing process. While most healers focus on the positive aspects of prayer and intention, he noted that there could be negative influences as well. The notion of employing negative thoughts is the basis of curses, a topic seen as a hoax by most scientists. (I'll have more to say on the subject when discussing shamans in a later chapter.)

Beyond the inference that thoughts, either positive or negative, can influence healing, Larry coauthored a paper that proposed that intercessional prayer can have a retroactive impact on a patient as well. This paper was based on a signal study by Leonard Leibovici and published in the *British Medical Journal*.[26] The abstract reads, "Leibovici published an intriguing study questioning conventional notions of time, space, prayer, consciousness, and causality. The randomised, controlled, double blind, parallel group study (prayer versus no prayer) included 3393 septic patients and considered the hypothesis that 'retroactive' prayer, offered 4-10 years later, affects outcomes. Of the preselected outcomes, mortality was similar in both groups, yet length of stay in hospital and duration of fever were shorter with prayer ($P = 0.01$ and $P = 0.04$). Leibovici, with humour befitting his style, concluded that remote, retroactive intercessory prayer should be considered for clinical practice."[27]

The mind-blowing significance of this finding is that retrocausality, which has been confirmed in more recent physics experiments,[28] is real. If true, that means the past can be altered. In the case Larry reviewed, it meant that for reasons inexplicable to modern medicine, prayer applied years *after* the patient had fallen ill and recovered, changed the healing process for the better.

Silva Mind Control

"Can I have access to the raw data," I asked. While working on my master's degree at Pepperdine University, I needed to produce a term paper for my courses in Education. Still stationed with the 25th Infantry Division at Schofield Barracks, Hawaii, I devoted all my weekends to studying. Having already taken both the basic and advanced courses, I was convinced that the Silva material could assist in the educational process. My request was sent to José Silva's corporate headquarters in Laredo, Texas. The response was far from what I expected. Not only could I have their raw data, they said, but they asked me if

I would be willing to take over as their representative for the state of Hawaii.

Obviously, that was only a part-time job. It consisted mostly of organizing courses to be taught by qualified instructors who flew in from the mainland. In the process, I learned a lot about José, and the direct relationships his method had to healing. José was very young when he quit school to help support his family. While working in a barbershop sweeping the floors, he asked the owner to complete some extension courses for him. The owner got credit, but José became very knowledgeable about electronics. Drafted during World War II, he tested high in electronic skills and was assigned to the Signals Corp. Though an enlisted man, he was sent to a communications school where most of the other students were officers with college degrees. He understood electronics but was short on formal math qualifications. However, José had found a way in which to sense electronic circuitry weaknesses by touch. Today, we would call this psychic skill psychometry. From that discovery, he made a trade with the lieutenants. They would teach him math, and he would teach them how to locate and fix electronics using their fingers to sense the site of the problem.

It was not a big step from fixing things electrical to the diagnosis of medical problems. What evolved was a process he called Silva Mind Control. That turned out to be an unfortunate choice of terminology. For José, who was altruistically inclined, it simply meant learning to control one's own mind. However, conspiracy theorists took the term to be far more sinister. Furthermore, with nepotism prevalent in its corporate structure, and insistence on keeping the headquarters in the dusty border town of Laredo, Texas, the growth of the Silva Mind Control method was limited, at least in the U.S.

Silva Mind Control focuses on having the student learn how to induce a dominant alpha brainwave state. This is based on a medical discovery, which associated creativity with the alpha frequencies of 7-14 hertz, that was popular at the time.[29] They also trained people to use theta brainwaves, which are even lower and are associated with deep sleep. The Silva Method basically uses self-hypnosis to enter states of meditation and maintain control of your consciousness.

There are several reasons why one might choose to explore the Silva method. Healing is only one of them, and many students have found it beneficial in both their personal life and with employment that rewards intuition and creativity. At the time I worked with them, I never imagined I would be writing any books, let alone one about experiences with spirituality and healing. Regrettably, I did not document either the healings I witnessed nor the many accurate diagnoses that students accomplished. What I can attest to is that the process was successful in many areas, including alternative medicine.

Other Healers

Over the years I have been privileged to interact with a number of other alternative healers. In some cases, I have personally witnessed their results. For example, at a conference in Honolulu, a visibly mentally disturbed woman, the wife of a speaker, kept interrupting presentations by talking loudly, but not in the context of the subject matter. Also attending was the 3HO founder, Yogi Bhajan, who has now changed his name to Harbhajan Singh Khalsa Yogiji. Sitting just a few feet away, I observed Yogiji, dressed in his flowing white robes, quietly walk up behind the woman. Saying nothing, the bearded guru simply placed his right hand a short distance behind her neck. Instantly, the woman fell silent and remained so for the rest of the session.

At that same conference, Sivaya Subramuniyaswami, a Hindu advocate, unexpectedly entered the banquet. His spiritual influence overshadowed the gathering, which included some of the biggest names in the field, such as the author of the then-recently released *Jonathan Livingston Seagull*, Richard Bach. Never again have I literally felt the essence of a room change as happened when Subramuniyaswami joined the dais that evening. Years later I was shocked to learn he had been born Robert Baker in Oakland, California. His impressive demeanor certainly suggested that he was an Indian yogi and reincarnation a real possibility.

At another event, the renown healer Olga Worrall captivated my attention. She was quite frail, and by then her husband, Ambrose, had transitioned. The couple had treated thousands, and their successes were regaled in a number of books. As a scientist, I found the laboratory experiments in which she had demonstrated her prodigious healing capabilities with bacteria in petri dishes most intriguing. As with Bengston's mice, it was impossible for these unicellular organisms to be experiencing a placebo effect

Then there was Hiroshi Motoyama, who is not well known in America although he founded the California Institute for Human Science (CIHS). Located in the coastal desert town of Encinitas, his school attracts a small number of students interested in studying human consciousness. A Shinto priest, Motoyama gracefully incorporates spirituality with the scientific method. Having been the benefactor of acupuncture treatments, I was drawn to his research.

After being shot down in Vietnam, my back and neck have never been the same. Periodically, my neck would stiffen and greatly restrict my ability to traverse from right to left. Surprisingly, it was a unique Army flight surgeon who applied alternative Chinese methodologies and repaired me. Acupuncture was one of those methods. I would not argue with success, but did wonder how the process worked, especially when acupuncturists refer to organs like the Triple Heater, which have no physical correlates.

What Hiroshi Motoyama had done was to develop a mechanical device that could actually measure the flow of ki/chi, the life force that flows through all living things. What he discovered was that they could measure the flow patterns. Further, they found that energy points physically existed on twelve invisible meridians. This was just as Chinese doctors had indicated for more than a thousand years, but here Motoyama produced the proof. Properly placed, the acupuncture needles could manipulate the flow of ki. While Western medicine remains skeptical of the efficacy of acupuncture, Chinese physicians for decades have even conducted open heart surgery using the needles in place of, or with greatly reduced doses of, chemical anesthesia.[30]

The prevailing medical model is that the human body is like a machine. As long as each of the parts functions properly, health is maintained. While some deference is paid to the psychological predisposition of the patient, the importance of nonphysical interventions are generally disregarded. The prevalence of that belief system is not accidental. At the core is the funding of medical schools. Study after study reveals the impact of the pharmaceutical industry with their grants to medical schools.[31] With those grants goes the implied message that the answer to medical issues is using yet more of their products. Similarly, study after study demonstrates that consciousness plays a significant role in the healing process. Unfortunately, those findings tend to be ignored as they represent a significant challenge to science.

CHAPTER 5
DOWSING, HOT COALS, AND MORE

Some of the strange things I experienced over the years were one-of-a-kind events, which often occurred without warning. Still, they seem to defy simple explanations. Here are a few examples.

Perceived Levitation

I joined the U.S. Army as a private in 1956, and after basic training I was assigned to the newly reactivated 101st Airborne Division. That division was the vaunted Screaming Eagles that had jumped into France on D-Day in World War II. After completing jump school, I was selected, based on my test scores, for assignment to the 326th Medical Company. That was an unusual organization, as our company commander was a lieutenant colonel and all of the medical doctors for the division reported to him.

Life in the barracks in the 1950s was very different from what soldiers experience today. As junior enlisted-men we had double-decker bunk beds in platoon bays. That meant about 30 or so men were all housed in the same room. The lights went on and off at designated times and everything was highly regimented and orchestrated by the First Sergeant, who held a rank next to God.

Dining was very different as well. Today, those using the Army dining facilities go to the equivalent of a restaurant that is run by civilian contractors. But in our dining situation, the cooks were assigned to the company and lived with us. There was a "mess hall" for each company, and while the basic menu was determined from on high, everything was cooked in the company kitchen and the variety at any given meal very slim. We could choose to eat what was served, or not eat at all. Older Army veterans may fondly remember their rotating duties on kitchen police, more simply known as KP. That was a group of about five guys, selected daily from a roster, and assigned to assist the cooks. Everyone hated KP duty, as it involved getting up early so as to prepare breakfast for everyone else.

Despite the fact that our mess hall was located in the building we slept in, to enter it you had to exit and come in through the designated external door.

The chow line, as it was called, opened at a specified time and closed on schedule. Troops literally lined up down the sidewalk; gaggles were not allowed. As an airborne unit, physical fitness was a very high priority. Every morning we had physical training (PT) and that often began well before daylight. In addition, there was a pullup bar located in front of the mess hall door. Normally there was a sergeant posted outside the door to keep order. Each man was required to do pullups before he could enter the mess hall. That routine happened three times a day, including weekends.

While I was in great physical shape and could run for many miles, upper body work has always challenged me. Six pullups were a minimum requirement and I could handle that. At eight or ten repetitions, I usually struggled, even after years of practice. Airborne units required full pull-ups, palms out, and arms extended after each one. There were no half curls with legs flailing that you often see on TV.

Since I wanted to eat, I bit the bullet and did my pull-ups three times a day. This had gone on for many months and I knew the routine well. Suddenly, one evening a strange thing happened. As I jumped up to the bar, it seemed as if my body had lost all its weight. At the time, I probably weighed about 145 pounds. But this night I felt light as a feather. Effortlessly I did 18-20 pull-ups in rapid succession and stopped only because others were waiting to get into the mess hall. This appeared to be a change in my physical state, but I have no idea what brought it on. It was a totally unique event and has never happened since. The feeling of weightlessness was so dramatic that I have remembered it clearly for the last half century. The effect was as if I was levitating, but that would not have been noticed by observers. There is no scientific explanation for why or how my physical state could change so unexpectedly—and so briefly—and it has not happened since then.

Fire Walking

The U.S. Army Intelligence and Security Command (INSCOM) Jedi Project was an attempt to learn how experts accomplished their tasks and determine how those skills could be transferred to others.[32] Through a rigorous selection process, INSCOM had very good people with IQs generally well above the Army standard. Our mission was to determine how to take good people and make them better. For that objective, we used Neuro-Linguistic Programming (NLP), which is addressed another chapter.[33]

One of the people under contract to us was Tony Robbins, who would later become a mega-guru in personal development and empowerment. At the time, Robbins was conducting fire-walks in which participants attending his workshops would have the opportunity to walk over hot coals. Since we were already working with him and John Grinder, a co-founder of NLP, we decided to experience the fire walking ourselves. In hindsight, I doubt that any human subject review board would approve such an activity today. This was before political correctness became pandemic, and although we recognized the potential for serious injury, we decided to hold the session.

Historically trial-by-fire has been used to symbolize a rite of passage, often for acceptance as a tribal warrior. In many situations, such as religious ceremonies, there are preparatory requisites such as fasting, mediation, prayer, and even temporary celibacy. What we were about to embark on did not entail any of the prescribed strictures. Being in a hurry, we stopped at a local McDonald's and gulped down a Big Mac en route. Admittedly that was not very aesthetic, but it would call into question the need for the established protocols that religious devotees often follow.

A site was selected near Annapolis, Maryland, well outside the Beltway, where having a fairly large fire would not attract undue attention, or the local fire department. It was on a small farm, at the home of one of the participants who lived in a semi-rural area and who had warned the neighbors about the bonfire that would rage for several hours.

The day had been quite unique for this group of approximately 20 people. That morning, using karate techniques, we had taught novices how to break boards with their bare hands. In the afternoon, we engaged in a psychokinesis metal bending (PKMB) exercise, a process that I discuss in detail in the chapter "Bend, Bend, Bend." Then finally, it was this group's turn to experience fire walking firsthand.

With substantial amounts of wood assembled, we began by starting a large fire. Given the amount of coals that would be needed, it would take a couple of hours to burn down. After starting the fire, we went inside for a mental preparatory process in which issues of fear were addressed. According to those who believe that fire walking is achieved through a mental state, it is necessary to prepare adequately before making the attempt. At the time, we understood the process and were ready to make the attempt. As humans naturally fear fire, and fear was a factor that we wanted to better understand and control, fear is what we discussed. Our process included identifying the mental state change and then, using an NLP anchoring technique, locking that into our consciousness. To be successful, practitioners must hold all thoughts of burning effects in abeyance.

It is important to note that there are serious physical consequences if fire walking is not done correctly. As recently as June 2016, *CNN* reported that more than 30 people were injured, some seriously, in a fire-walking seminar conducted in Texas by the same guide we had that night in 1983, Tony Robbins.[34]

Before the fire-walk, the hardwood fire was raked into a pattern four-feet wide and twelve feet long. That length insured that everyone who attempted the walk would take more than a single step on the coals. The heat that emanated from the glowing coals was a stark reminder that this was for real. In later tests, we used pyrometers and found the temperature levels to be about 1300 degrees F. Each participant would determine whether or not to enter the pit.

One of the fundamental misunderstandings concerns pain management. That is wrong. Pain is not an issue. If fire walking were pain control related, then physical injury would have occurred and just be mentally blocked. Everyone in our group eventually chose to walk across the coals that night. No one received even the slightest burn, and several of us chose to make multiple trips.

There has been considerable controversy regarding fire walking. A popular response has been that there are no burning effects due to what is called the Leidenfrost effect. You will be familiar with this effect if you have ever have seen water strike a very hot pan. What happens is that the water bounces as soon as it hits the heated area. The skeptical assumption is that the body's sweat would produce water and thus serve as an insulation between the foot and the coals. Jack Houck tested that concept by placing thermocouples on the feet of fire walkers. He determined that the wet area stayed under 300° F for less than a quarter of a second before rising rapidly, which indicates there would be no water left for insulation of the foot during the remaining steps on the coals. As I wrote in The *Warrior's Edge*, "temperatures above and below the maximum and minimum for the Leidenfrost effect have been recorded during fire-walks in which no walker was injured."

There are other skeptical explanations. One is that the short duration of the encounter means the contact with the hot surface is too minimal to cause burning. Yet people with very brief contact have been burned. In addition, some people who successfully walked on one occasion were subsequently burned on another. As discussed later in the chapter on voodoo, some individuals manage to maintain direct contact with the fire, or heated rocks, for several seconds or even minutes with no adverse physical effects.

My personal perception is that a distinct mental state change occurs. It is ineffable, thus impossible to describe. Like riding a bicycle, or swimming, you will know it when it happens.

As a final warning, do not try fire walking without instruction from a trusted and experienced leader. The consequences for getting it wrong can lead to serious injury, or even death.

Dowsing

There is much controversy about the efficacy of dowsing. There is no reliable scientific theory that explains how the observed effects occur. That is especially true for remote applications such as map dowsing. To be fair, controlled experiments in laboratories have not yielded positive results. There are, however, many examples in which dowsing has been employed successfully in the field and with great benefit for the dowser or the community.

Over the centuries, there have been countless tales of using willow sticks, or other dowsing devices, to locate underground water sources. The United States Geologic Service claims it is hard not to find water at some depth just about anywhere.[35] While popularly associated with finding wells, dowsing has been employed to find many other substances.

Victoria, Uri, and the author.

Our friend Uri Geller, while best known for spoon-bending, has made a lucrative business out of mineral exploration using dowsing techniques. "Out of 11 clients that have used my services so far," he writes, "four have struck big, another four did very respectably and only three had lacklustre results."[36] I learned of his successful exploits supporting the Mexican state-owned oil company, PEMEX, from an unusual source, a U.S. Customs Agent (Uri later confirmed the story). After being given a Mexican passport and a magnificent pistol, Uri was stopped passing through the U.S. at JFK Airport in New York City. A U.S. Customs Agent, who now lives in my area, confirmed to me the incident and that he had assisted Uri in retrieving his weapon. In addition, he credits Uri with his support in solving what was known as the Son of Sam serial murder cases in New York City. The shooter, David Berkowitz, was arrested and convicted of six homicides. That arrest came after Uri correctly identified his location using a variation of map dowsing.

A personal example involves my brother, Don, a former Metro-Dade County Fire Rescue Department lieutenant in Florida. Firemen often work on a 24-hour shift, which allows them consecutive days off, thus allowing many of them to hold second jobs. Don became an independent contractor and decided to build houses. Such construction requires the builder to know where buried pipes and wires might be located. Often working in the blind, reliable information was not always available. Don's solution was simple; metal coat hangers. Routinely he would take the wire coat hangers and bend them into an L-shape. He then placed the wires into empty Coke bottles, which he would hold instead of the wires.[37] The procedure insured that no one could claim it was the small muscles of his hands that actually created the motion of the wires. Holding one bottle in each hand, he would walk across the land, watching for a reaction. When he passed over the items he was trying to find, the wire coat hangers would spontaneously cross. Marking the spot, he would carefully excavate the area and confirm the location.

Zaboj Harvalik was a physicist who became extremely interested in dowsing. I had the good fortune of meeting him at his home in Northern Virginia and discuss his work with the U.S. Army. During the Vietnam War, finding hidden weapons of the Viet Cong was a perplexing problem. It was well known that there were many people who were traditional farmers by day, and Viet Cong by night. They would stash their small arms and ammunition in a variety of places, often concealing them in commonly frequented places such as in haystacks or under the earthen floors of their homes.

Working with U.S. Army engineers at Ft. Belvoir, Virginia, Harvalik helped construct a Vietnamese-like village that was used for pre-deployment training. Harvalik would train young soldiers in the art of dowsing, and then send them into the Virginia village to find weapons that were dispersed in various hidden spots. Anecdotal reports indicate they were quite successful both in Virginia and in Vietnam. Unfortunately, I have been unable to find any official documentation to support his claims. But I can state that Vietnam veterans, who happen to know about dowsing, believed it worked.

At Harvalik's home was a field that he used for training civilians interested in dowsing. He once told me that if he shielded certain areas of the body from electromagnetic (EM) radiation, the dowsing capabilities would be extinguished. He believed that there was an internal triangulating mechanism that facilitated the phenomenon. That suggests that dowsing is mediated by EM radiation in some unknown manner. While he had done experiments to support that thesis, his assertions seem to be contradicted by those who make claims for the efficacy of remote map dowsing. These are important issues, but they are ignored by traditional scientists.

Chasing Bigfoot

In July of 2015, I had an opportunity to join a small Bigfoot expedition. Headed by James Collier, the expedition's purpose was to obtain film for a sizzle reel to support a television series proposal. While there have been sightings of hairy hominid-type creatures all over the world, there is stretch of land from Eastern Oklahoma through East Texas and down through the Louisiana bayous that records more than its fair share of reports.

Our first stop was in Honobia, Oklahoma, which hosts an annual Bigfoot gathering. That event attracts hundreds to thousands of people, which is many times the normal size of this unincorporated village. On arrival on Indian Highway in the rolling Kaimichi Mountains, we were greeted by a "Home of Bigfoot" road sign. The area is unlike any other part of Oklahoma I had ever passed through. Instead of vast grain farms were lush forests that covered hundreds of square miles. Traveling on foot, I had little doubt that large beasts could be within close proximity without ever being spotted.

Our host was Troy Hudson, a Choctaw descendent with both military and law enforcement experience. Extremely capable, he was very familiar with the woods and had heard many tales of encounters with large hominids that are believed to live in the area. To get to the more remote areas, Troy arranged for us to travel via all-terrain-vehicles (ATVs). Our nights there were spent following logging trails and observing the woods. We recorded some unexplained sounds, but that was the extent of our personal interaction with whatever was out there.

What did impress me was the information provided by our ATV operator. He hailed from Dallas, Texas, where he held a professional position, but he had had such an amazing encounter that he returns to Honobia every chance he gets. In a matter-of-fact tone, he told us about the incident that changed his life. One evening a couple of years prior, he drove his ATV up to an abandoned cabin deep in the woods. Despite the twilight, he could still see objects quite clearly. In front of the cabin was a grassy field that had been cleared of trees. As he stopped his ATV, he saw a figure crouching near the corner of the cabin and only a few meters away. Suddenly, the creature stood and let out a call. When erect on its legs, it stood over six feet tall, he estimated. He took this creature to be a male hominid, covered in dark hair. It was certainly not a bear rising up from all four legs.

The creature's alert was answered by another he thought to be about 100 meters away near the wood line. Situated across the field the ATV operator saw another adult hominid, probably a female, and accompanied by a smaller animal he took to be their offspring.

The sighting lasted only a short period, probably less than a minute, but had profound impact on this lawyer. While sounding dramatic to us, the story he relayed is echoed by many people in the area. Later that evening, as I was walking alone I encountered some local teenagers who often go as a group to see what is happening. Convinced of the reality of Bigfoot, they seemed shocked that I would venture through that area by myself and not use a flashlight.

While our experience in Oklahoma was interesting, it was not nearly as convincing as the encounter we had north of Shreveport, Louisiana. Our guide there was Webb Sentell, a local neuropsychologist, whom I had introduced at the Society for Scientific Exploration (SSE) conference in May of that year which had been held in Rockville, Maryland. The title of his talk had been, "Why does the tree cross the road?" Provocative, his presentation focused on anomalies that he had found in the forested areas in this vicinity: small trees had apparently been physically manipulated by a sentient force. Webb also had evidence of something interacting with materials he placed in obscure locations. Of particular interest were jars of peanut butter that had been opened. That was significant as it would take an opposable thumb to unscrew the lid. His premise was that the local Bigfoot that had done it.

Accompanying Webb, we met some local people who had encountered Bigfoot. But it was our personal experience that was far more telling. We stayed on private land and set up camp very close to a bayou. One tent was located within five feet of the water, and the one I stayed in with movie producer, Chuck Parker, was about 20 meters further inland. Night fell and we heard the enchanting sounds from the chorus of denizens that inhabit the deep swamps. Hours after slipping into our sleeping bags, at about 2:30 a.m., I was awakened to see lights flashing near the other tent. James and his research partner, Kman Miller, were frantically searching the immediate area. Just minutes before something had made a massive roaring sound from just a few feet from their tent. Though separated by the fabric of the tent, they guessed it had originated less than a meter away. James said it was so loud that it physically shook them in their sleeping bags and air mattresses.

Being very hard of hearing, I was not aware of the noise. At night, I always remove my hearing aids. Still, the lights got my attention and I went over to see what the commotion was. At this point the situation got even stranger. The dense wet wooded terrain was replete with spiders. Nocturnal hunters, their webs are everywhere. Surprisingly, most of the webs in the immediate area appeared to be undisturbed. Based on the proximity and volume of the acoustic signal, James logically assumed that whatever the source, it must have been quite large. The conundrum was the lack of physical traces of a large hominid, those that should have been present if this were a physical creature. Yet the incident did happen and certainly got our attention.

The Torture King

Tim Cridland makes a living by demonstrating resistance to pain. He bills himself as "Zamora, The Torture King" and almost daily punctures himself with sharp objects.[38] We met through a set of coincidences. I saw Tim perform at one of Jeff McBride's monthly Wonderground gatherings, where magicians from around the world come to appear before their peers. Intrigued by what I had seen, I contacted Jeff and obtained Tim's contact information. Before I could get in touch with him, I was scheduled to give a presentation at the National Atomic Testing Museum. There, in the audience, was Tim looking to contact me, but unaware I was looking for him.

Having many interests in common, we became friends and remain in contact, even when he is abroad. As Zamora, Tim pierces various parts of his body with long needles, much like meat skewers. I had also watched David Blaine on a television special, *Real or Magic*, as he pushed a single long needle through his arm while Ricky Gervais sat inches away, grimacing.[39] Knowing that was not a trick, I wanted to know how it was accomplished.

During a long conversation at our home, I asked Tim if he was someone who did not feel pain. There are such people; the inherited condition is known as congenital insensitivity to pain or CIP. This can be very dangerous, as some people with CIP have experienced serious injuries, including broken bones, and not realized they were injured. Tim's response was that he did feel pain, but that he processes it differently from most people. After appearing on Stan Lee's television show *Superhumans*, Tim was tested at the Los Angeles Medical Center. An fMRI screening revealed that it is the unique mental processing in his brain that allows him to perform his act. Tim also has extensive knowledge of anatomy and physiology, which is important: he knows where it is safe to penetrate the body, avoiding major blood vessels and critical organs.

There is a religious component to what he does, which he alludes to in his biography. It's based on how he acquired these rare capabilities. Tim performs a brief private ceremony that is not displayed to audiences.

Besides skewering himself, Tim has also explored other dangerous feats. At one point, he learned fire-eating, as well has how to control reflexes when standing on extremely hot surfaces.

The importance of better understanding of pain mechanisms cannot be overstated. Somehow Tim, like a few others, mentally deflects pain and allows himself to engage in activities that seem unnatural. Because of inadequate pain management protocols, Americans are becoming addicted to opioids in astounding numbers. If, as Tim has suggested to me, these skills can be learned, it would provide critical alternatives to the current pharmaceutical treatment modalities. While the answers so far have eluded medical researchers, this does seem like an area worth considering.

Orgone Energy

Trever James Constable was an iconoclast if there ever was one. When we met at his home in Long Beach, California, he was a communications officer in the U.S. Merchant Marines, serving on ships that sailed between that port and Hawaii. Constable brought a unique perspective to UFOs, which he believed were living entities. But what led me to meet him was not UFOs but his work with orgone energy devices.

The existence of orgone energy was hypothesized by Wilhelm Reich in the 1930s. Reich, an Austrian psychoanalyst, was renowned for his work on human sexuality. Reich claimed that this energy system flows freely around the earth and can be tapped into and used for health benefits, weather modification, and other applications. Reich invented orgone accumulators and made claims about their therapeutic capabilities. The response from conventional science and medicine was harsh and led to his arrest and an eventual jail sentence. Reich died in prison in 1957.

Today few Americans remember him or his research. Even those people who were alive in the 1950s are not aware that not only was he convicted of a crime, but the courts ordered his materials destroyed and his books burned! What made that so significant is that we had just come out of World War II in which Nazi book-burning was widely condemned for suppression of free thought. Yet, here it was happening in the U.S.

Having heard of Constable's research, I was most interested in his weather modification experiments. According to Reich's theory, orgone energy had some unique characteristics. While seeking homeostasis is a norm in most energy systems, he claimed that orgone flowed from low potential to the higher potential. There was also an affinity for attraction to water sources. The orgone weather modification systems consisted of a series of long tubes, usually anchored in water.

Constable showed me the system he had at his home. But of more interest were the experiments he conducted while sailing. The videotapes he gave me were very convincing. As the communications officer, he had a lot of free time and the ship's captain approved of his efforts. What he repeatedly demonstrated was the ability to create rain—and do so in specified locations. For example, as his cameras panned the entire cloudless horizon, Constable would say that he would create showers off the bow. The ship would then sail into a series of small rain storms as they proceeded forward. Another sequence showed the panning of a cloudless sky followed by a declared intention to develop rain off the starboard side. Within minutes, clouds showed up—and only off the starboard side—followed by rain, exactly as he had predicted it would.

He also claimed that orgone guns could be used to block prevailing weather systems. He established that quite persuasively with a land-based system. In that demonstration, he filmed clouds moving with the standard west to east flow pattern for the area. After establishing this baseline, Constable turned on the orgone energy system. Almost immediately the clouds that had been moving toward the cameras stopped their forward easterly progress. Fortunately, within the video frame was a pole with which one could orient the action. The clouds directly in front of the guns stopped their forward motion and moved to the north. But once those clouds were clear of the orgone energy path, they again resumed their easterly flow. It was clear that Constable's system was causing these weather perturbations.

Even if one believes that the orgone systems work for weather modification, there are some major ethical questions raised by their use. Most of us who have observed the process think the weather systems are not really being *created* but that they are being *engineered*. Therefore, if rain is moved to one area to irrigate crops, it is being taken away from another. There are also conventional means of weather modification such as seeding existing clouds with silver iodide crystals or dry ice in order to increase precipitation. Such technology has been used to cause rain to fall early so that a country can manage when it arrives and prevent heavy flooding at a later date.

Because of the implications of major weather modification, there are international treaties regarding how it may be employed. Aware of those constraints, Constable actually filed weather modification documents, especially before he undertook major projects. He did provide me with documentation of such an experiment with systems located in the Salton Sea in southern California where existing weather patterns area well known. Normally the moisture comes north from the Gulf of California, then sweeps north and east, bringing the annual monsoons to Arizona and New Mexico. On command, Constable blocked that weather pattern and moved an unexpected storm to Los Angeles that statistically gets 0 (zero) mm of rain in that month of the year. The recorded television news weather reports expressed shock at the downpour and noted they had not predicted it.

For me the treaty issue became important in 1983, when Constable advised me that he was going to conduct another experiment of that magnitude. Forewarned, as a lieutenant colonel at INSCOM, I asked the people in charge to more closely monitor the weather satellite data before, during, and after his event. That request was denied for fear it might look like the military was involved in the project. The topic of weather modification was mentioned in a U.S. Air Force document projecting technology for 2025.[40] Some researchers concluded that "owning the weather" could be the "ultimate weapon of mass destruction." The evidence I saw for the employment of orgone energy as a means of weather modification suggests that it is imperative that further research be conducted on the concept. Unfortunately, that runs counter to conventional scientific wisdom.

Trever James Constable died in 2016. A leader in contemporary orgone energy research is James DeMeo who lives in Ashland, Oregon.[41]

CHAPTER 6
THE CRYSTAL SKULL

As psychic emanations radiated from the unique object before us, we were totally unprepared for what would follow. Those events, to this day, remain without rational explanation. I could easily discount the story of these events had it not happened to me.

It was early 1983 and Andrija Puharich was his quintessential self. Unceremoniously Andrija informed me that the famous crystal skull had called for me. He went on to note that one didn't ask to see the skull; it beckons those it wants to meet. I'm not sure I even believe the part about being called by the skull, but it was an interesting twist to what turned out to be a most intriguing encounter.

The crystal object referenced was the classic Mitchell-Hedges skull, the most famous of the lot. Andrija instructed that if I wanted to follow up with the mysterious artifact, I should go that weekend to a specific hotel in Toronto, Canada, and wait to be contacted. That was both interesting and convenient as we had just learned about some filmed experiments that appeared to show anti-gravity being demonstrated there. One of the main researchers involved in that project was electrical engineer George Hathaway, who was working with John Hutchison. The application would go on to become known as the "Hutchison Effect," which is the subject of a subsequent chapter. While Hutchison's laboratory was located in Vancouver, British Colombia, Hathaway lived in Toronto, so I could fully justify the trip.

This legendary crystal skull was reportedly found by Anna Mitchell-Hedges when she was a young teenager. According to this narrative, Anna was accompanying her adoptive father, Frederick Albert (F.A.) Mitchell Hedges, on an expedition in what was then British Honduras (now called Belize). F.A. Mitchell-Hedges was a British adventurer of the colonial period. He was not always successful in his explorations, and at one point while looking for remnants of Atlantis, he was captured by the prominent Mexican revolutionary Pancho Villa. It has been suggested that he was at least in part the model for the adventurous movie character Indiana Jones.

The origins of this crystal skull are murky at best. Even those who accept the written version of the skull's provenance widely believed that F.A Mitchell-Hedges actually found the artifact and planted it where Anna would find it. The exact history surrounding the find is vague and very controversial. He claimed the discovery took place on expeditions near the Mayan ruins of Lubaatun in the 1920s. But there are no records of that skull before the 1940s. In his writing F.A. Mitchell-Hedges dubbed the item "the Skull of Doom." It was used by priests, he professed, to will death on their victims, and he suggested that this skull was the embodiment of evil.

Adding to the confusion are investigations that suggest that Mitchell-Hedges bought the object at auction from Sotheby's and that it has no connection to Mayan ancestry. Some researchers note that it is unlike any other artifact that has been found in the broad expanse of Central America's Mayan ruins. Certainly the physical characteristics of the skull raise serious questions about authenticity. Experts note that the typical Mayan hierarchy had their heads elongated and sloping back. This skull has a rising forehead, a feature not associated with the area. The questionable attributes and facts were sufficient to cause Zig Zag Productions to conduct an elaborate experiment for the National Geographic television program *The Truth Behind Crystal Skulls & Crop Circles.*[42] For that episode, they hired a forensic artist to recreate the actual face that would have belonged to such a person. This technique is frequently use to help identify murder victims and add details to archeological finds. What Zig Zag discovered was that the facial reconstruction appeared to be that of a European woman and clearly not a Mayan.

Still, the legends persist. Adding to the mystique of the skull are the stories about the inhabitants of the area. To this day, the extent of the Mayan civilization, which may date back to 11,000 BCE, remains unknown. When traveling in the Mesoamerican area one is constantly aware of mounds everywhere, most of which were actually buildings of one sort or another. As I have witnessed, there are thousands of them and for the most part still unexplored. What is known is that the Maya were highly advanced in education, and well known for the complex hieroglyphs that adorned their monuments. Institutionally they had developed a number of city-states and engaged in commerce and periodic conflicts. The last large Mayan city, Nojpetén, continued to flourish until it was conquered by Spanish invaders in 1697.

Along with general mysticism associated with the Maya was fascination with their famous calendar. In the 1970s and '80s, popular New Age prophecies proclaimed that the Maya saw that the end of time was in December 2012. It was also generally believed that the Mayans had mysteriously "disappeared," leaving behind only enigmatic traces. In reality, the population did diminish after the Spanish came, but they never ceased to exist. As our guide told us repeatedly, "We are still here—just ask us."

It was under this mystical backdrop that we began our adventure. There are several crystal skulls in existence, but this one is unique in complexity. Beautiful to behold in person, it is about five inches high, seven inches in depth, and five inches across. It is quite heavy, weighing 11 pounds 7 ounces. It has clearly delineated zygomatic arches and the orbits of the eyes suggest a connection to the optic nerve rather than the round holes seen in most such skulls. Also, the Mitchell-Hedges version has a detachable mandible (lower jaw), which is unlike all other carved skulls that have been presented.

It should be noted that later scientific analysis indicates that the skull is not of Mayan origin, and that it was professionally polished. That aside, as time passed, legends grew about psychic powers and mystical events associated with the increasingly famous skull. The provenance of the object is not related to the events that would unfold.

It was chilly in the late Saturday afternoon on the 26th of February when we boarded the flight from Baltimore-Washington International Airport. My former wife, Dr. Jan Northup, accompanied me as we dutifully headed north wondering what might be in store. At that point, little did we know that a mystical experience awaited us in Canada.

Sunday morning found the cloudy skies breaking and rays of sunshine peering through. About 10 a.m. the phone rang, and we were instructed to be in the hotel lobby at 1 p.m. There, we would be picked and taken to another, as of yet undisclosed location. Adding to the mystery was that we did not know who would be meeting us. Our guide turned out to be Alan Neuman, an established television producer from Los Angeles.[43] Perhaps his most popular series was *Person to Person,* during which he interviewed such luminaries as Edward R. Murrow, Marilyn Monroe, Frank Sinatra, Elizabeth Taylor, and John F. Kennedy. Not as well-known is the fact that Alan had directed a series called *Inner Sanctum* and had personal interest in exploring psychic phenomena.

Previously, I had met Alan when he was producing a special for NBC attempting to capture metal bending on camera. (The details of that episode are covered in the chapter on spoon bending parties.) Alan was accompanied by an assistant, and he informed us that we would be driving to the town of Kitchener, about 75 miles away. So, in his chauffeured car, we took off across Canadian Highway 401. The trip took about 90 minutes and we conversed about various psychic experiences. We still knew little about the destination or what would transpire.

The white frame home belonging to Anna Mitchell-Hedges was located in a very middle-class area of Kitchener. Vibrant for her mid-70s, she courteously invited our small group into her home. The initial impact was stunning. While we expected to see the crystal skull, to our surprise a variety of museum-quality artifacts adorned the rooms. Frankly, I wondered how such a collection could be safely housed in this area of town with no obvious security. I suspect that her neighbors had little clue as to the value of her assembled belongings.

Also present was a modest, middle-aged woman. She was a medium who worked with Anna and the skull. Regrettably I did not record her name. Soft spoken, the medium began slowly to evoke lengthy messages ostensibly from a spiritual entity associated with this skull. The tone was conspiratorial in nature and provided warnings of dire events that might occur. It should be noted that during that period there were many such messages being delivered and popularized in New-Age literature. We already had heard a plethora of psychic warnings about severe environmental disasters that would soon follow. These messages went on to warn about changes in governance that were not for the betterment of mankind. And there was an admonition about the introduction of mind control technologies that would have a detrimental impact on society.

According to the medium, the mission of the skull was to provide protection and bring salvation for humanity. The claim was that this was one of a group of crystal skulls that, once brought together, would reveal the secrets of the great skulls of Atlantis. Specific information regarding required actions, the medium relayed, would come at a later date.

She then asked if we would like to participate in healing. Jan opted to go first. Standing in front of the crystal skull, which was located a small coffee table in Anna's modest sized living room, the medium placed her left hand on the crown of the object and slowly waved her right hand near Jan's head. Almost immediately Jan collapsed, seemingly unconscious. Standing beside her, Alan and I caught her and gently lowered her onto a couch immediately behind her.

After a short period of time, maybe a minute, Jan opened her eyes. She reported having an experience of hands doing some sort of medical procedure on her mid-section. Within a couple of minutes, having regained full consciousness, she sat up, fully aware of the situation. She described the procedure as a psychic surgery complete with suturing. Of course, there is no way of confirming such an experience as it was almost entirely subjective, except for her apparent physical collapse. From long-term observation, I can report that there was no noticeable change in her medical condition.

But the most significant event was yet to come. While I am normally the observer, rather than a participant in experiments, I agreed to engage with the medium. Though I was not aware of any physical ailments that needed correction, I thought I'd just go along for the experience. Over the years, I have been close to numerous psychic healings and generally remain unaffected. After seeing Jan collapse, Alan, as a precaution, took a position directly behind me with his hands located about two inches from my back.

Anyone who has participated in *trust exercises* will be familiar with how easy it is, when prepared, to catch a person falling backward. These activities are commonly employed in team building sessions led by organizational development coaches in order to gain confidence in the group. From a physics perspective, even if the person falling is very heavy, by placing your hands close to the subject little momentum is built up thus making the transition safe and easy. Alan was strong of medium build and a bit heavier than me so catching should have been simple.

As I stood before the skull, the medium again moved her hands in a slight waving motion in front of my head. Almost immediately, as a reaction to her gentle movements, I noticed a minute shift in balance but nothing significant. Consciously, I decided not to step back and brace myself. My next awareness was lying on top of Alan with both of us on the couch. Unexpectedly and swiftly I had unconsciously fallen backwards. Alan, despite being prepared for such an eventuality, was unable to stop my momentum, which knocked us both over in such a manner and with sufficient force that we landed on the couch. Alan exclaimed loudly, "Alexander, get off me. I didn't know you weighed so much." In fact, I didn't. My weight at the time was probably less than 170 pounds.

From today's standard scientific model of the physical universe, what happened that day was fundamentally impossible. The medium had employed no physical force of any kind. She had neither physically touched nor pushed me. Under normal circumstances, Alan should have effortlessly stopped my backward movement, although he indicated that he had attempted to catch me. It was as if he was not even present. Some unknown force had suddenly knocked us both backwards. I have no recollection of what happened between the time I felt the ever-so-slight wavering and when Alan was pushing me off from on top of him on the couch. I was not psychologically tricked into falling, and such a theory would not account for both of us being physically affected. As indicated, under normal circumstances that event should not have transpired. Clearly, these were not normal circumstances.

Shortly thereafter we got back in the car and returned to Toronto. We discussed what we had experienced but had no rational explanation. What happened seems to be in conflict with the conclusion in the Zig Zag television exposé that the skull "has no special power except the power to captivate us." For the record, we were not aware that any physical healing had taken place from that incident.

CHAPTER 7
THE TRAVELING POLTERGEIST

Poltergeist, or noisy ghost, stories have been around since antiquity. They are often regarded as malevolent, though sometimes benign, and being either lost, trapped, or tied to emotional events from their lives in human form. Of course, traditional scientists tend to dismiss the possibility of unseen external entities creating physical events in our world. However, once you have personally experienced these events, their reality becomes quite clear.

In 1974, I was assigned to the Tropic Lightning Division (25th Inf. Div.) at Schofield Barracks, Hawaii, and married my second wife, Diana. With her came three delightful children, Lena, Mary, and Connor (all pseudonyms) ranging in age from 4 to 12. While Mary and Connor observed some of the events that happened over the next few years, the events seemed to be focused on Lena, the oldest of the three.

Those who have studied poltergeist phenomena state that these interactions often center around a specific individual, often one who has mental instability issues or a teenager entering puberty. Lena would fit the latter category. For the children, there was plenty of emotional trauma and upheaval. Their mother had divorced their father, married me, and moved to the Hawaii. To make matters worse, their father was killed by a drunk driver in a head-on car crash shortly afterwards.

It was after they had been living in Hawaii for about a year that Lena started reporting unusual experiences. By then we were all living in base housing. Scofield Barracks comes with a long history, especially from World War II. The main troop housing area consisted of large quadrangles of red brick construction. Each quadrangle was assigned to a battalion, and I had just left as the company commander of Alpha Company, 1st Battalion 21st Infantry (Gimlets). The Gimlets had been stationed at Schofield since 1921 when they were reassigned after fighting in the Philippine insurrection. During the infamous raid on Pearl Harbor, Scofield Barracks had also been attacked, and up to our time in the 1970s bullet pockmarks from the Japanese strafing could still be seen on the buildings.

Soon, Lena began feeling an unexplained presence in her bedroom. The base-housing we lived in was relatively new, and there was no reason to believe discarnate spirits might be lingering there. Rather, the most likely response was that Lena had an active imagination, which was true. However, Lena kept suggesting that something generally unseen was following her and sometimes would sit on her bed at night. Since nothing physical or serious seemed to be occurring, Diana and I wrote it off as a passing phase.

In 1977, I was transferred back to the mainland, having spent nearly five years assigned in Hawaii. The posting was to Fort McPherson near Atlanta, Georgia. However, en route we would spend several months at the Organizational Effectiveness (OE) course at Ft. Ord, California. With the Pacific Ocean as its western boundary, Ft. Ord then occupied some of the most prime real estate in Central California. Even with fog present almost every day, and knowing a jacket would be needed at some point daily, Ft. Ord was considered to be part of the Army's sought after "Golden Triangle" for assignments.

While I was attending the school, we rented a three-bedroom apartment in the town of Seaside, located just south of the sprawling Army base. Technically, we had an ocean view, meaning that from one small window we could see the waves of the Pacific continuously rolling onto the sandy shore.

It did not take long before Lena was again complaining about invisible visitors. Sharing a bedroom with Mary, Lena told us that periodically during the night she felt as if someone was sitting on her bed. Since they had a night-light in the room, she was sure it was not Mary. Lena told us that whatever the entity was, she was sure it had followed us from Oahu, Hawaii. While Lena did not appreciate having this visitor, at that point it did not invoke fear. That would come later. For now, all we had to go on was Lena's description of what she was experiencing. Whatever was happening, Diana and I now tended to believe her and thought it was more than a matter of adolescent psychological misgivings. Neither Mary nor Connor reported any strange encounters at that time.

After graduating from the OE school, I took leave for several weeks. Upon my return to the mainland, I had bought a GM van that best fit our transportation needs. The large blue vehicle was ideal. It had plenty of room for the kids, swiveling captain's seats up front, and adequate space for all the camping gear and our baggage. It was June 1977, when we departed Ft. Ord heading north and camping through Oregon and Washington before turning east. For over a month, we meandered from one National Park or campsite to another, all of us sleeping in two tents. Some of the highlights included stops at Mt. Shasta, Crater Lake (where snow was still on the ground), and the Great Salt

Lake. At Yellowstone, we watched the geysers and buffalo, then crossed the Badlands of South Dakota, and came down to Mammoth Cave before swooping into Atlanta. No psychic events occurred during the trip. But that soon would end.

In July, I signed in and assumed my duties at Ft. McPherson, located in East Point, Georgia, a part of southwest Atlanta and very close to Hartsfield International Airport. Since there were very few quarters on post, and having a U.S. Army Forces Command (FORSCOM) four-star command on base, housing was at a premium. We were fortunate to find a house to rent on Huntsman Bend, which is located in the suburbs east of Atlanta outside of I-285 and south of I-20 that bisects the metropolitan area.

The house was tri-level, meaning there was a portion lower than the ground floor with bedrooms above it. Except for my long daily commute, the area was great. The tree-covered yard provided plenty of play space and general privacy. The spacious brick house, probably about 20 years old at that time, was well maintained. Entering the front door, there was a good size living room immediately on the right. Directly to the front of the main door was a modest kitchen and a connecting small dining room. Near the entrance to the kitchen were stairs leading both to the bedrooms above and down to a large sunken family or entertainment room. Though separated by a wooden railing, the area in the family room was clearly visible from the kitchen, a point that becomes important in this story.

Not long after our arrival the poltergeist events began again in earnest. Lena said something was staying with her in the bedroom. She described it as a large misty, or cloudy-like, being that generally remained across the room from her. Over a few weeks, as the entity came closer to her, she became increasingly concerned. It seemed that the apparition that followed us from Hawaii to California had now made its way to Georgia. Still, at that point, we had only her description of the presence. No one else in the family actually saw the entity Lena was reporting.

But that changed. One evening Lena, Mary, and I were standing in the kitchen. Connor was known to be in the living room and Diana was upstairs. Suddenly, we heard a fairly loud thud in the dining room next to us. The lights were on and we ran into the room to determine what had caused the noise. There we found a bag of chocolate chip cookies on the floor next to the wall. The bag had been sitting in the middle of the table moments before and there were no humans near it at that time of the incident. Obviously, something—nonhuman and unseen—had picked up the bag cookies and thrown them against the wall.

From a scientific perspective, this event could not happen. For an object to move requires that energy be applied. In this case, there had to be sufficient energy to levitate the bag of cookies and then accelerate it towards the wall with enough force to cover the distance from the table to the wall (about four feet), and without gravity first pulling the object to the floor.

That was not the only instance of an object being thrown without human physical force being applied. Our entrainment area had the usual items—couches, a television set, and beanbag chairs—which were popular at the time. Also in the room was a stereo system. The record player was the standard (for the time), 33 and1/3rd rpms. As with many stereos of the period, there was a detachable plastic cover that could encase the entire playing surface, probably about 18-inches square, four-inches high, and a bit heavier than the bag of cookies previously mentioned.

Again, while we were standing in the kitchen and no one was in the family room, we heard another rather loud crashing sound. At that point, the family room was dark. Once illuminated, we saw that the top for the stereo had been thrown across the room, a distance of about eight feet, as I now recall. As with the cookies, the levitation and throwing of the stereo lid without some physical force being applied is literally impossible. Yet, that is exactly what happened although no one was in that room at the time of the incident.

Lena reported multiple other incidents, but their validity relied solely on her testimony. She often claimed there was that dark amorphous form that seemed to watch her from across the bedroom. She grew concerned because it seemed to be moving closer to her.

The next physical incident occurred a short time later. Atlanta is hot and muggy in the summer, and Lena kept a large fan in her bedroom. It was about 36 inches in diameter and rested firmly on the floor across from her. One evening she reported that the apparition had knocked over the fan, which was running at the time. There were no other witnesses to this incident, but based on our prior observations of physical poltergeist activity we believed her. Note that the fan had run for months without ever spontaneously tipping over. If Lena was correct, and something intentionally knocked over the fan, there was no source of energy that could account for that activity.

In a later chapter, "The Flame," I will address exorcism in a bit more detail. In this situation, I was generally familiar with the process and even carried a copy of the Catholic rites of exorcism in my briefcase. While attributing any priestly qualities to me would be a huge mistake, there were several occasions when I employed some of the basic principles. The bottom line is that they seemed to work. In Lena's case, the entity did not leave but did maintain a greater degree of physical separation.

These events spanned several years and multiple locations. The common factor was Lena. She later married and has not reported any continuance of psychic events. However, the bottom line is that physical events did occur, and there is no conventional scientific explanation that can account for the energy that would be necessary to facilitate them.

What I just described challenges both science and the Christian religion. Of course, most scientists don't believe in poltergeists or evil demons and would tend to reject our observations out of hand. On the other hand, the Catholic Church, which does believe in evil forces, specifically states that the rites of exorcism can only be conducted by an ordained priest. I, therefore, was unqualified by their standards, yet the application of the rites was effective in obtaining our desired result. Trying exorcism without adequate training or support is not recommended. Also note, in this instance I did not perceive that I was going up against any of the big boys, but rather an entity that was a nuisance.

While Lena's encounters were very strange, there was a historical precedence in my family. At a very young age we moved from New Jersey to La Crosse, Wisconsin, and moved in with our maternal grandmother, Mary Bradfield. Her deceased husband, my grandfather, John A.L. Bradfield, had been a very successful medical doctor who was able to buy a three-story house that was more than adequate by the standards of the day. That said, the house always had a spooky feeling to it, especially in the partially furnished attic. We three boys had our bedrooms there.

Due to the sharp angle of the roof, these rooms had sloped ceilings. At night, the incessant creaks and groans could easily set one's imagination ablaze. Also, each night there was near-constant yelling and fighting between our mother and our abusive, alcoholic father. At the time, getting a divorce in the state of Wisconsin was extremely difficult, so we just had to put up with it. Constantly embarrassed, as children our solution to minimize contact with our father was to get to bed before he returned home and the inevitable conflict began. It was there in the attic that my brother Don had an experience that lies outside the bounds of conventional reality.

What happened was much as Hollywood portrays in houses haunted by evil demons. One night, as Don was falling asleep, he felt the bed begin to move. This was a fairly heavy old wooden bed, so movement of any kind required a substantial force. Soon, the bed began to rise, albeit without any known physical means. This was just like a scene out of *The Exorcist* but more extreme. The bed continued to levitate upward until it approached the eight-to-ten-foot ceiling and was about to crush him. Don resisted by placing his hands on the smooth painted slats. That took such force that it left his hand-prints on the ceiling for us to see. Then, just as it had begun, the bed slowly descended to the floor again.

Shaking with fright, Don leaped from the bed, ran from the room, and bolted down the steep stairs to the second floor. It took more than a week before he could be convinced to return to his assigned bedroom. This incident raises questions that are impossible to answer. Why did it happen? Why only at that time? Why did it happen to him, and not to me or our younger brother? Was there a purpose to it (as there was no physical damage done to him, the bed, or the room)? This instance of levitation defies all existing models of physics.

As usual, our father did not believe Don's story about how his palm prints got on the ceiling. But there was a second poltergeist-like incident that almost brought Don undue punishment. This also involved a flying object, a bottle of ink. This was well before ballpoint pens were commonly used. Fountain pens were filled by carefully dipping the point into the bottle, and then a lever was slowly raised sucking the ink into the pen. It was always a potentially messy proposition.

Dr. Bradfield had left us several desks, one of which was a carved wooden secretariat that resided in a small hallway between the kitchen and the living room. The desk held the normal complement of writing instruments of the day, which included a bottle of ink. Though the house was appointed with shiny hardwood flooring, he had also collected several large Persian rugs that could be found in every room. Today they would be invaluable, but unfortunately they were totally destroyed when Category 4, Hurricane Donna hit Islamorada in September, 1960. The rugs are pertinent because of what happened when Don passed by the desk. Without warning or reason, the ink bottle spontaneously flew nearly 20 feet across the room, smashing into the wall, and splaying the midnight blue ink onto both the wall and the carpet below, causing irreparable damage to a Persian masterpiece.

It reminds us of the experience with the cookies in Atlanta. There is no viable scientific explanation for such events. One does have to wonder how many children have been blamed for spontaneously flying objects for which they had no responsibility.

Psychic researchers have suggested a link between emotional stress and poltergeist activities. Our home environment fit the bill. It was fraught with fear instigated by our father. The stress we were living under had to be released and expelled in some way. Poltergeist activity may be a unique but powerful tool to release the constant state of anxiety. As such, it may be a potent coping mechanism but one that is poorly understood.

CHAPTER 8
TRIPWIRE

Move! Now!

"Have you ever known you have to move? Just get out of where you are? Then see the place where you had been lying explode?" The questions came from then-Lieutenant General Robert "Barbed Wire Bob" Kingston during a presentation I made at Readiness Command Headquarters at MacDill Air Force Base in Tampa, Florida. A highly-decorated hero, he had served in combat in both Korea and Vietnam and was awarded the nation's second highest honor, the Distinguished Service Cross, and two Silver Stars. With his multiple tours in both theaters, he had been in extremely intense situations, ones where survival was not assured. But he had survived and was well aware that sensing danger and premonitions were partially responsible for that. The year following my encounter, he was promoted to four stars and became the first commanding general of U.S. Central Command and was responsible for all of our military actions in the Middle East.

Up until my presentation, the meeting had not gone well. Whoever set it up had badly misjudged the general's interests, thus we experienced firsthand how he had acquired the nickname Barbed Wire Bob. When I innocently mentioned that we had paper copies of the briefings, he snapped at me and angrily grumbled, asking if I wanted to take his notes as well. He left the room to answer the phone and was gone for about 15 minutes. I had serious misgivings about what would follow as I was the next presenter.

My prepared topics were on remote viewing and our metal bending experiences at the Army Intelligence and Security Command (INSCOM). To my great relief, his mood changed dramatically and for the better. Based on his personal experiences in combat, these and other phenomena were what he was interested in hearing about. Though somewhat generalized, he did recount how, on several occasions, he had sensed danger and was fortunate enough to react in time. As I recall, I touched on the subject of near-death experiences as a point of common interest as well. As we were leaving, General Kingston inquired if I had a laboratory in which to continue my experiments. He strongly encouraged that work be done to explore the intangible, lifesaving senses that he had encountered.

From my own personal experience in the Mekong Delta in Vietnam, I understood what Kingston meant by his question about the feeling of having to *move*. There had been plenty of close calls. As an example, I can tell you that there is a significant difference between a bullet whizzing by and when you hear it crack sharply. That distinctive crack means the bullet was millimeters, not inches away from your ear. The scientific explanation is that the acoustic wave in close proximity produces a crack, as the bullet goes supersonic. In my case, I'm thankful the Viet Cong sniper tried to take my head off, instead of shooting for my body, which he would not have missed. Unseen in the jungle, and closer than we expected, he actually made a decision that saved my life. An old French-era trench was located a meter away in the forest. Instinctively I dove into it. The sniper's second shot was right on target and kicked up the dirt immediately above me. Though I had been isolated in the trench, with a little help from my artillery friends, we were able to convince that sniper to get out of the immediate area and allow us both to fight another day.

There are numerous stories about the point-men who sense danger better than others. When patrolling in combat the lead person is called the point man. His job is to go first and alert the rest of the troops of impeding danger. Normally soldiers rotate that duty, as it is potentially the most hazardous place to be when the shooting starts. Even so, it is not uncommon for a unit to learn who possess the innate ability to sense danger and avoid getting ambushed. Yes, observational skills and local situational awareness can be learned as well. However, most combat veterans believe that some soldiers have an intuitional ability that exceeds the physical senses of sight, sound, touch, and smell.

In the movies, we sometimes see time depicted as slowing down so that the detailed action is clearly visible. As an example, you might think of Keanu Reeves bending backwards as the bullets slowly fly past him in *The Matrix*. Since then several other films have employed similar computer-generated imagery. In combat, however, there are instances when such time distortion becomes real. A close friend and fellow consciousness explorer, Dr. Cecil B. "Scott" Jones, had just such an experience. Scott was a U.S. Navy carrier pilot flying F9F Panthers during the Korean War. While the United States Air Force (USAF) was contending with advanced MIG fighters in the northwestern sector, the Navy was flying missions on the eastern side of the peninsula. At the time, the Air Force was frequently losing aircraft in what became known as MIG Alley.[44] Almost forgotten today is that during that Korean War, 224 USAF F-86 fighters and many other American aircraft were shot down in that area, mostly by Soviet pilots. That is a far cry from later engagements when American air superiority became a norm. It should be noted that the Korean War was the first conflict in which jet aircraft engaged in air-to-air combat.

The Navy pilots were glad they did not have to contend with the superior Soviet jets. But the North Koreans also had excellent ground anti-aircraft guns. New to aerial combat were their 37mm radar-controlled guns that would predict the flight path of U.S. aircraft with devastating results. To attack targets, the Grumman Panthers with their 20mm nose cannons would fly flack-suppression missions immediately prior to the arrival of the less agile Corsairs, which were laden with heavy bombs to strike the main objectives. Needless to say, these were harrowing missions.

The phenomenon Scott describes took place on one such mission. Initiating his attack from about 10,000 feet, he saw the black puffs of smoke created by the exploding 37mm shells. Suddenly, he was aware of his consciousness being located as if sitting on his left shoulder, an out-of-body experience (OOBE) as he now labels it. Time seemed to slow dramatically. The flack was intense that day, and yet he flew deftly through the dark clouds created by the explosions. Sights and sounds were temporally distorted, enhancing his ability to respond to each impending danger.

Scott and the other pilots flew many such dangerous missions. It required a rapid learning curve. Dramatic changes were occurring in tactics for air combat. They were based on the advances in technology that had taken place since World War II, but had never been tested before. In that environment, Scott and his fellow pilots often flew two missions a day against those heavily defended targets. He now credits his "higher self" for navigating him safely through his combat experience.

Scott said he never told anyone about his OOBE experience until after he retired from the U.S. Navy many years later. That may have been a wise decision. He left the service after his superiors refused to accept his explanation about how he was able to derive specific information regarding a sensitive intelligence target in another area of the world. (That part of the story is covered in the chapter "Psychic Spies.")

As fellow military veterans have learned of my interest in phenomena, many have come forward with personal stories of strange things they encountered during the stress of combat. In several instances, they have described having out-of-body experiences similar to the one Scott relayed. When engaged in intense fire-fights, they said that they left their physical body and would hover above the scene. If you accept that statement as true, there are two possibilities supporting the efficacy of that notion. One is that it provides a vantage point from which they can more clearly grasp the situation. The other is that an OOBE may be a safety, or survival, mechanism. The sense of being out of one's physical body takes away from the sense of physical danger that one is confronted with.

During my deployment to Vietnam, I had operational responsibility for an area of the Mekong Delta near the Cambodian border known as the Seven Mountains. The enemy in that area at the time was comprised of Viet Cong (VC), as opposed to North Vietnamese (NVA), who were concentrated further to the north. While we would engage in fire-fights fairly regularly, we generally did not have pitched battles.

The prime exception to that was the infamous Tet Offensive of 1968.[45] That time my intuition did not work well. There was to be a truce. Previously, truces had been honored by all combatants. Therefore, I thought it was an appropriate time to fly to Can Tho, where my higher headquarters was located, and get some administrative paperwork out of the way. Yes, we had paperwork even in combat. That day a Cobra gunship had sunk a large sampan in the Mekong River, just a short distance north of the regional capital. They suspected it was an arms shipment and wanted to verify the cargo. Since I was qualified in underwater operations, I was asked to make a dive on it to determine what was on board. But it grew late, so we decided to postpone the dive until the following day.

However, January 30, 1968, was not a good night in Southeast Asia. That night, across the entire country, the largest offensive the of the war began. Unlike the large, conventional American units north of us, we had no warning from Saigon. Suddenly awakened in a borrowed bed, I saw green tracer rounds going by the window. American tracer rounds are red. These being green meant only one thing—the VC were already inside the perimeter of the airfield. A vicious fight ensued. If that was how the Vietnamese wanted to celebrate Tet, I'd just as soon they did it without me.

In the Mekong Delta, unlike other areas of the country, it ended relatively quickly, and quite badly for the VC. Despite inflicting heavy casualties on the enemy, we were shocked at their ability for sustained battles in urban areas. That was something we had not seen before. Previously, most of their attacks started at night and usually ended before dawn. Normally in our area, the VC would fight for a few hours, then break contact and disappear back into their homes. Many of them were VC by night and farmers in the day. The Tet offensive was a major turning point in the war as we engaged VC units of unprecedented size and capabilities.

The following day I caught a helicopter back to Ba Xaoi, the camp I commanded. While nearly every city and village in the country had been attacked, my camp, which was on a hill and not near a city, was spared. Our camp, unlike many Special Forces camps, had not been collocated with political headquarters. The VNA/VC objective was to destabilize the South Vietnamese Government; thus, all those other camps became targets. While we only had 15-18 Americans on the team at any given time, I employed more than two battalions of indigenous mercenaries, Civilian Irregular Defense Group (CIDG). That made my camp the strongest fighting force in the area.

For readers unfamiliar with the Vietnam War, it is important to note that the circumstances of the conflict varied greatly based on time and location. The units we faced in the Delta were very different from our adversary in the Central Highlands, or certainly the intense the battle for Hue. That is offered only to alert people who think the movie version of the war was what everyone there encountered. This backdrop is provided to make sense of the situation I will now describe.

The VC we faced fought in an unconventional manner. To that end, they relied heavily on mines and booby traps. These were precursors to the improvised explosive devices (IEDs) that we have heard about in the wars in Iraq and Afghanistan. The VC would use anything they could find to make their devices. However, many of the ones we encountered were unexploded American ordnance, mainly the remnants of cluster bomb units (CBUs).[46] These CBUs were submunitions that contained round metal pellets that would have a devastating effect on a human body. The CBUs were dispersed out of larger bombs, called the CBU-75, or Sadeye, and were scattered widely in the target area. They were designed as antipersonnel systems to target the VC in areas where they were not well protected.

During the war, the USAF indiscriminately dropped millions of these bombs. The problem was that a substantial number of the CBUs did not explode on contact with the ground. The VC would collect the unexploded CBUs and reconfigure them with a new firing mechanism. They were also very good at hiding these booby traps, sometimes within a few meters of the main camp. The VC also employed their devices in areas that they suspected we would be patrolling. On one operation alone, three of my sergeants were wounded by these devices. All survived, but one lost his leg; he was standing immediately next to the grenade held on a stick just about level with his calf.

My distinctive intuitive experience occurred several months later. We were on patrol in the thickly wooded transition zone that rose up from the ubiquitous rice paddies. It led to Nui Gia, a mountain that was one of the most contested pieces of real estate in the area. The dominant rocky terrain afforded the VC areas where they could hide and operate safely. It was the same general location from which the sniper incident, described previously, took place. Caution was mandatory when traversing this territory as the VC always had access to it, while we did not. Concerned about what was developing in front of me, I was slowly backing up when I froze instinctively. A lieutenant from the Vietnamese Special Forces who was near me started yelling. We had entered a mined area. In my case, the tripwire from a mine was in contact with the back of my left boot. Worse, I had already put tension on the tripwire and begun to extract the trigger mechanism. Had I continued even a few more millimeters, it would have detonated.

To this day I cannot explain why I stopped moving at that instant. I just did. That intuition saved my legs and quite possibly my life. But more importantly, this is not a unique story. If you ask almost anyone who has been in direct combat, you will hear of similar events. The challenge for science is to explain the mechanisms involved in these lifesaving experiences. The military too has a challenge—they must recognize the authenticity of intuition and find a way to teach it to everyone they will be placing in harm's way.

CHAPTER 9
PSI AND THE MARTIAL ARTS

For more than six decades I have been involved in martial arts of one style or another. Most of them concentrated on physical fitness and pure fighting skills. Those are not the focus of this chapter. The martial arts of interest here are those that have elements that seem to defy conventional wisdom and science as well.

Aikido

The elderly Japanese man smiled when I collapsed instantly onto the wooden floor. He had delivered the move with a deft downward flick of the wrist, small fingers striking near my neck behind the clavicle. It was not physical force that had dropped me, but I sure wanted to find out what it was.

The scene was an auditorium in downtown Honolulu, Hawaii. Most people in attendance were of Asian descent, many of whom were Japanese. The attraction was the appearance of Koichi Tohei, 10th Dan,[47] at the time an heir apparent to Professor Morihei Ueshiba,[48] the progenitor of Aikido. This was one of Sensei Tohei's rare excursions outside of Japan, and anticipation of his martial arts demonstration was palpable. It was already apparent that a divergence in philosophy would split the school, but this master would dominate the future, and adherents of aikido wanted a firsthand experience with him. They would not be disappointed.

As the name implies, aikido employs the use of ki, or chi, as it is called in other languages. This energy is considered to be the essence of life and flows through all living things. It is the principle upon which acupuncture is based. Important to the martial arts aspect, it can be projected beyond the physical body. Equally significant is the concept of centering the One-Point, which means mentally placing one's center of gravity at a spot about one fist below the belly button. With all movements flowing from that point, the accomplished aikido practitioner can do some amazing things.

My executive officer, Lt. Rich Haake, had introduced me to this martial arts discipline, which had been adopted by some Hawaiian police departments. Rich was also a Special Forces soldier, and possessed an inner strength I rarely saw in fellow officers. He, like his father, a captain in the police department on Maui, were native Hawaiians. While the ethnic Hawaiians tend to be physically large people, those from Samoa are huge. At 5'8" in height, and about 250 pounds, one Samoan sergeant who worked for me was considered to be a runt at home. While I was stationed in Hawaii, an international tug-of-war contest was held on the Big Island. Each team could have six people, but they could not have a total weight of more 1800 pounds. The Samoan participants had trouble getting five people and staying under the weight limit.

Why was aikido important in this setting? When drinking, which was very common, the Samoan community tended to become rather boisterous and feisty. That often led to police intervention. Looking for an effective and safe means to handle large, noncompliant individuals, the department came upon aikido. Uniquely, this martial art has no offensive moves but takes advantage of the offensive moves by the aggressor. It also relies on a lot of wrist locks, which, while effective, are fairly benign and a great pain-compliance tool. Rich had taught me a bit about the basics, such as the unbendable arm, and centering the One-Point. Still, I wanted to learn more from the master, and this opportunity was very unique.

During the first segment of the demonstration, I saw Tohei do things that might be considered physically impossible. He was not a large man by any standard. Yet, he invited several bigger men to join him on the stage. Mentally focusing his One-Point, he dropped his center of gravity and asked the men to push him backwards. Try as they might, he remained unmoved. It was not as if he was actively resisting; he just stood there calmly, unmovable. He then sat in a gray metal folding chair, the kind you often find at outdoor events. He raised his feet and sat cross-legged in the chair. Again, he asked the men to push him over, and again, they could not.

That demonstration was of particular interest to me from a scientific standpoint. Mentally lowering the one point while his feet were planted on the ground was one thing. But, in this demonstration, he was not in contact with the floor, thus from a physics perspective he was not in control of the center of gravity. If you take a vertical object and push on it at an elevated position, it is easier to move. That is simple mechanics. Yet somehow, Tohei was not moved.

He then invited several aikido black belts to attack him on stage. And just like in movie fight scenes, he was able to counter them all. But unlike what you see in the movies, Tohei was throwing people without any physical contact with them. The process involved raising their center of gravity and using their energy against them. He also demonstrated the use of a jo, or wooden staff. Tohei was able to project ki through the jo and affect the person attacking him. His very impressive moves defied gravity and inertia. From a scientific perspective, and allowing that ki exists, how can a bodily force be transmitted through the jo?

Later in the seminar, he placed one member of the audience on his back, face up, across two men on their hands and knees. Tohei then made a quick movement that he claimed aligned ki so it would flow linearly throughout the person's body. Next, he had three men, each well over 200 lbs., sit together astride the prone man's exposed stomach area. The person never moved despite the weight resting on him. What impressed me most about this demonstration was that I was the person with more than 600 lbs. sitting on me. It was as if those men sitting on my stomach area seemed weightless.

After that demonstration, we started exercising in the auditorium. The move described at the beginning of this chapter was provided by a kindly old Japanese man who had been practicing aikido for several decades. He was about 5'6" in height and could not have weighed more than 120 lbs. He made no rapid moves, nor did he use physical force such as punching. Patiently, he showed me wrist locks, much as Rich had done. Having previously broken bones using hard martial arts forms, including Taekwondo, I found the flowing movements of aikido very appealing.

In time, Rich would tell me about a few very advanced aikido skills, some of which defy accepted scientific principles. One involved using a round bamboo bokken as if it were a sharp sword. With it, the master would slice through rice paper like a razor without shredding it to pieces. The most amazing description was using one's mind to stop flowing water as it fell from above. Rich stated that when the water fell in chunks, instead of continuously, the master would quickly pass his sword between the chunks of water so that it emerged dry. While everyone knows that water flows in a stream and cannot be interrupted by thought, that is exactly what appears to happen. He also mentioned that *dim mak*, also known as *the death touch*, was whispered about in the upper circles. He believed it to be real, but it was never a topic to be made public.

I also learned about the healing aspects ki. Near the end of World War II, Tohei had been sent to China as an infantry leader. He found that adequate medical assistance was not available for his unit. Having already begun training in judo and aikido, Tohei began exploring the use of ki to heal wounded soldiers. From that wartime experience, Tohei would create Kiatsu, a healing art, using the same energy source used in fighting. The technique involves mentally projecting ki through the fingers and into the wounded area. It is based on the notion that the wound has interrupted the flow of energy and can be rebalanced with this method. Personally, I have found this useful on many occasions, particularly in treating headaches in others.

Qigong

Another extremely interesting demonstration I witnessed took place at the 2001 meeting of the Society for Scientific Exploration near the University of California, San Diego. The complex experiment used qigong masters to demonstrate that physical responses to the remote application of ki/chi were possible and verifiable.[49] In this case, the qigong master who would apply the force was located on the fourth floor of the building. The recipient was located on the ground floor at the opposite end of that building. Instrumentation ran through a middle office in order to record and time synchronize both the application of chi by one master and the physical response in another master. The setup was such that there was no possible communication between the two masters at the time of the experiment.

Demonstrated was a detectable biophysical response being transmitted over a distance of several hundred feet and through various layers of building material. Both qigong masters were instrumented during the experiment, and the results seemed to be instantaneous, or at least closely correlated within a second.

There were other demonstrations involving students interacting with their teachers, known as sensei. Several were quite underwhelming, but offer useful examples of what to watch out for. These included a master ostensibly projecting ki and impacting their students. But, since they were in visual proximity of each other, it seemed clear that the students were simply responding to the master's movements in an anticipated manner. Just keep the sensei happy and you'll do fine.

Other qigong demonstrations deserved more attention. They took place in a gym and involved the sensei projecting ki through an opaque object and generating significant physical effects on the recipient. By that I mean physically knocking them backwards, or in some cases to the ground. While the previously mentioned experiment involved biophysical responses that were detectable by sensitive electronic instruments, this entailed clearly visible effects on a macro-scale. Placing cameras in a position where both the sensei and the target could be viewed—*though they could not see each other*—the causal relationship between the action and impact was clear.

Advanced martial arts take into account the use of energy systems that are not generally accepted by modern allopathic medicine or traditional scientists. The Asian origins of qigong date back more than four millennia and are based on the concept that there exists a flowing life energy circulating throughout the body. Although it is not a unique idea, it has not been explored by Western scientists. Qigong practice often involves breathing and meditation, while it acknowledges the relationship between matter, energy, and spirit. In reality, qigong is far more than a martial art discipline or a healing method. It also is a philosophy that can be integrated into one's way of life.

Many varieties of qigong have evolved over time and have been incorporated into several religions such as Buddhism, Daoism, and Confucianism. Qigong's popularity in the West largely can be attributed to the entertainment industry. David Carradine's character, Kwai Chang Caine, in the hit television series *Kung Fu*, greatly enhanced awareness and interest in these arts. Since then many movies have been made with qigong derivative arts. Unfortunately, they tend to emphasize violent martial arts applications and totally miss the essential underlying philosophical basis of qigong.

There have been periods throughout history in which governments have sought to suppress the practice of qigong and tai chi. The concern appears to be that, as practitioners learn about a universal flow of energy, they would be harder to control. That did occur in mainland China from the time of the Cultural Revolution until recently. However, the art forms always manage to survive, and these practices are spreading globally.

On several occasions, I have had the opportunity to observe very sophisticated demonstrations of qigong. The performances often include extreme acrobatics, ones that require great skill. Of most interest to me have been acts that seem to defy what we know of physiology or the laws of physics. One that got my attention involved a traveling troop from Taiwan who lifted heavy objects in a most demanding manner. With large hands, some basketball players can hold a ball from the top without dropping it. That requires both long fingers and sufficient strength with which to grip it. The Chinese qigong demonstration I refer to exceeded such control by a wide margin. The performer took two large, multiple-gallon liquid containers and successfully lifted them with his hands placed only on the top of the jars. Whatever they contained—maybe small brightly colored plastic balls—they were probably light. But it was the ability to raise the items that should have been effected by gravity that was impressive.

Also impressive are feats involving metal spears and swords. One event that has been demonstrated on television includes placing the point of a spear against the throat and the moving forward so that the spear bends and does not penetrate the throat. I have seen that demonstrated several times. While visiting the Beijing branch of the Shao Lin monastery, I both saw that performed and had a chance to try it myself. While the point of the spear was not very sharp, it was still capable of perforating the body. With minimal training, I was able to bend the spear without injury to myself. This is not recommended for novices who have not been involved in martial art forms generating ki.

Hammering Hank

My first martial arts instructor came from a unique military background. At the end of World War II the death penalty was carried out by hanging, a technique that actually had a specific skill identification. Command Sergeant Major (CSM) Henry Slomanski had been one of those assigned to execute some of the Japanese who had been convicted of war crimes. When we first met, "Hammering Hank," as he was nicknamed, was the senior noncommissioned officer at the 101st Airborne Division Jump School. In 1958, fresh out from graduation at Ranger School, which brought a promotion to sergeant, and at only 20 years of age, I was selected to join the Airborne School cadre and wear the dreaded black jacket.

Of course, the only thing I would say to Slomanski was "Yes, sergeant major," or "No, sergeant major." Even before my assignment to the school, I, like everyone else on the base, had heard of the karate legend. He had been stationed in Japan for several years and taken up the chito-ryu style of karate. He rose through those ranks to become the highest-level Caucasian ever to win the Golden Fist award at that time, and be authorized to test and promote black belts. His acclaim came from an infamous match in which karate students fought, full-contact, in a round robin with only the winner advancing. As a foreigner, he initially did not garner a lot of respect from the other fighters. The match lasted two days, and Slomanski kept winning. In the end, after defeating more than 110 opponents, he won the tournament. With that came recognition of his amazing fighting capabilities. In 1956, he was named the International Commissioner for Karate by his Japanese counterparts.

Later, in 1960, it was CSM Slomanski who would promote Elvis Presley to his first-degree black belt. For the record, Elvis had an excellent reputation, both in the Army and in karate circles. It was under Slomanski that I started training, and acquired a fair number of bruises. It was during discussions at the Airborne School that I learned about his training as he had advanced through his black belt levels. He spent a year studying anatomy and physiology, just

80

to understand the effects of blows. His master also required him to take up painting and floral arrangements, as a means to better understand the philosophy behind the art. That is something I have never heard from any American martial arts school. From the beginning of my training, it was made clear that the mental aspects of martial arts were more important than the physical ones.

In a most interesting turn of events, Slomanski, upon his retirement from the U.S. Army, entered the Maranatha Eastern Orthodox Bible Seminary, and later became an ordained minister in the Eastern Orthodox Church of the East and earned a doctor of theology degree. For seven years before his death in 2000, he served patients and staff at New Hanover Memorial Church in Wilmington, North Carolina, and as a chaplain at Henrico Doctors' Hospital in Richmond, Virginia. I mention all this as an indication of the spiritual nature at the foundation of many martial arts.

Guy Savelli

As part of the Jedi initiative at INSCOM, the group pursued several areas of excellence, martial arts being one of them. Along with fire walking and spoon-bending, we had already proven that wooden boards can be easily broken with little training with nothing more than bare hands. There was nothing of scientific significance in striking boards as it was purely a matter of concentrating energy in a small area. It was the mental aspect of convincing novices that they could do it that was important.

However, we were aware of advanced martial arts skills that were more challenging, both from the standpoint of application and results. From Special Forces members from Ft. Bragg, North Carolina, we learned of a black belt who was teaching remarkable skills; his name was Guy Savelli. Based near Cleveland, Ohio, Savelli primarily practiced Kun Tao karate but was also trained in Shotokan, Tai Chi, and Goshin Jitsu Kyo Jujo. In addition, he was conversant with the concept of psychokinesis (PK), and believed PK was involved in many of the advanced martial arts effects. That is what we believed was important and needed to be studied.

We were able to train with Savelli for a few days, and what we observed was compelling. There was no doubt he was a real deal, not one of the commercial martial artists who are all show but short on delivery. Savelli had been tested at several university laboratories, and the anecdotal evidence supported his conjecture about use of PK as a primary source of energy. We learned several skills that suggested that there was a mental component to striking a designated target that went beyond convincing the student they could do it. In generating ki, speed of attack was vitally important. One of our first exercises was to develop a snapping motion that could deliver a blow with amazing power. For that, Savelli set spring-loaded rat traps (not mouse traps). We had to set off the trap and get our fingers out of its path. The consequences for failure could really hurt. Next, we used the same technique to break wooden boards. The actual contact would be initiated with only one or two fingers, not a fist or the knife edge of the hand.

The thesis was that PK energy was being deposited and actually causing the fracturing. In most karate strikes on boards, the hand or foot continues through the object. But in this case the hand was actually being withdrawn as the PK force continues through and breaks the board. Even more difficult was breaking a board that was not secured. Typically, pine boards are held firmly by another person, or lodged against hard objects, when the demonstration takes place. The loose board technique relies on a concentration of energy at a single point. Done improperly, the board will simply fly across the room. Savelli indicated that one must project PK energy to successfully accomplish this task.

One of the lessons we practiced was penetrating an orange using just one or two fingers. That may be safe for you to attempt, but you'll find it is far more difficult than anticipated. The flexibility of the orange provides strength and resistance to penetration. Our work involved projecting ki or PK ahead of the fingers, thus facilitating the penetration slightly before physical contact was made.

Much of our training involved being able to anticipate an attack. The idea was to mentally intercept the intent of the attacker before there were any physical cues, such as a squint of the eyes or the twitch of the shoulder. Quickly, we learned that by the time any physical cues are detected, it is too late to evade the blow. Of course, this suggests that there is a telepathic, or precognitive, aspect to this technique. As I wrote in *The Warrior's Edge*, Samurai warriors had adapted this skill. Their very survival was predicated on knowing what an adversary would do, even if they had their backs to each other.

We also practiced using ki projection to protect our bodies. In that exercise, we would center our attention and move ki throughout the body, mentally making it as rigid a tree trunk. Once prepared, we were struck with a heavy metal pole; it was hollow but still retained great strength. The result, if done properly, was a bent metal pole without damaging the body.

Another of the advanced techniques Savelli showed us he called "The Mind Stops." This was designed for specific situations, such as when you are confronted by a thug with a gun pointed at you. The idea is to mentally block the opponent's mind so that they are not aware of your movement. Saville showed a video of this being done. In it, the assailant remained focused on where Savelli had been standing, while he was able to circle the target and attack from his rear. Although nothing more than a demonstration, it appeared as if the attacker had no perception of Savelli's movement. This is reminiscent of the Jedi Mind Trick popularized in *Star Wars*. Remember: "These are not the droids you are looking for."

Mind blocking techniques are neither new nor unique. There are many stories about their application. One involves Joseph Stalin, who was allegedly interested in psychic phenomena. He had invited a famous Russian psychic, Wolf Messing, to visit him in the heavily guarded country home. But Messing had to enter the house without getting caught by the guards. Reportedly, Messing had a mental projection technique that could cloud the minds of observers, thus creating a real cloak of invisibility, as seen used in the Harry Potter movies. Messing supposedly convinced the guards that he was really Marshal of the Soviet Union, Lavrentiy Beria, the head of the secret police. While not known in America, Messing's mind reading and prognostication capabilities frightened both Hitler and Stalin.

It was yet another skill that most fascinated us. We heard that Master Savelli knew how to apply *dim mak*, also known as the quivering palm or death touch. This was the same technique that Rich Haake had told me about years before. The interest in *dim mak* from a military perspective is obvious, yet it has not been aggressively researched.

During our training with Savelli, we were joined by two senior Special Forces NCOs who had worked with him at Ft. Bragg. They were Special Forces medics by training, which meant they knew a lot about anatomy and physiology. When the Army created their Survival, Evasion, Resistance, and Escape (SERE) program, they chose Colonel Nick Roe to lead it. Roe was an obvious choice, as he had been captured by the Viet Cong (VC) in the Mekong Delta in 1963. In late 1968, he managed to escape during an attack on a VC encampment near the almost-impenetrable U-Minh Forest.

This story was personal for me. My camp, Ba Xaoi, was located in the Seven Mountains area of the Mekong Delta. From time-to-time, we would hear of the sighting of a round-eye prisoner being held by the VC. Every time we thought there was a chance, we would launch a rescue operation. All of them were unsuccessful—until December 1968. Roe's recovery was accidental and nearly fatal. After a bombing strike, helicopter gunships rolled in as the VC were seen scattering. One of them, however, was wearing black pajamas and hobbling toward the helicopters. Recognizing a heavy black beard, something an Asian would not have, the gunships held their fire. As they closed, they saw he was an American. Swooping in they snatched him to safety, and just in the nick of time; the VC had grown tired of his resistance antics and had set his execution date a few days hence. He had been captured near Le Coeur in An Xuyen Province, along with Captain Rocky Versace, whom they had quickly executed.[50] Roe, in reality a Special Forces lieutenant, convinced his captures that he was a civilian engineer, not a military officer. It was not until several years later, when a list of American POWs was provided to North Vietnam by a peace advocacy group, that the VC learned who he was. By then, his intelligence value to them was depleted.

But, back to SERE. Who better than someone with five years of personal experience as a POW to run the program. During his captivity, Roe had tried to escape several times and paid a price for each attempt. He learned a lot from his experiences, including the use of his mind to influence his captors. Thus, when he took over the SERE program, he tasked these NCOs to search out alternative capabilities in general, and *dim mak* in particular. They were the ones who found Guy Savelli and brought him to Ft. Bragg to teach martial arts courses.

Special Forces medics get very advanced training. One exercise includes treating a goat that has been shot. It was not desirable for the first gunshot wound a medic treated to be an American on the battlefield. Not widely advertised, and to support that medical training activity, there was a goat laboratory on the base. The medics arranged for Savelli to apply *dim mak* to two goats. Located in front of time-lapse television cameras to document the results, the goats were clearly hobbled.

Dim mak is not a severe blow, as one might expect. It is not the same as a fatal strike that compresses the chest and stops the heart, or a hammer-like hit to the side of the head. Rather, the contact aims to disrupt the flow of ki throughout the body. Also, death does not occur at the time of the strike. It usually occurs hours later and is near instantaneous when death finally does take place. In this experiment, the first goat died approximately twelve hours after the *dim mak* blow was administered. The second one died another twelve hours later. The video cameras showed the goats just suddenly collapsing.

The results of the necropsy that I saw were even more intriguing. The goats' ventricles were full of blood. That seemed to indicate that onset of death was so rapid that the heart did not have time to contract. There was another anomaly observed as well. Internally, across the thoracic region of the body, a line of energy could easily be seen. It appeared very similar to what occurs when a bullet passes through a body and deposes a pattern of radial energy. The difference in this case was that there was neither a wound of entrance nor wound of exit. There can be no doubt that such a deposition of energy is a challenge for conventional science.

There were experiments done with staring as well. The results were far from conclusive, yet interesting. As a POW, Roe had used the techniques on the VC.[51] He perceived that he could influence the guards to walk further, or look longer, in a certain direction. All he wanted was a little extra time not being observed so as to complete his task.

For anyone who saw the George Clooney movie, *The Men Who Stare at Goats*, this may sound familiar. No goats ever died from being stared at, but they did die from *dim mak*. Unfortunately, Jon Ronson, who wrote the book, took a small amount of truth and added about 90 percent fiction. And then they made the movie.

Shihan Gary Alexander

Not all martial arts surprises come from psychic phenomena. My cousin, Grand Master Gary Alexander, exemplifies this other facet of the arts. Gary is a Shihan, 10th Dan, in Isshinryu, an Okinawan style of Karate. At 25 years of age, in 1962, he became the North American champion by beating all challengers in open tournaments. He does not understand, nor does he rely, on psi. As I have learned from experience, he just hits really, really hard. He rose through the ranks fighting without pads and with full contact. That is a far cry from today's matches in which trophies are awarded to completely padded contestants just for showing up. Over the decades of his fighting career, Gary amassed a record of over 1000 matches and went undefeated. There are photos of him as a contemporary with Bruce Lee, Chuck Norris, and other notable karate masters.

But the real story is his background. As a young child, he and his brother, Ed, were bedridden or incapacitated for more than 12 years. Rheumatic fever has just about vanished in America today, but like polio in the 1940s, it was a relatively common disease, and a very debilitating one. This was an acute illness that causes fever, inflamed joints, and heart valve damage. During the time of their infirmity, neither Gary nor Ed could participate in sports of any kind. Running and jumping, like most children do, was out of the question. School teachers came to their home, and their father carried them to the car whenever they had to go somewhere. Importantly, muscle development was greatly inhibited for all those years.

Mentally banishing pain, Gary exercised his joints and eventually was able to become ambulatory again. Everyone who knew him was amazed, and upon graduation from high school, he joined the U.S. Marine Corps and became a qualified infantryman. While assigned in Okinawa, he began training in Isshinryu. That's when the tolerance he had developed for withstanding pain paid off. In 1962, he accomplished a knock out in Madison Square Garden in a record five seconds. His next match went about 60 seconds. Within a few years, his instructors asked him to refrain from formal competition so that other fighters had a chance.

Gary is an example of what can be done when one is determined and chooses to persevere against the odds. It is the kind of story worth retelling as there is evidence to back it up. Today, Gary is disenchanted with most of the karate schools he has seen. Too frequently they are commercially oriented, and some even guarantee a trainee will get a black belt within a designated period. He does not think much of the hype. Inducted into the *Black Belt Magazine* Hall of Fame, his approach to gaining respect is simple. As he always stated, "The mat doesn't lie."

Conclusion

As with many sports, when you look very closely at extreme performances, there seem to be elements that defy conventional wisdom. These examples go beyond excellence and training and enter the realm of the physically impossible. For instance, some researchers believed that the famous Russian ballet dancer, Vaslav Nijinsky, was actually levitating because he could stay in the air so long. When performing, Nijinsky sometimes entered an altered state of consciousness, one in which he said "there were moments in which gravity disappeared."

In my experience, there are aspects of certain advanced martial arts that support the notion that psychic phenomena play a significant role. Participants in Aikido and qigong demonstrate the use of ki, sometimes extending well beyond the physical body of the performer. And what if *dim mak* is real, as the goat necropsies seem to suggest? The totality of evidence does beg the question as to the relationship between ki and psychokinesis. Are they related, or are they one and the same? Based on laboratory research on PK, I believe there are some differences, but that question deserves serious research. First, science must accept that there is an unseen energy system that regulates the human body and can be manipulated. Second, they must accept the existence of PK. Only then will we be able to address these more complex issues.

Some skilled martial artists have also learned to apply precognition in order to know what an opponent will do next. Then there appears to be an ability to influence the mind of another in order to allow actions to take place. While rarely considered by researchers of psychic phenomena, the martial arts offer a complex and intriguing venue for exploration.

PART II

MILITARY EXPERIENCES

CHAPTER 10
BEND, BEND, BEND

A child is trapped under a car. Her mother runs out and lifts the car, saving the child's life. Whether urban legend or real event, this story has consistently caught peoples' imagination. Certainly, feats of great strength have been recorded throughout history. There are two classic responses. One is, of course, it didn't happen. The second is, once triggered by a critical event, the adrenaline starts pumping and provides the burst of energy necessary to accomplish the lifesaving task.

While the secretion of adrenaline, or epinephrine, is instrumental in preparing the body for "fight-or-flight" when under threat, it cannot account for dramatically increasing muscle strength to lift objects weighing a ton or more. As an example, *ABC News* reported the story of a 22-year-old woman from Virginia who allegedly lifted a BMW off of her father after the car he was working under slipped off a jack. Another is a *Fox News* story of two teenage daughters in Oregon who lifted a 3,000-pound tractor off their father's chest after it had flipped and pinned him to the ground. *Scientific American* described the case of a bicyclist in Tucson, Arizona, who was struck and dragged under a Chevrolet Camaro. To save the badly injured biker, a man lifted the car and held it up for about 45 seconds while the driver pulled the victim to safety. These anecdotes go on and on. The events, while rare, do occur and defy simple explanations. The scientific basis for producing the energy necessary for the movement of these heavy objects is missing. But similar feats can be observed at smaller scales.

Employing one's mind over matter is one of the fantasies that has been discussed for centuries. One of the enduring challenges to science is the evidence supporting the reality of psychokinesis (PK). There is no conventional scientific theory that can account for the energy that would be required to move objects purely by mental power. Yet, PK happens!

My personal encounters with PK really started when I met Jack Houck, an aerospace engineer then working at McDonnell Douglas in Huntington Beach. Houck heard about the spoon-bending exploits of Uri Geller and designed a model for creating PK on an observable scale. His events became known as spoon-bending parties, though he called the process psychokinesis mental bending, or PKMB.

Of course, we were highly skeptical at first. Based on his day job, a highly-classified project for the CIA, Houck had reason to travel to the Washington area quite frequently. Bob Klaus, a friend that I worked with on Neuro-Linguistic Programming, better known by the acronym NLP, arranged for a PKMB party to be held one evening at his home. What we observed at that time was sufficiently intriguing to be worth a closer look. After that session, I reported to my boss, Major General Albert N. "Bert" Stubblebine,[52] that we had seen some fairly heavy metal objects bent in a manner we couldn't explain.

Stubblebine wanted to have a firsthand experience, so I set up another evening session, this one at my apartment in Alexandria Knolls West, in Alexandria, Virginia. The eclectic group included Andrija Puharich, a medical doctor who had been studying strange phenomena for decades and had been instrumental in bringing Geller to the U.S. a few years prior. Also present was an impressive medium, Anne Gehman, who that evening would play a pivotal role in our involvement with PKMB. Another was U.S. Navy Captain Joe Dick, who was exploring alternative approaches to locating unrepatriated prisoners of war from the Vietnam conflict. Ann Armstrong-Dailey, who worked for the National Hospice Organization, was present as well, along with a few other people.

Houck introduced the PKMB process and continued to use it up until his death in 2013. He began by dumping a box of previously bent forks and spoons on the floor. They made a clattering sound as they impacted the surface. Then he provided some background about his prior experience and how he had discovered that PKMB could be experienced by almost anyone. Most important, Houck found that PKMB does not take a person with special skills, like a Uri Geller, just a willingness to participate with an open mind.

Having fun was also a key element to the process. For reasons not yet fully understood, there does appear to be an emotional component to PKMB. In some ways, that is similar to the situations in which extraordinary strength is displayed. Of course, the PKMB parties generate but a tiny fraction of the emotional stimulus of saving a loved-one's life, but it does play a significant role.

That night, in Alexandria Knolls, a critical incident took place. Members of the group were mostly sitting on the floor in roughly an elliptical pattern. Serendipitously, Stubblebine was seated directly across from Anne Gehman. The PK party evolved from what Houck called "kindergarten" levels, in which participants were allowed, even encouraged, to use their hands in assisting the bending process, to the "graduate" session. Here, in the final stages, participants held a pair of matched forks, touching nothing more than the base of the cutlery. Absolutely no physical force is allowed at this point.

Suddenly, the fork that Gehman was holding in her right hand dropped over with about a 90-degree bend. That's right, with no physical force applied, her fork just wilted. Both Stubblebine and I witnessed that amazing incident right before our eyes. There was no doubt this was the real deal. A macro-PK event had happened that was witnessed by several people.

Gehman herself was extremely surprised. Although she is a professional medium who had seen many unusual occurrences, never before had she participated in a PK party. Hastily, Stubblebine and I huddled near the apartment door to discuss what we had just observed. Clearly, this was significant. If PK was real, and what we had just observed suggested it was, it had huge implications for the military. This was something that needed to be further explored. But we also knew that convincing others of the reality would be a tough sell.

There were more surprises to come. The day after that PK party I was driving to an International Association for Near-Death Studies (IANDS) board of directors meeting in Storrs, Connecticut. As we headed up I-95 through New Jersey, Jan Northup, my wife at the time, said her hands felt very warm, much as she had experienced at the party the night before. When she picked up a couple of spoons in the car, they quickly bent into knots. Arriving at the University of Connecticut, where IANDS was founded, we described the PK party to the assembled board members, all of whom were interested in the details. The obvious next step was doing demonstrations. Much to the chagrin of our host, Ken Ring, a number of his home implements quickly became unusable. Although Jan was using her hands in this process, she was able to contort the bowls of several very heavy serving spoons. Those spoon bowls were so thick that it would have been extremely difficult for the average person to cause that kind of damage with their bare hands. Yet, it happened repeatedly, and with extreme ease.

We maintained contact with Houck and learned how to replicate the PK party environment. Stubblebine was very excited about the prospects for PK parties, and we held a number of such events as a means to demonstrate to senior leadership the implications that psychokinesis had for the military and intelligence agencies. These continued for several years during which we bought a house and moved to Springfield, Virginia. We held many PK parties there. On occasion, the dignitaries attending wanted their identities protected. Some were reluctant to admit that they had ever participated in anything as crazy sounding as spoon-bending. To ensure that protection, Stubblebine even dispatched a counterintelligence team to sweep the house looking for electronic bugs. I'm not sure I understand their report even today. They told me there "was nothing there that wasn't supposed to be there." I always wondered if they had installed something of their own.

The U.S. Army Intelligence and Security Command (INSCOM) had units scattered all over the world, mostly targeted against the Soviet Union. Each quarter Stubblebine would bring his subordinate senior commanders together for what became known as "Love-Ins." For about three days each time they would meet at a sequestered site and discuss ongoing and future operations. At several of these meetings, Stubblebine had me brief on the more unusual topics I was exploring. He had given me a great deal of freedom in which to operate. When asked what my job was, I often jokingly replied that I was a freelance colonel. There were some of my contemporaries who were not amused, but as long as Stubblebine was flying cover for me, there was not much they could do.

Among the snide remarks I often heard was, "What are you going to do, bend tank barrels?" The answer was: no, the target will be electrons. In the early 1980s, computers were just becoming mainstream in the military. And I noted that as we became more reliant on computers for decision-making, there was a vulnerability we had not experienced before. Today, most people have heard of cyber-warfare as a serious threat. At that time, the concept of fighting with computers was almost incomprehensible. As I pointed out to the detractors, the adversary did not have to crash a computer. All they had to do was to make them unreliable. Obviously, moving electrons would require far less energy than the deformation of physical objects.

At one Love-In, Stubblebine ordered that a PK party be held; Jan and I would conduct the event. Attendance was not optional. Skepticism was rampant. A few were overtly unhappy, if not hostile. Little did I know that one of the most spectacular PK events I would ever witness would happen with that cloistered group of generals and colonels. The scene was a horseshoe shaped meeting room at the Xerox conference center in Lansdowne, Virginia. The room contained two tiers of desks. About 30 people were present when I dropped the previously bent spoons and forks unceremoniously on the floor. The crashing sound was intentional and managed to get everyone's attention. For about an hour, we conducted the typical PK party in which people are encouraged to have fun and use their hands to assist in bending. It is known that on many occasions a tactile perceptual change takes place when an object is about to bend. Words like heat, or even cool, or plastic would be reported as these naive participants noticed a change in consistency of their fork or spoon. When the change took place, they would feel it and find that the object became extremely malleable. For a few seconds, the implement could be rolled up or twisted with minimal force.

Finally, we hit the graduate session; the one that does not allow for any physical force to be employed. Each person was provided a pair of matched forks. That meant we fit them together so that any perturbation would be detectible. On several occasions in the past (other than the Gehman incident), we had seen the tines of forks visibly change shape. That was pretty amazing in and of itself, but that was nothing like what was about to take place.

The configuration of the room restricted my vision of everything that was happening. There were small clusters of officers at various stages of interest and participation in the PK party process. As I turned to my right to watch a noisy group, someone behind me yelled out. It was a colonel who was sitting next to an officer who was a liaison to our European units. A lieutenant colonel, one of the few lower ranking participants, was holding a fork in his right hand, bent at a 90-degree angle. He stated he had looked away when the fork self-deformed, and was surprised by the event. I did not observe that action, and frankly I was a bit skeptical and thought that one of the less supportive officers might be setting me up. Therefore, my initial response was quite non-committal.

But that would change quickly as what followed defied all scientific explanation. Without any physical force, and with many people watching, the fork returned to the original upright position. It then folded over once again. Spontaneously, from the right-angle position, it moved back upwards to about a 45-degree angle and stopped.

Seemingly stunned, the lieutenant colonel dropped the fork on the desk and stated, "I wish that hadn't have happened." Since we were all sequestered, it helped that the staff psychologist was present. Before we sent him home, that officer needed some counselling and assistance coming to grips with his experience.

Normally at PK parties, participants take their bent objects home with them. This person wanted nothing to do with his bent objects, and I still have them on display at my house. I have shown them a few times for television interviews. Stubblebine visited the lieutenant colonel a few months later. The officer told him that he had successfully done that once more, just as a reality check. But since it ran counter to his personal religious belief system, he never tried another PK experiment.

Among the key witnesses that night was Ed Speakman, the INSCOM science adviser, who was a distinguished scientist in his own right. Independently wealthy from his 1930s invention of the car antenna, Speakman was legendary for his assistance in several special projects. He had participated in several of my PK-parties, and on this occasion he was seated directly behind the officer when this happened. That night he saw everything.

While that was the most spectacular bending of the evening, it was not an isolated event. Across the room another colonel experienced substantial bending of a spoon he was holding. This was about a 30-degree bend near the neck of the spoon. At any other PK-party, that bending would have been declared as the truly amazing event it was. But on this evening, it was overshadowed by the single most impressive bending I have ever personally encountered.

Readers should know that I consider Uri Geller a personal friend. We have known each other for several decades, and I appear in the film about his life entitled *The Secret Life of Uri Geller*.[53] I also wrote an article about his impact on the U.S. Army, which appears on his website. During the time of our friendship, I have observed him bend many objects. There was one incident, however, that stands out in my mind as more critical than all others. That is because it took place in the U.S. Capitol Building, and I was seated only about four feet away when it happened. From Scott Jones, who was working for another friend, Senator Claiborne Pell, I had learned that Uri would be speaking there. I also invited Major General Stan Hyman, then the INSOM commander, to go with me. Hyman was open-minded and had been supportive of the psychic programs when I was still in INSCOM. Although some time had passed since the demise of those programs, Hyman was interested in the promise of the psi experience. We both knew that it would be politically impossible to resurrect such efforts in INSCOM, but the potential threat from psi still existed.

There is a Sensitive Compartmented Information Facility, called a SCIF, located in the Capitol Building. That is where the meeting was held. In the 1980s, with the Cold War still raging, Geller, an Israeli, was concerned about the plight of Jews in the Soviet Union. Attending the presentation were a few congressmen and dozens of staff members who had heard about Uri's exploits. Although he was there to talk about international relations, members of the audience insisted he bend something. As no cutlery was available in the room, someone went outside and obtained a spoon from a guard's coffee cup. That is important as it proves that Uri had no means to prepare the object ahead of time.

Obligingly, Geller held the spoon by the bowl with two fingers of his left hand. With his right forefinger, gently he stroked the neck of the spoon from above. Expecting this spoon to bend, I watched very carefully and noted that at no time did he touch both sides of the neck of spoon, as magicians do when faking the process. As Uri continued, the handle of the spoon visibly bent upward. Clearly, there was no force being applied that could account for the movement. Uri placed the spoon at the top of the back of a chair next to him. He then continued with his discourse about relations between Israel and the Soviet Union. As he did so, with an unobstructed view, I could tell the spoon was continuing to bend, even though Uri had no physical contact with it. In fact, he was no longer even paying attention to the spoon. At some point the spoon fell on the floor. Discretely, it ended up in my pocket. That spoon remains on display in my office, along with the INSCOM forks.

There are, of course, a number of different methods for faking spoon-bending. In fact, it has become a signature act for my friend, mentalist Alain Nu, "The Man Who Knows." Early in our research we knew that consulting magicians would be important. Skeptics of PKMB have frequently been critical that magicians were not involved. That is simply not true. Initially, it was Doug Henning, a world class illusionist, who helped me. At that time, Henning was at the top of his game and on par with David Copperfield. Henning had headlined in Las Vegas and had television specials to his credit. Based on his association with Maharishi Mahesh Yogi and Transcendental Meditation, he was personally interested in phenomena and had a belief system that could accommodate mystical events.

We were introduced at one of his shows on The Strip, and I invited Henning to our home in Springfield to participate in a PK-party. He accepted, and arrived with his manager, but admitted being skeptical about these events. At our event, two things basically blew him away. The first person to experience spontaneous bending was his own manager. He knew there was no way we could have set that up. The second was bending by a slight, eleven-year-old girl who, like Henning, had never previously attended a PK-party. After he demonstrated some interesting card tricks, we discussed the ways in which an illusion of bending might occur. Once you know what to look for, catching the trick is pretty simple.

There were other infamous PK-parties along the way. In 1982, I attended the centennial celebration for founding of the Society for Psychical Research

(SPR) in the UK. That was held at the SPR birthplace, Trinity College, at Cambridge University. Coincidentally, it was also the 25th anniversary of the American Society for Psychical Research (ASPR) so they held a joint meeting. Trinity College is revered by scientists as it was once the home to Sir Isaac Newton.

It was there that I met John Hasted, an experimental physicist at Birkbeck College in London, and his assistant, Julian Issacs. They had heard about PK parties that were being held on our side of the pond and were interested in getting details.

Hasted had already worked with Uri Geller and publicly pronounced him to be authentic. Hasted had also examined a number of British children who he thought had psychic abilities. After discussing the basic PK experiments, Hasted and Isaacs showed me a heavy metal bar that was bent in a 360-degree circle. As I recall, the bar was about three feet in length, about three quarters of an inch in diameter, and half an inch thick. With all my strength, I could cause the bar to flex slightly, but was unable to create any permanent bending. According to them, the bar had been contorted in their presence by a young boy. That bar is the heaviest item I have ever seen allegedly perturbed by psychic means.

Hasted asked if we could hold a PK party for some select attendees at the conference. I agreed, provided they would hold the number of participants down to no more than 20. Word got out, however, and they literally had to bar the door once about 50 people were in the room. There was a very limited amount of cutlery available for that session, and some modest bending seemed to happen, but nothing extraordinary.

Professor Hasted became excited by the results. The next day, he openly announced there would be another session that evening and everyone was invited. There was one significant caveat; each attendee would have to provide their own metal implements. In those days, stores in the UK generally closed about 5 p.m., and the conference sessions ran much later. As fate would have it, there was a scheduled formal dinner that night. You might guess where participants acquired their forks and spoons. The problem was that they were all stamped TCK, for Trinity College Kit. Yes, real silverware, not the cheap stuff we usually used. A lot of them were bent, but I must confess I saw a lot of white knuckles, meaning physical force was being applied. I will not attest to anything bent that night, but I can report the college was not amused.

Based on his research of young psychics, John Hasted wrote *The Metal Benders*.[54] It was not well reviewed by the scientific community and his peers did not take his work seriously. While the PK parties exemplify popular interest and the efficacy of PK, there is an entire body of literature on scientific research into micro-PK, the psychokinetic movement of very small objects. The work of Bob Jahn and Brenda Dunne at Princeton University is premiere in the field. Jahn was the dean of the School of Engineering, with an impressive and impeccable résumé. He was challenged by a pair of graduate students to be their faculty adviser and oversee a proposed experiment in psi, as no other professor would accept to do so. While extremely skeptical of the outcome, the students had created an exquisite protocol. Keeping his promise, Jahn supervised the research project. To his amazement, positive results were achieved.

Many faculty members would have failed the students and destroyed any papers or references to the positive results. But to his great credit, and despite later buffeting by the scientific community, Jahn recruited Brenda Dunne and created the Princeton Engineering Anomalies Research (PEAR) laboratory.[55] Although their work is far too voluminous to summarize here (they have published many articles and books on micro-PK experiments), the bottom line is that with trillions of decision trials, they have demonstrated conclusively that small, but detectable, psi effects are real. As with Houck, most of their participants were naïve subjects, generally students needing credit for experimental participation.

Visiting their lab at Princeton, I had an opportunity to attempt to influence one of their classic experiments. This consisted of a wall device that contained a large number of pegs. Each peg was a decision point as a ball could either go to the right or left as it cascaded downward. As the experiment started, hundreds of BBs were dropped from the top of the device. The goal was to influence the balls to move in a designated direction. To determine if actual psychic influence was being generated, Jahn and Dunne created a trinomial protocol. That is, the subject would be randomly instructed to attempt to move the objects to the right, to the left, or to have no influence on each specific run.

As I recall, I did not perform better than chance as I attempted to influence the rapidly falling BBs. It should be noted that my trial was not included in their data collection, as PEAR strictly prohibited anyone but their naïve subjects from being recorded. That was to prevent would-be psychics from showing up, making a couple of attempts at the device, then adding "Tested at Princeton" to their business cards. As happened with me, roving psychics would get a friendly welcome, maybe a cup of tea, but no official sanction from the lab.

Unbeknownst to Bob and Brenda, my visit to PEAR was not my first encounter with the micro-PK device called a random mechanical cascade. Years before I had made a similar attempt, but at a place that has remained out of the spotlight that castigates most psi research efforts. Redstone Arsenal is contiguous to Huntsville in northern Alabama. It is home to some of the most exciting research and engineering projects in the country, and yet it gets little public attention. Redstone is a huge facility with over 38,000 acres. At NASA's Marshall Space Flight Center, you'll find Space Camp located there. It has also been home to the U.S. Army's missile development and testing commands, which has existed under a number of different names. This is one of the main sites where Werner von Braun, and his cadre of German rocket scientists, were brought to create the US space program at the end of World War II under the infamous Operation Paperclip.

After departing INSCOM, while assigned as the chief of the Technology Integration Office at Army Materiel Command, I visited Redstone Arsenal on several occasions, dealing mostly with the burgeoning field of smart munitions. However, I did learn that there was a tiny secret program exploring PK going on there. This was very fundamental work, or what is called basic science. Basic science is working at a theoretical level, long before any technology might be integrated for development into a weapon system.

The research was conducted in a small outlying building many miles from headquarters. It was very remote, and I thought I had lost my way attempting to find it. The experiment they were conducting resembled what PEAR was doing. The men heading the experiments were quite welcoming and allowed me to try it out. Sitting across from the device, I then attempted to move the BBs to the right or left as they fell from the top. I commented on how physically exhausting these experiments were, which seems strange as all I was doing was sitting still and mentally attempting to interact with the falling balls.

The scientists informed me that my feeling physical exertion was not unusual. The issue seemed to be that people don't really know how to move the BBs. Therefore, test subjects create body tension during the experiment. An analogy would be the way many bowlers employ body English after they have released the ball, in an attempt to influence the course of the ball before it strikes the pins.

It was not until about two decades later that I met the progenitor of that project. While working with the Army Science Board 2006 Summer Study at the Beckman Center in Irving, California, I met Randy Clinton, who was the former director of the Missile and Space Intelligence Center located at

Redstone. Clinton, like Stubblebine, had become interested in psi phenomena and had a budget that was large enough to initiate the small program without causing any commotion. Like many military psi-related projects, this one was personality dependent and died when Clinton moved on and budgets got tighter. Clinton also knew and appreciated the work of Jack Houck.

The U.S. Army was not alone in their interest in psychic phenomena and PK in particular. One was a remote viewing project director named Dale Graff, who worked at both the U.S. Air Force Research Laboratory at Wright-Patterson AFB near Dayton Ohio, and later with Defense Intelligence Agency at Bolling Air Force Base, Anacostia, Maryland.

I also frequently interacted with several U.S. Navy officers interested in psychic research. For the most part, their participation appeared to be predicated on personal interest. However, there was also interest at the Naval Research Laboratory (NRL). I attended one important meeting that was held at their headquarters in Anacostia, Maryland. Several of the people mentioned in this chapter were present. There were also a number of the NRL première scientists, ones who normally would not grace such a gathering.

The emphasis of the meeting was on what concerns were relevant to the military, assuming PK was real. At that time, my main threat issue was the potential for perturbing computers. As the discussion wore on for hours, as usual, Bob Jahn, who was also there, just sat back and listened. His propensity of patience was exemplary, as the folks new to the topic reiterated the fundamentals as if they had just discovered something extraordinary. Finally, he interjected what I believed to be the most cogent comment of the day. Many of us involved in PK research had noted a relationship between events and emotion. Bob noted that the electronic systems in fighter aircraft were often functioning very close to the limit of their capability. Since air-to-air combat was extremely stressful, that added emotional component might push the operational capability of their systems beyond their limits. As pilots were flying very expensive aircraft, Jahn suggested it would be wise to include additional testing of psi to ensure that they could operate safely in a high-stress environment. I have no idea whether or not the Navy followed up on that suggestion. While he rarely speaks, when Bob Jahn does, you should listen.

CHAPTER 11
JOURNEYS OUT OF THE BODY

Turning onto county route 634, I experienced a surrealistic feeling, far different than when I had driven on it about a week before. The rolling green hills that lead up to the Shenandoah Mountains had a unique glow that I had not been noticed on arrival. But in the intervening period, it was I who had changed, not the terrain.

The Monroe Institute

It had been a nearly week of Controlled Holistic Environmental Chambers (CHEC) and vegetarian diets at the Monroe Institute in Faber, Virginia, that made the difference. In the CHEC units, we had experienced Hemi-Sync sessions several times a day, and the combined effects were amazing. The process was a series of tapes with increasing intensity in a program now called Gateway.

The creator of the program was Robert A. Monroe, an electrical engineer, who had risen to be a vice president and member of the board of directors of the Mutual Broadcasting System (MBS). Now defunct, MBS at one time was on par with the NBC, CBS, and ABC radio networks. At the time, June 1982, Bob was best known for his unique mode of travel as detailed in his book *Journeys Out of The Body.*[56]

While studying various aspects of human consciousness, Bob became interested in sleep-learning, a process in which the individual could acquire information while sound asleep. But during his exploration, he had suddenly found himself fully awake, yet located outside his physical body. Initially he just went wherever the phenomenon dictated. It took considerable practice to gain control of what was happening to him. He was aware that such out-of-body events had been reported for a very long time, at least centuries. Still, they tended to be one-time experiences often precipitated by a traumatic event, similar to what is described in near-death experiences. But Bob's experiences were different as they occurred repeatedly.

His exploits came to the attention of Charles Tart, a psychologist at the University of California, Davis, who had coined the phrase Out-Of-Body Experiences (OOBE) and produced a book entitled *Altered States of Consciousness.*[57] Under the watchful eye of Charley Tart, Bob participated in a series of experiments to determine whether this was a real state or simply a hallucination. In some of those studies, Bob was monitored with an electroencephalograph (EEG) so that Charley could examine Bob's brainwave activity while he claimed to be in an OOBE state. The EEG charts looked like Bob was dreaming, but one unexpected difference was that Bob reported OOBEs shortly after entering a sleep state. Sleep states have well-known cycles, and normally one does not enter a dream period until they have been asleep for about 90 minutes.

Charley made attempts to prove that Bob was actually outside of his body and maneuvering about, not just imagining these events. One approach was to place objects at specific locations and ask for Bob to identify them. But when Charley asked Bob to read numbers that were placed in a hidden place, he was unable to do so. At that time, Bob indicated he could not control where he went while having an OOBE. His control of out-of-body travel would come later.

Over time Bob and I became friends, and I visited the institute on several occasions. In fact, we were close enough that my former wife, Jan Northup, became one of Bob's "facilitators," as the staff was called, for the Gateway Program. Bob had assembled an amazing staff. When I first attended the Gateway Program, Melissa Jaeger and Bill Shull guided us through the sessions and helped integrate our experiences into the real world. Melissa was an early participant and one who willingly experimented with Bob, researching various technologies to alter states of consciousness. Hemi-Sync was not his only approach, but the one he settled on for the commercial program. Bill was a licensed psychotherapist and willing to push the limits in the exploration of consciousness.

Bob's private description of his involvement in OOBE was a little different from the published version. What he told me was that, when he was born, they "didn't put in all the pegs." As a result, "he just slipped out of his body more easily than most people."

Having engaged in various forms of meditation, and being technically oriented, I was captivated by his engineering approach to altered states of consciousness. The development of Hemi-Sync involved the auditory stimulation of the brain. Through earphones, the system puts one audible signal in the right ear, and a slightly different signal in the left ear. Sometimes the frequencies are about ten hertz different. What happens is that the brain tunes to the beat frequency, i.e. the difference between the two. In the early 1980s, there was considerable research being done on alpha and theta level brain waves. The alpha range is 8-to-14 hertz, and theta 4-to-8 hertz.[58] These were of interest because it had been discovered that when dreaming, and rapid eye movements (REM) detected, the electroencephalograph (EEG) patterns indicated the brain was operating in alpha. Theta is found in deeper sleep levels. The 10-hertz signal is right in the middle of alpha and a place in which Bob believed attendees could work.

In learning meditation, I found that one had to spend a lot of time in trial and error, trying to find the right frequency, even when just clearing the mind. My analogy was that meditation was like tuning a radio when you didn't know what frequency the desired station was on. You just had to tune up and down the dial until you found the signal you wanted. Then, you had to find a method to return to that station on demand. Radio stations have designated frequencies you can write down. It is a bit trickier with the mental processing of altered states of consciousness.

Bob's approach was different, with Hemi-Sync he could take you right to the desired frequency. There was no searching for the right place. Interestingly, he noted that his early research appealed more to men than women, even though many women would go on to take the program and be quite successful.

Bob insisted that acquiring an OOBE should not be a designated outcome for success. Rather, he thought that the participant should explore the altered states of consciousness and take whatever information or experience came to them. Some attendees did have OOBEs, but others did not. That did not, however, take away from the experience.

A friend of mine, Frank Burns, experienced a full-blown kundalini experience during a Hemi-Sync session. At the time, Frank was a lieutenant colonel assigned to the Pentagon. An organizational effectiveness officer, he reported to the top levels of the Army. Frank was the creator of Task Force Delta, an Army think tank that was far, far ahead of its time, exploring a wide range of alternative areas to create high performing units. It was Frank who really brought Neuro-Linguistic Programming (NLP) into the Army.

This trip was an exploration for both of us. It was early afternoon on a Thursday, when we found Frank sitting in his CHEC unit in a highly-altered state. He told us about seeing a very bright light, even though he was in a darkened chamber. According to him, he had felt energy rising from the base of his spine, flowing up through his chakras and out the top of his head.

At this juncture, I should digress and briefly discuss what the kundalini is. It will not be readily accepted in Western society, but it is well-known in Eastern religions. The kundalini is described as the primal energy that resides at the base of the spine. It is sometimes represented as a coiled serpent; safe when left alone, but once activated it is capable of producing awesome experiences, though controlling it can be tricky. There are yogic practices that are designed specifically to release this form of energy. Through meditative techniques, the kundalini can begin to move up the spine. When totally unleashed, it is said to lead to enlightenment.

The kundalini experience can be overpowering and unstoppable, causing severe mental issues. Gopi Krishna described being incapacitated for a month when it first happened to him. I have encountered other people who were having such experiences. Unfortunately, most in the medical profession would assume the person was having a psychotic break and treat them with drugs.

While Western science will have problems accepting the concept of an unseen and undetectable energy source residing inside everyone's body, the concept has been around for millennia. It is mentioned in the ancient Hindu Upanishads, which date long before the Common Era. While kundalini events can happen spontaneously, an experienced yogi master should be involved in any attempt to deliberately awaken the serpent.

To facilitate the training, we each had a CHEC unit assigned. This consisted of a soft mattress located in an isolated chamber that prevented visual contact with anyone else during the recorded exercises. It was not complete sensory deprivation, but about as close as you could come in that setting.

Like many Americans, especially for those in the military, I was constantly operating in a sleep-deprived state. Therefore, my first few sessions in the CHEC units resulted in some pretty sound sleep. Within a day, I was able to focus my consciousness while listening to the Hemi-Sync tapes. Awareness of time evaporated. When beginning a tape session, one does not know how long it will last, and the length of the sessions vary. Each session began with an affirmation, one that I completely agree with: "I am more than my physical body." Since I underwent the Gateway experience, more has been added to the affirmation, but the notion that we are spiritual beings having a physical experience remains fundamental.

INSCOM had several contracts with the Monroe Institute, but many of us were specifically interested in Bob. Several remote viewers attended the programs to see if that would enhance their capabilities. One even went on leave to attend the course. That guy, and the one who gained the most from those interactions was renown Remote Viewer 001, Joe McMoneagle.[59] He married Bob's adopted daughter, Nancy, better known to us as "Scooter." After more than three decades, they still live together on the mountain, just down the hill from where Bob and his wife, Nancy Penn Honeycutt, used to live.

Bert Stubblebine also used the Monroe Institute's basic program as a means to expand the awareness of some of his staff members. As with our efforts in spoon-bending, the main reason for taking these courses was to convince people to think more broadly in their jobs as analysts. One of the most interesting applications took place at a group session the day prior to returning to Arlington Hall Station where INSCOM Headquarters was located. Most of the group had just come out of a Hemi-Sync tape that took people to a very deep level.

Stubblebine had assembled the group, but instead of using Monroe facilitators he led the session himself. The mission of INSCOM was to gather and evaluate broad categories of data from which analysts tried to predict the actions of the Soviet Union and other threats around the world. Taking advantage of the fact that the participants had just come out of an altered state of consciousness, Bert asked each of us to predict what would be the main story the following year, one that was not currently foreseen.

I was attending this session as an observer or monitor. The intelligence community is very sensitive about the mental condition of its people. Since we were intentionally altering their normal states of consciousness, my job as a monitor was to ensure that nothing classified was revealed, as the Monroe facilitators were not all cleared, and certainly not to the levels at which INSCOM operated. Even though I had not been using the tapes, the environment was such that it seemed to have some impact on me.

For this session, the facilitators were specifically excluded, as Stubblebine had no idea what might come through. Even though this was highly speculative, we did not want to take any chances. The participants put forth a wide range of responses. I chose to join in and I remember to this day what I projected. In hindsight, it may sound like a blinding flash of the obvious, but in 1982, it was not. My response was that there would be massive famine in East Africa, on a scale not previously experienced. Yes, there were periodic food shortages in the area, but in 1983-1985 Ethiopia experienced an epic drought, one that brought death to over 400,000 people. Maybe it was a lucky (or unlucky) guess I my part, but a weather-related famine in East Africa was not on our scope at that time. Exacerbated by ongoing civil war, that Ethiopian famine is ranked as one of the great tragedies of the 20th century.

It should be noted that not everything we tried worked, and Bob sometimes pushed the limits of credulity. One such example was a contract initiated by Bob Klaus, a civilian organizational effectiveness practitioner from Army Materiel Command. Klaus worked with us on numerous projects, and like Frank Burns he was deeply into Neuro-Linguistic Programming. Klaus and Bob Monroe cooked up a scheme to try to use Hemi-Sync for weight loss. For those not acquainted with the Army, weight management is a very big deal. Having a body-mass ratio above a certain limit can sometimes get you kicked out of the service.

The basic idea was to "decalorize" food using the tapes. That's right, they wanted to take calories out of food that had been ingested, purely by mental processing. As might be expected, the project was a dismal failure. You cannot just think your way thin and still eat prodigiously. Had it worked, the use of Hemi-Sync would have expanded exponentially, but frankly I'm still not convinced it was worth trying and said so at the time.

We learned the hard way that participation in the Gateway Program was not without danger. To attend the program for INSCOM required an evaluation by the staff psychologist. Everyone had to be cleared before going down to the Monroe Institute. As it turned out, on one of the programs, a member from a distant command failed to make it to Arlington Hall Station on time to catch the bus. In the wings was a lieutenant who wanted to attend, but he had not been processed and cleared. General Stubblebine relented and let him get on the bus and head down to Faber. That was a grave mistake, one that would cost Stubblebine dearly a few months later.

While attending the program the lieutenant had a psychotic break. Bill Shull, who happened to be facilitating this program, gave me the informal diagnosis: "He was not wound too tight to begin with." Not exactly clinical, but it did describe the lieutenant pretty well. I had not gone down to the institute on this occasion, but I was at the headquarters when they packed him up and sent back him to us. While not harmful, he was ranting and raving in an incoherent manner. He was sent to Walter Reed Army Medical Center where they put him in the psychiatric ward. A few days later, he was released and seemed fairly normal.

Although Stubblebine initiated a formal investigation, the incident haunted him later. Unfortunately, members of the U.S. Army have fatal accidents several times a year. On rare occasions troops get run over by tanks. We know that, on occasion, fatalities happen when jumping out of planes. Though the lieutenant was only hospitalized for a couple of days, the repercussions were greater than any fatal accident. Shortly after this event, there would be a bloodbath over who would become the first three-star general to become the Army's deputy chief of staff for Intelligence. Stubblebine was one of two candidates. But the opposition used this episode to keep him from the job.

It should be noted that the Monroe Institute does screen attendees. We also know that these types of programs often attract people who are not mentally stable to begin with. A firm grasp on consensus reality should be a prerequisite for attendance.

Research into the Hemi-Sync process has continued, and the Monroe Institute publishes reports periodically. A few years ago, I located another source that was doing similar work. The near-death experience of Eben Alexander[60] will be covered in the chapter "On Being Dead." It is, in my opinion, one of the most significant NDEs on record. Important at this point is the work of his associate Karen Newell. She has produced a series of CDs that employ the binaural beat concept. Eben became attracted to the work, as he claims it is the closest thing to the sounds and states that he experienced while in his week-long comma.

Research on Out of Body States

From a scientific perspective, proving that a person is really out of their body, versus transmitting their imagination, is difficult. Generally, scientists dismiss the notion as impossible and would not give it further thought. That is certainly counter to a vast amount of anecdotal evidence from thousands of personal reports. Another possibility is that the person is using remote viewing, or clairvoyance, to gather the information. Even if true, that also would challenge the current scientific paradigm, which would not accept that as valid means of gathering information either.

One man I've met who seemed to have unique talents along those lines was Alex Tanous. Tanous became involved in very innovative experiments at the American Society for Psychical Research in New York City. In the late 1970s, Tanous conducted a series of out-of-body experiments involving what he called astral travel. The concept has been around for a very long time. It suggests that collocated with the physical body lies a second form, the astral body. It is believed that the astral body is what becomes detached and can travel much as Bob Monroe described. Most of the experiments with Tanous involved accessing data from a distant location that could be subsequently independently verified. Tanous claimed that he could provide that information through astral travel. Of course, that explanation did not rule out remote viewing techniques, in which the person doesn't actually detach from the body.

Dr. Karlis Osis designed a complex experiment that attempted to measure whether or not some part of Tanous (his astral body) was actually at the location of the observation. There were two aspects to the experiment. One included the creation of the target at a remote spot, in what they called an Optical Image Device. That insured that the only possible place the composite picture could be viewed was from a known specific location. The Optical Image Device contained three components of the target pictures: form, position, and color. Only when viewed from the designated location would the components merge to produce the actual target. The second aspect involved placing strain gauges at the designated spot, with the expectation that there would be at least minimal physical perturbation of the site. A researcher also physically observed the site in an attempt to catch sight of the astral body during the experiment. The results were impressive but far from 100 percent accurate. However, when compared against chance, Tanous proved to be startling effective. In 197 attempts, Tanous correctly identified the visual target 114 times. In addition, the strain gauges recorded movement, indicating a physical presence at that time.

Sensory Deprivation and John Lilly

The Monroe Institute was not my only encounter with out-of-body experiences, or those researchers who explored altered states of consciousness. While attending the Organizational Effectiveness School at Ft. Ord, California, I availed myself of some of the offerings by the nearby New Age organizations. That included traveling to Big Sur, where huge pine forests merge precipitously with cliffs that met the Pacific Ocean, and visiting an idyllic conference center, the Esalen Institute. An ancient site, hot springs interrupt their journey to the sea as they feed the legendary communal baths at the Institute and offer healing to all who enter. At that time, Esalen also attracted world-class scientists and consciousness explorers.

One workshop that I chose to participate in was with John Lilly. Lilly was already world-famous and had written a number of books on consciousness studies, one of the best known being *The Center of the Cyclone*.[61] Lilly was a leader in the field of interspecies communications (mentioned previously in the chapter "Speak to Me"). The meeting at Esalen introduced me to one of the most brilliant men I have ever known, and I have had the privilege to meet many. John's wife, Toni, assisted, and also present was Heinz von Foerster, who is considered to be one of the architects of cybernetics. They had amazing conversations as they openly explored the relationship between the burgeoning fields of cybernetics and human consciousness.

Lilly was a hands-on explorer, which sometimes led to unpleasant circumstances. As a medical doctor working for the National Institute of Health (NIH), Lilly was one of a handful of people to have legal access to LSD. In addition, he was a co-inventor of the sensory deprivation tank; I found the subject of sensory deprivation fascinating. A few years later, when assigned at INSCOM, I would buy my own tank and reconnoiter altered states for hours.

The sensory deprivation tank eliminates as many physical sensory inputs as possible, leaving the mind free to explore. The tank is completely enclosed, with only a sliding door for entry. Epsom salts are used to increase salinity, which enables the body to float and distributes the person's weight evenly so that tension at any given point is minimal. The water temperature is carefully controlled to that of the external skin temperature. The tank takes away all sight, sound, and as much touch as humanly possible. I can attest that one can easily lose track of time in that environment. Lilly recommended taking things a step farther, albeit raising hygienic issues; he said that in this totally relaxed state the bladder would tend to void. The participant, he suggested, should become used to that function and ignore it. Even in my private tank, I did not follow that advice.

During my mental travels in the tank, I experienced several mystical events, including what I perceived to be partial OBE. Rather than being autoscopic, or looking down at myself, it seemed as if there was a separation of part of my body from the physical counterpart. This involved the distinct sensation of my arms being outside the body and not in contact with the buoyant water that supported my physical self.

Possibly the most bizarre encounter occurred when I lost all sense of direction. I could not distinguish up from down or right from left. This was somewhat frightening, even though all one has to do to escape the tank is simply raise the door. The problem was that in that mental state I had no idea where the handle was located. Strangely, although I could think very clearly, all of the physical cues that are normally present were missing. We locate our relative position in space, such as being upright or lying down, based on gravity, sight, and organs of balance such as the semicircular canals of the inner ear. At that moment, all of those were failing, or not reporting their input to my brain.

Finally, I mentally determined that if I could touch behind my back, then the shallow solution would tell me where down was. From there, my hand was close enough to the bottom of the tank to touch it. With that as a point of reference I was able to locate the handle and open the sliding door. As soon as that happened, there was enough light to see and my other senses returned immediately. I admit that a complete failure of your senses to respond, which is the basis of every physical movement you make, is an extremely strange sensation.

That experience did cause me to question our approach to some types of mental illnesses. There are fundamental inferences we make about how others sense their environment. This event proved to me that such an assumption may be incorrect.

CHAPTER 12
PSYCHIC SPIES

Knowing the enemy's intent has been the objective of intelligence opera-tives and military commanders since the beginning of conflict some twenty millennia ago. To gain this knowledge, they have employed a wide range of tools, including human spies and technical means such as signals intercepts and photography. Today, with satellite-based systems, an observer can look down almost anywhere in the world with amazing accuracy. Sophisticated computer algorithms, coupled with metadata, allow for locating and identi-fying targets with a high degree of certainty. But no matter how good these technical systems become, there are still hidden things of interest the satellite systems cannot access.

During the Cold War era, both the United States and Soviet Union be-came involved in the use of human consciousness as a means for collecting data at a distance. In the U.S., a program, best known as Star Gate, created a process that has become known as *remote viewing*.

Many books have been written on the topic, so I will provide just a brief overview. My intent is to demonstrate that not only is such a capability pos-sible, but that it provides fertile ground for scientific exploration. In 1987, I participated in a study by the National Academy of Sciences to evaluate re-search in a wide range of human technologies the U.S. Army was employing. Remote viewing was one of the topics, though it was not given much credence by the panel. On one hand panel scientists were stating it was impossible, while on the other hand the U.S. Army had put it into operation.

The International Remote Viewing Association (IRVA) defines remote viewing as "a mental faculty that allows a perceiver (a 'viewer') to describe or give details about a target that is inaccessible to normal senses due to distance, time, or shielding." It is a discipline that allows for data acquisition at a dis-tance, and incorporates what psychics once called clairvoyance, with aspects of precognition and retrocognition. This has been done for centuries. The new overlay from Star Gate was formalization of the process, and more recently, branding.

Here is a bit of history of the military application of remote viewing.[62]

Known under various names and organizations, this program was first called Gondola Wish, then Grill Flame, Center Lane, Sun Streak, and finally Star Gate. The intelligence community's interest in a remote viewing program began in 1972, when Stanford Research Institute (SRI) theoretical physicist Hal Puthoff, a former National Security Agency analyst, wrote a paper about how a remote viewer had influenced a carefully shielded magnetometer. At that point, some scientists in the CIA were already concerned about the substantial efforts the Soviets were making in the field of psychic spying.

Conventional wisdom suggested that the Soviets would not continue to spend significant amounts of money unless they were achieving results. That year the CIA funded a very modest research program at SRI. Initially Puthoff, and his co-researcher Russell Targ, conducted a series of basic experiments using people with known psychic ability. Most prominent among those chosen were artist Ingo Swann, photographer Hella Hammid, and a former police commissioner named Pat Price. The early research had many success stories, and the results of the initial experiments were sufficiently promising that they continued for the next several decades.

The subjects of the experiments were always totally blind as to the nature and location of the targets that were selected for them. In one unique experiment conducted on April 27, 1973, Swann was directed to mentally leave the controlled environment at SRI to explore a target that turned out to be the planet Jupiter. He only had been given one of a set of numbers, all of which referred to targets on Earth, except for one; he did not know his assignment was extraterrestrial. During the session, he "observed" that a set of rings was circling a planet. Everyone knew that Saturn had rings, but not Jupiter, so the validity of his remote viewing session was questioned. Being the iconoclast that he was, Swann remained adamant when he learned that the target had been Jupiter: there were rings around Jupiter, he insisted. It was not until after March 1979, when Voyager I traveled close to Jupiter and sent back photos of a ring, that Swann's observation six years prior was validated. Most importantly, that knowledge could not have been obtained in any conventional manner and ran counter to conventional scientific knowledge.

Chief Warrant Officer Joe McMoneagle, later known as Remote Viewer 001, demonstrated the potential for strategic applications of remote viewing nearly three decades ago. Early satellite coverage of a facility near the port of Severodvinsk on the White Sea close to the Arctic Circle had gotten the attention of the intelligence community. The building under scrutiny was very large but its contents was shielded from reconnaissance satellite observation. It was obvious that some form of construction was occurring there, but conventional-intelligence failed to provide answers about what was happening inside the huge building. McMoneagle and other remote viewers were always totally blind as to the nature and location of the targets that were selected for them.

At the time, then Lieutenant Commander Jake Stewart was assigned to the National Security Council, and was a supporter of the remote viewing program. He decided to task the detachment at Fort Meade, where McMoneagle worked, to see what they could produce. Over several days McMoneagle and another remote viewer were assigned to examine the facility using only their mental remote viewing skills. Given only geographic coordinates as a targeting mechanism, McMoneagle first accurately described an immense man-made structure. Then, after being shown a satellite photo of the roof, he was asked to describe the contents of the building. McMoneagle indicated the presence of several submarines. One, which was under development, was portrayed as extremely large and having features previously unknown for the Soviet Navy. He described a missile boat, with a double row of 20 launching tubes, and a new drive mechanism. The tubes, he noted, were forward of the sail, a position never previously observed on ballistic missile submarines. McMoneagle also detailed an unusual double hull and the use of special welding techniques.

None of the remote viewing material made sense to submarine experts, and professional intelligence analysts scoffed at the report. The analysts noted that they would have picked up intelligence reports of such a dramatic change in submarine architecture. Besides, U.S. boat builders had determined that a submarine of that size would be crushed when diving. Over a series of sessions, McMoneagle provided 12 sketches. Not only did he accurately describe the exterior and interior of the building in question, but also predicted the general timeframe when the submarine would be launched. Again, his predictions were rejected since conventional wisdom suggested that the Soviets were constructing their first full-size aircraft carrier.

The dynamiting and excavation began just as McMoneagle had predicted. An artificial channel had been created and the submarine was floated to the sea. When satellites passed over the area again, a massive boat appeared in the images, nested next to an Oscar-class attack submarine; that boat would become known as lead ship in the Typhoon class. McMoneagle had been right. The new double-hulled titanium boat exceeded everyone's expectations, and it would not crush while diving as the experts had predicted.

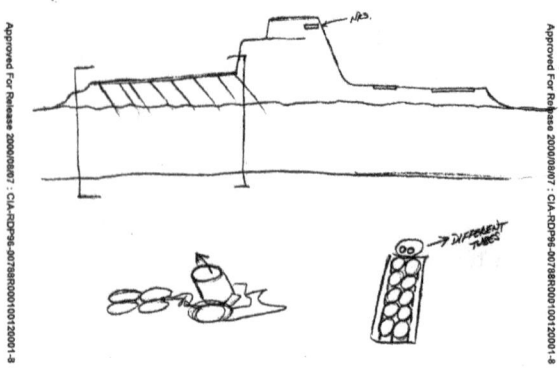

*One of twelve drawings of new class of Soviet submarines made by
Joe McMoneagle via remote viewing. (CIA)*

*Photo of the Typhoon class Soviet submarine. Note the missile tubes forward of the sail and the
double hull, as McMoneagle had indicated. (Department of Defense)*

Swann, for his part, was contracted by INSCOM to train a select cadre
of the military personnel who did not share his innate capabilities. He made a
major contribution by developing a mental model that allowed his students to
acquire the desired capabilities. Over the following two decades, members of
the detachment performed both training and operational missions, employing
their skills based on Swann's model of consciousness. Their successful missions
included the targeting of narcoterrorists and locating missing persons. While
the program was officially declassified in 1995, a significant number of remote
viewing documents remain classified. And while many of the Army's remote

viewers have become known publicly, others wish to remain in the shadows. Some of them still are concerned about retribution from those they exposed.

Unfortunately, most clients in the intelligence community saw remote viewing as the court of last resort. They used the techniques only when no other means of getting knowledge of the target existed. Although some successful remote viewing projects produced positive evaluations from intelligence community consumers, many other projects could not be validated. Because of the location or nature of some of the targets, ground truth was difficult or impossible to obtain. Thus, validation was denied. However, the very fact that users kept coming back with new targets for the remote viewing unit to explore attests to the success that the detachment enjoyed.

Remote viewing has a Catch-22 association. Nobody can provide an adequate scientifically acceptable theory to explain how the data were obtained at a distance. Attempts to formulate electromagnetic models have been made, usually involving extremely low frequency radio waves as a carrier for the data from the target to the remote viewer. However, controlled experiments have conclusively excluded electromagnetism as a possible mechanism to explain remote viewing. Furthermore, under certain conditions remote viewers have demonstrated the ability to perform accurately in both precognitive and retrocognitive sessions. While accepting that some wave might carry information over great distances, perturbation of time is another matter.

Supporters of remote viewing in the military comprehend the significance of the capability and believe it could have strategic implications. Most of them have a personal interest in the subject and appreciate being kept informed. At times, they accept input from the retired practitioners on difficult issues. These officials rarely make public comments for fear of ridicule. But some have. After retiring, the former Defense Intelligence Agency (DIA) Star Gate project manager, Dale Graff, wrote a book about his experiences and lectures publicly on the topic.[63] Attending the Marine War College in 2001, then-Commander Rick Bremseth, a U.S. Navy SEAL with a long and distinguished career, wrote his thesis on remote viewing.[64] After careful study and interviews with many of the former Star Gate participants, he concluded that the evidence supported continued research and application of remote viewing. Now retired, Captain Bremseth continues to advocate for further research and the military applications of remote viewing. He believes this valuable strategic capability has been ignored to the detriment of the intelligence community. While remote viewing is far from perfect, its significance lies in providing options when nothing else can accomplish the mission. Under proper techniques, it can provide information about inaccessible redoubts and advances in technology. More importantly, once the process is more thoroughly understood, those who have carefully developed these skills should be able to determine an adversary's intent and be predictive about future events.

Since the Star Gate program's formal declassification, remote viewing has gained popularity in the civilian sector and become fraught with unsustainable claims made by overenthusiastic supporters. Still, the basic tenets are sound, and a large body of credible scientific and military literature is available in the public domain. Some of the operational sessions remain classified and accessible only through the CIA.

The program has always had its detractors, however. Religious objections came from very senior individuals who believed the skills to be possible, yet saw them "as the work of the devil." A favorite tactic of detractors was ridicule and ad hominem attacks against proponents. Some scientists who remained casual observers complained about the lack of adequate scientific theory. But some scientists were willing to become intimately engaged in the projects and tried to understand how the process worked. To quote one of those researchers, "Anything that does happen, can happen," as we noted in the Introduction.

In many cases, while Star Gate was active, officials from the agencies that used the remote viewing intelligence product were quite supportive. However, that following was limited due to excessive compartmentalization of information. In short, the project failed to gain wide acceptance by senior officials. Most of them had been barred from access to the program and thus had no idea about the concept or its successes. It was also rejected by other officers whose worldview the program offended. When large budget cuts finally hit, Star Gate was put on the chopping block. The end came in 1995, with the release of the AIR report.[65]

The story of the remote viewing program is typical of many creative endeavors. It began through personal inquisitiveness backed by a need. Initial results proved worthy of further research and application. Individual senior officials, both in the military and from Congress, took an interest and provided resources and protection. Concurrently, resistance grew at several levels. As long as the program remained small, and was seemingly of little consequence, detractors paid little heed. However, when large rice bowls, or conventional orthodoxies, were threatened, opponents reacted vigorously.

That's exactly what happened when it came to the American MX intercontinental ballistic missile (ICBM) system based on a race-track concept that was formulated in the late 1970s. The proposal was to have MX ICBMs mounted on mobile platforms, then shuttled from shelter to shelter in random fashion, so that an enemy could not predict which shelter actually held the missile at any given time. But, while this expensive project was under development, a well-executed experiment demonstrated that remote viewing could dramatically narrow the margin of error in choosing the correct shelter where the missile was hidden. The possibility that Soviet remote viewers might increase the vulnerability of the ICBM system in this way raised significant concern. The MX supporters were not at all happy about hearing of any technique that might reduce the effectiveness of their program. Eventually MX became Peacekeeper, a 20-billion-dollar program, sans the racetrack basing concept.

The lesson from remote viewing, for those involved in creative endeavors, is that demonstrable results are not sufficient to keep a project alive. Even pressing requirements will not overcome personal biases of casual observers who are always willing to provide negative comments. Too frequently, supervisors use such unsubstantiated comments as justification for killing projects they do not like or understand. Too many scientists employ the premise, "If the data don't fit, ignore it." Such was the situation with remote viewing.

There is no doubt that remote viewing challenges our scientific paradigm of time and distance, as the work of Bob Jahn and Brenda Dunne at Princeton makes clear. As the Dean of the School of Engineering, Dr. Robert Jahn had semi-reluctantly been sucked into the world of psi research. He deserves kudos for following experimental data that ran counter to his belief system. While the PEAR lab may be best known for their work in PK, they also conducted premiere research in remote viewing.

In one case, they showed that a remote viewer could not only obtain data more than a thousand miles away, but also precognitively, i.e. before it happened. The target selected was the Bratislava Bridge in what was then known as Czechoslovakia and is now the capital of Slovakia. The remote viewer was situated in Wisconsin and had no knowledge of the target's location. In fact, at the time the remote viewing session was conducted, the site had not yet been selected.

At a distance of 5,600 miles the viewer stated, "I have a feeling the (on-site observer) is near water. There might be boats. Several vertical lines, sort of like poles. They're narrow, not heavy. Maybe lampposts or flagpoles. Some kind of circular shape. Almost like a merry-go-round or gazebo. A large round thing. It's round on its side, like a disc, it's like a round thing flat on the ground, but has some height as well. Maybe with poles. Could possibly come to a point on top. Sensing vertical lines again. No idea what they could be… a definite sensation of being outside rather than in. Water again… To one side where (the observer) is I get the feeling there's a small building. Could be a shed… Predominant colors are blue and green…Water again… Some very quick impression of a fence, a low fence…Steps. I don't know where they are leading to. The steps lead up to like a path or walkway. Like a boardwalk. And there's a fence along it. There's people walking along it, and there's vertical lines along that walkway." [66]

The Bratislava Bridge. Described by remote viewing before this target was selected. (Robert Jahn and Brenda Dunne)

During that session, the person who would become the on-site observer was still en route to Czechoslovakia. The viewing was conducted about 24 hours before their arrival. What the remote viewer was describing was a future event, what the observer would see upon arrival.

There are also reports of spontaneous intuitions that have many of the characteristics of classic remote viewing. Previously in this book, I covered the lifesaving, combat-related, out-of-body experience by U.S. Navy carrier pilot Scott Jones. But he had other experiences that were almost as amazing and eventually would lead to the end of his career. [67]

An intelligence officer, Scott was assigned in India for two and a half years during the Vietnam War. While we had cordial relations with India, they were also close with the Soviet Union and often purchased equipment from them. As observers of international affairs are aware, India is almost paranoid about their relations with Pakistan and vice versa. That is not without cause as they have engaged in four violent wars, and still have frequent skirmishes on the border in Kashmir.

While Scott was serving at the American Embassy in Delhi, the India Ministry of Defense began buying SA-2 anti-aircraft missiles provided by the Soviets. As could be expected, the first instalments were introduced around the capitol. Although an ally, the U.S. still had an intense national interest in keeping track of this significant development by the Indian Government. While military attachés could fly over India, they were required to get flight plans approved prior to any trips. The Indian MOD took pains to insure those routes did not go close to their sensitive sites, including those of the SA-2s.

But one day something strange happened when Scott took off on his assigned flight path. It began with some uneasiness in his stomach, enough that he wondered about being able to finish the flight. That physical discomfort soon gave way to very clear thoughts that he chose to act upon. Despite a minor protest from the copilot, Scott intentionally strayed to the right of their designated route, a violation of restraints placed by the Indian Government. Then, somewhat to their surprise, they spotted an SA-2 site. Based on his psychic intuition and responding to it, Scott provided the first solid confirmation, photographed from the air, of the SA-2 in India. This proved to intelligence community that India was then installing these anti-aircraft missile sites.

Scott was later able to locate all of the missile defense sites. But at a cost. His photos were so good that he was called in by his supervisors to explain how he had obtained the data. Please note that this all occurred well before we had extensive satellite coverage of the world, and spies often risked their lives to get such data. His superiors demanded that he reveal the source that provided him the information about where the sites were located. He adamantly maintained that there was no secret Indian agent working for him. Rather, when flying he would sense the location and go to it. Interestingly, he notes, this sense would only occur once he was airborne. His superior officer was not amused by his explanation. Unconvinced, and despite the quality of his work, his rater "damned him with faint praise," meaning it was unlikely he would be promoted again. With the handwriting on the wall, Jones opted to retire. This is but one of many examples of how admitting to a psychic sense could have negative consequence.

Civilians Use

Some civilians conducted remote viewing research as well. Stephan Schwartz founded the Mobius Group and engaged in some very persuasive experiments.

Interestingly, he employed some of the same remote viewers who were being tasked by the military. One of the early hypotheses about how remote viewing might be possible involved some form of as-yet-undiscovered electromagnetic (EM) waves. While perturbation of time would eliminate that possibility, it was a reasonable place to start. It was later learned the Soviet researchers posited the same premise.

Based on an earlier appointment as a special adviser to the Office of the Chief of Naval Operation, Schwartz had access to resources not available to most researchers. To test the theory, he created Project Deep Quest, which entailed the use of a submersible craft that would hold the remote viewers. Sea water effectively shields all EM emanations. That is one reason why communications with submerged submarines is so difficult. The first phase of the experiment had remote viewers descending in a submersible craft and mentally accessing unknown targets on the surface.

But just as he prepared for the experiment, he lost his trusted psychics at the last minute. Aware of the work at SRI, Schwartz contacted them and asked for the assistance of their remote viewers. One of those involved was Ingo Swann, who would attain legendary status in the RV community. Hella Hammid was the second person involved and accurately identified the target selected by the surface team from SRI, located about 375 miles away. The results answered two questions. The mental projection penetrated the sea water, thus eliminating the EM theory of transmission. The other was that the effect could occur over long distances, at least hundreds of miles.

Schwartz then engaged in an even more difficult task, locating a wreck somewhere off Catalina Island, California. True, there are numerous wrecks in that area and many had been charted. But the task presented to Ingo and Hella Hammid was to locate a wreck that was previously unknown. This is what Schwartz terms a triple-blind study; there could be no intentional leakage of information as no one knew where such a craft might lie on the sea floor. Again, dropping below the surface of the Pacific Ocean, Ingo actually directed the pilot to an area where his psychic impression told him the object would be located. With Schwartz, they successfully found the heavily-encrusted, long-lost, sunken boat.

Schwartz continued his research and created the field of psychic archeology, which he describes in his book, *The Alexandria Project*.[68] The book's title comes from the time he took psychics to Egypt and searched for several sites. One target was the fabled Pharos lighthouse in Alexandria, the now submerged city that was home to Mark Anthony and Cleopatra. In 1979, the expedition successfully located the lost city. This was documented in a television program made at the time.

Obtaining the needed documentation was difficult as the waters were so polluted that divers were prohibited from being in the water for long periods of time. But sufficient film was obtained to prove the location to be accurate. Amazingly, more than three decades later, in 2013, another diving team would take credit for the find with great fanfare. Before their divers arrived, the waters had been substantially cleaned up, making it safe to remain underwater for longer periods of time. They gave no credit to Schwartz or his team, even though he beat them by decades.

That was not the only time in which Schwartz's effort would encounter resistance from scientists and Egyptologists. He set out to explore another target, this time on land. As with the sunken craft, he wanted to locate a site whose location had been lost. Again, his team made psychic impressions of such a site. To document the effort, Schwartz had all of the papers date-time stamped and notarized by Egyptian officials. To confirm their work, an Egyptologist who worked for the government would accompany them when they began to excavate the target.

Schwartz and his team went into the desert to a location that met their criteria. Walking the area, his psychics determined the parameters of the site and put pegs in the ground indicating where the dig should occur. That task was finished late in the afternoon, so it was agreed that everyone would converge there the following morning at 10 a.m. Intuitively, Stephan took the team to the site before the appointed hour. When they arrived, they caught the Egyptologist moving the stakes they had carefully placed the prior afternoon. This is indicative of the opposition that psychic researchers can expect to encounter. Archeological data that contradict established timelines, or published history, are officially not welcome.

Much later, Schwartz conducted an even more amazing experiment, but this time rather than relying on people with special skills, he used people who had attended his remote viewing workshops. The construct was brilliant. As the invasion of Iraq wore on, the search for Saddam Hussein was a top priority. Certainly, coalition forces had no idea where to find him. Seminar participants were asked to identify the location and other information surrounding Saddam's capture. His workshop participants had varying degrees of expertise with remote viewing, including some who were complete novices. Their drawings and comments were collected, and again marked with times and dates, so that no one could claim they were made post hoc.

When Saddam was captured on December 13, 2003, the remote viewing results were examined. The accuracy of some of the comments was simply amazing. Participants had drawn a building that definitely described that location. It was so detailed that it could not fit just any house in the area. Some of the correct hits were counterintuitive. As an example, intelligence operatives always assumed he would be well protected by members of his inner guard. The remote viewing report indicated that only one or two people would be accompanying him. They accurately depicted the underground hole he would be hiding in; that he was armed, but would not resist, and that he had money with him.

What made this experiment so unique was its emotional component. Researchers have long surmised that numinous qualities are important, especially when engaging in precognitive targets. It was anticipated that Saddam's arrest would be accompanied with a global response. That was true. As with the memory of my location at the time of the Kennedy assassination, I can describe being in the dining facility of the military compound in Kabul, Afghanistan, when the news came on television. Because that degree of emotion is hard to predict, creating a similar test has proven to be very difficult.

Military Competition
During the Cold War, there was considerable competition for control and implementation of psychic capabilities. A book titled *Psychic Discoveries Behind the Iron Curtin* by Sheila Ostander and Lynn Schroeder did much to bring the issue into public awareness.[69] My article, "The New Mental Battlefield," appeared in the December 1980 issue of *Military Review*, a mainstream Department of Defense publication.[70] It was the first military article to openly mention remote viewing and other psychic phenomena. That article brought down on us the wrath of counter-establishment columnist Jack Anderson, who wrote in the *Washington Post* that we were "The voodoo warriors of the Pentagon."

Recently a unique book entitled *ESP Wars: East and West*[71] has been published in which participants from both sides of the Cold War contributed their views. While examining the roots of the so-called ESP wars, the authors correctly note that the use of psychics is nearly as old as conflict itself. Mystics, oracles, and other religious leaders were often consulted before battles in attempts to divine the outcome and to seek advice from external sources regarding the advisability of engaging in war. Recounted are stories of the Oracle of Delphi asking Apollo for guidance, the efforts of King Cyrus, founder of the

Persian Empire, and even biblical quotes detailing the use of psychics prior to combat. Russian traditions tell of employing shamans for the support of operations, a practice that continues with indigenous people to this day. The book's historical overview, which is not generally known outside of mythologists and a few conspiracy theorists, even mentions the Nazi fascination with the occult.

In 1992, my former boss, retired Major General Bert Stubblebine, and I went to dinner in the Washington area with the head of a Russian organization called the Institute for Theoretical Problems. He told us that he had been directing remote viewing research for many years. At that time, Russia was in a very tough spot economically, and he was authorized to sell anything to keep his organization fiscally viable. Bert and I were both retired from the Army and not in a position to assist with his funding problems. Still, at dinner that night we discussed issues that a decade earlier would have been unimaginable. Times certainly have changed.

Not All Roses

The remote viewing enthusiasts like to point to their successes but rarely admit their failures. That is a serious shortfall. When interviewed by reporters, my comment has always been, "Sometimes it works." From a scientific perspective, the hit and miss aspects are confounding. In reality, many of the products were not nearly as good as proponents often claim.

A couple of glaring examples come from Courtney Brown and his Farsight Institute. Brown, a professor at Emory University, has given several presentations at the annual conferences of the Society for Scientific Exploration (SSE). At the June 2008 meeting at the University of Colorado, Brown proclaimed that according to his remote viewers, the Los Angeles airport (LAX) would be physically destroyed by December of that year. Now, some nine years later, LAX is still up and running. In order to explain this obvious remote viewing failure, Brown informed us at a presentation the following year that LAX was in fact destroyed; it just happened in a parallel universe.

In June 2010, at another SSE conference, Brown claimed they had evidence that the U.S. military had an underground base on Mars. According to his remote viewer, this was an operational facility, and the photographic evidence showed ejecta being spewed forth from that location. In his talk he stated, "There are unregistered flights going out of Cape Canaveral all the time that never get recorded." That is utter nonsense. When there is a launch from Cape Kennedy, half of Florida is aware of it. Obviously, his people have no concept of the logistical requirements to support an extraterrestrial base.

While I take issue with scientists who fail to accept hard data, these examples are some of the reasons why they don't. I admit that I was a peer reviewer who blocked his article on this topic that Brown submitted to the SSE's *Journal of Scientific Exploration*

I would be remiss not to mention that the field of remote viewing has been invaded by people making unsubstantiated claims about their background. In Las Vegas, I encountered one such individual who claimed he was a heart surgeon, an SR-71 pilot with the U.S. Air Force, and a remote viewer in the Army's Star Gate program. One problem with the secrecy that surrounded the Department of Defense's remote viewing program is that people believe they can make claims that no one can check. Internally, the list of participants was pretty small, and most were known to each other. My best advice to anyone wishing to be trained is caveat emptor. High visibility does not equal credentials.

IRVA and Training

In March of 1999, meeting at Lyn Buchanan's home in Alamogordo, New Mexico, we created the International Remote Viewing Association (IRVA). As a founding board member, I had great hope that it would evolve and establish standards and ethics for the rapidly emerging field. Unfortunately, it has devolved into a trade organization, with the main focus being on publicity and marketing. There are still some good people associated with IRVA, but the IRVA's imprimatur should not be mistaken for capability or quality.

There have been many discussions about the nature of remote viewing and whether or not it is a trainable skill. Commercially, there are a number of instructors who are dependent on the answer being "yes, it can be taught." The debate is similar to the nature-nurture controversy. There are those who believe that these psychic capabilities are innate—either you are born with them, or not. In support of that thesis are the few individuals who exhibit extraordinary capabilities.

Ingo Swann would argue otherwise. One of the major contributions he made to remote viewing involved his concept of the matrix. Much as in the Keanu Reeves movie of the same name, *the matrix* was a mental construct that allowed the practitioner to move about independently of consensual time and space. Most of the military remote viewers who were specifically trained for that assignment were taught employing Ingo's concept. Therefore, most of the second or third generation remote viewers who were trained by former Star Gate personnel use the matrix concept, whether they know it or not. This exacting method is both time and labor intensive. It is not a trick you pick up in an afternoon. To really engage in remote viewing takes a lot of dedicated effort.

There is also debate concerning whether it is better to rely on one strong remote viewer or look for consensus among several remote viewers. Joe McMoneagle argues in favor of a single viewer. He contends that when multiple viewers are involved, there can be a strong attachment to the wrong target; he feels the others will follow the false signal rather than operate independently on the real one. Stephan Schwartz, however, prefers the multiple viewer approach in which the analyst looks for consensus in reporting and suggests that is more reliable than the one-person method.

My belief is that psychic abilities are just like other human endeavors: everyone is endowed with some level of skill, and with training and practice improvement can be made. My own experience demonstrated to me that some data can be acquired. I know I lack the artistic acumen to transfer mental observations to recognizable form on paper, as I have problems drawing simple lines, and stick people are about as good as I get.

Most people can walk or run. With physical education in school, students run faster, jump higher or farther, etc. Still, most of them could never reach Olympic performance, no matter how hard they trained. With remote viewing, most practitioners will never approach the skill level of Ingo Swann or Joe McMoneagle. That doesn't mean you shouldn't try.

CHAPTER 13
WHITE CELLS MATTER

You probably have never heard the name Kangchenjunga, unless you are an avid mountain climber. Located on the India-Nepal border, it is the third highest mountain in the world, behind Chomolungma/Sagarmartha, or to Westerners, Mt. Everest, and K2. I mention it here in reference to giants, many of whom are unknown. As Kangchenjunga is to the Himalayas, so was my friend Cleve Backster to the world of psychic research. Very few people are aware of his many contributions to the field, and how he inspired many other projects, not the least of which was the remote viewing program popularly known as Star Gate.

Near the end of World War II, Cleve, then a U.S. Navy ensign, was in the South Pacific waiting to participate in the impending invasion of Japan.[72] The intervention of the only combat use of atomic weapons to date cancelled that requirement. A few months after being discharged in 1946, Cleve enlisted as a master sergeant in the U.S. Army Counterintelligence Corps. Keenly interested in human behavior, his objective was to explore the use of hypnosis from a national security perspective. A year later, as the CIA was formed, Cleve joined the new organization as an interrogation specialist. There, he developed the Backster Zone Comparative Technique for analysis of response to the polygraph.[73] That system is still the basis for such interviews today. After leaving the Agency, Cleve established his own school for lie detection, which is still running today, four years after his death in 2013.

Always inquisitive, Cleve engaged in many nontraditional experiments with his state-of-the-art equipment. He never married and was a bit of a recluse, but he loved playing with his sensitive instruments. In his New York apartment was a large dracaena plant. Cleve wondered how long it would take for water poured on the roots to reach the leaves. Galvanic Skin Response (GSR) is one of the measurements of the polygraph. The GRS sensor measures the amount of moisture on your skin and can detect when the person starts sweating. Out of curiosity, Cleve clipped a GRS detector to one of the leaves and then watered the base. He got his answer—and far more than he ever dreamed about.

Cleve forgot about the GSR device and just left it connected to the plant. The sensor was hooked to a graph that measured fluctuations in moisture on the leaves of the plant. It took a while, but Cleve began to note strange recordings on the graph; ones not associated with the periodic watering of the plant. There was nothing apparent in the environment that should be causing these variant readings.

To his great surprise, Cleve determined that the GSR chart seemed to be related to emotional events in the proximity of the dracaena. At the time, there was no rational explanation why a plant should show a measurable physical response to events occurring in its vicinity. Assuming the plant might be responsive to direct threats, Cleve cut a leaf. The chart indicated that the plant had an awareness of the cut. Was it pain? That was an unknown. But the assault on the plant was physical. The response he saw on the charts he labeled as "fainting." He wondered if this was the plant's response to danger. To test that hypothesis, Cleve took a cigarette lighter and burned a leaf. The plant fainted. Pushing the envelope further, he tried a series of experiments. What he found was astonishing.

Cleve then learned that when he approached the plant and just *thought* about burning a leaf, the plant would faint. That's right, the mere thought of harm, though no physical action was taken, was sufficient to cause a measurable response on the polygraph charts. He soon learned that the dracaena responded to threats to other life forms in its immediate vicinity. Boiling water close to the plant, Cleve dropped in a few live brine shrimps, causing their immediate death. Again, the plant fainted.

Knowing he was on to something important, Cleve went public with his findings. After all, he was a polygrapher, not an accredited research scientist. Naively, he thought that other scientists would surely jump on his embryonic but amazing results, and pursue more rigorous research. Instead, he was subjected to scorn and ridicule by most Western scientists. Our loss was a gain for the East, as the scientists in Eastern Europe under the Soviet Union took his work seriously. There were a few Americans who followed up, however. Hal Puthoff recognized the possibilities, and Cleve's work became part of the impetus for Puthoff's remote viewing research that began at Stanford Research Institute (later called SRI).[74]

It was Ted Rockwell, the nuclear engineer, who first introduced me to Cleve. At the time, I was assigned to INSCOM and exploring a range of unique topics, which I discuss elsewhere in the book. Ted assisted me in several areas, especially when it came to key introductions.[75] The work Cleve was then doing had moved far beyond exploring the reactions of plants, which had become publicly known through a book by Peter Tompkins and Christopher Bird entitled *The Secret Life of Plants*.[76] Cleve's new work involved monitoring oral leukocytes, or the white cells the permeate the mouth.

There are three types of blood cells. There are platelets that assist in blood clotting. Red cells carry oxygen to the body and are essential for life. White cells are known for fighting disease but sometimes get out of hand. When they do and multiply excessively, it creates a condition called leukemia, which is often fatal. The white cells in your mouth are called oral leukocytes.

The leukocyte study Cleve devised was relatively straightforward. The initial step was to collect and concentrate the oral leukocytes from the person. They did this by just spitting into a test tube. That tube was then placed in a centrifuge for a few seconds and then in a Faraday cage to protect it from external electromagnetic radiation. Silver electrodes were inserted in the tube, its wires attached to a device that amplified the signal, which was then sent to a polygraph. The results on the polygraph chart were videotaped with date/time data recorded. A second camera was used to record current events, and a split-screen generator captured both the events and the chart on a single tape in real-time.

Could these white cells respond to the emotional state of the donor even though they were separated in distance? To test the theory, the donor was exposed to potential threats, or situations that reminded them of a personal threat. In order to do that, test subjects would agree to watch specified television programs. These were frequently crime programs in which it could be anticipated that some threatening event would be seen, but neither the donor nor the researchers knew in advance exactly when such a scene would occur in that program.

What Cleve learned was that often there was an immediate and direct correlation between events portrayed on television and demonstrable deviation on the chart recordings. One striking example Cleve gave me was that of a young female volunteer. After contributing her white cells, she went to her home, which was located nearby. The specific TV scene she reacted to involved a woman being grabbed off the street and thrown into the trunk of a car. When that scene aired, the chart went wild. When Cleve inquired about what had happened, she informed him that something very similar had happened to her, but she had been able to fight off the attacker and run for help. Even though she had survived the kidnapping attempt, it was still a significant emotional event in her life. And that is exactly what the chart revealed.

From a basic science perspective, this was fascinating, as the data implied an ability to communicate in a manner never before anticipated. It raised many important questions: what was the mode of transmission, what were the distance constraints, and what was the reliability of the information? From an intelligence standpoint, we had some very pragmatic issues. In the 1980s there had been a number of high profile kidnappings. Among those was Brigadier General James Dozier, who was snatched from his quarters in Verona, Italy, by members of the Italian Red Brigade. Even more significant was the takeover of the American Embassy in Tehran the year before. The question I wanted to answer was whether or not the use of oral leukocytes offered a means to communicate, even at a basic level. The notion of inserting tracking devices in high-risk personnel was considered. The problem was that if an adversary suspected such a device, they would likely cut open the victim until they found the tracking device. The issue I wanted to determine first was whether the person was alive or dead. The second step would have been to attempt to send simple binary code transmissions, but unfortunately, we never got that far in the research.

After visiting Cleve's laboratory, I was able to hire Cleve as a consultant with approval from Major General Bert Stubblebine. The contract allowed me to replicate his device at my lab at Ft. Belvoir, Virginia. However, replication meant designing equipment that was beyond my technical expertise. Therefore, a senior scientist from the U.S. Army Night Vision Laboratory (NVL) was assigned to assist in creating the device. The director of NVL, Lou Cameron, was very open to the topics I was researching and had attended a couple of my metal bending parties.

The NVL representative and I visited Cleve in San Diego to obtain the specifications and see the system in operation. When I asked the engineer if he could build the device, he said he could, that the mechanical aspects were quite straightforward. But he noted, quite correctly, that there "was a piece missing." He was, of course, referring to how the signal got from the donor to the test tube. I told him that it would be my responsibility to handle that problem. Clearly, we had stretched his belief system too far. With his thumb and fingers, he formed a heart-shaped symbol in front of his chest, and said: "Look, I have carved out this much of the universe for me. You can move things about in here. But don't tell me I have to relearn physics, because I don't want to hear it."

I must give him credit. Despite serious concerns about the intent of my experiments, he built an exact replica of Cleve's device. He could easily have screwed me. One incorrect connection or a loose wire would be enough to completely stop what I was doing and would have been almost impossible for me to troubleshoot. I applaud his integrity for both telling me about his concerns and yet professionally completing the task.

In our experiments, we used materials other than leukocytes to detect emotions. Cleve used yogurt as it was easy to obtain and would last a long time. Yogurt is produced using a culture of Lactobacillus delbrueckii subsp. bulgaricus and Streptococcus thermophilus bacteria. This is living food in a form that was simple to handle for the experiments. Like the plants, yogurt seemed to be sensitive to emotional states in the immediate environment. Therefore, I followed his lead for the next year.

Not everyone was excited about the research. Several times, Stubblebine had me report the results to his council of colonels that met every quarter. Most of them were commanders of subordinate units dispersed around the world. They had already endured metal bending parties. Despite the demonstrated success of metal bending, many of them were still skeptical. Now I was telling them that we could record human emotional states from monitoring yogurt. A big topic for the U.S. Army in the early 1980s was a concept called AirLand Battle.[77] That had to do with fighting on multiple dimensions and focused on the defense of Central Europe. The military likes to use acronyms. After my briefing, the subordinate commanders came up with a new one, TY-ISALB, which stood for Talking Yogurt in Support of AirLand Battle. Cute, but I got the message. They did not see the relevance of the experiments that Bert and I did, but that was to be expected. The purpose in the briefing was not to gain support. Rather, it was a reminder that they should not disregard information just because it didn't fit what they already believed.

Working with Cleve was a delight. Not just because it meant trips to San Diego, but because we were really pushing the frontiers of science. In several experiments, I served as the guinea pig and was hooked up to one of Cleve's polygraphs. For that work, we devised a system using three cameras simultaneously. One camera recorded the chart from the oral leukocytes, while another registered the chart for the polygraph. The third monitored the environment where I was sitting. That method insured that we could time-synchronize my response to the graphs.

In some sessions, I attempted to fool the polygraph. In working with Dr. Richard Bandler, one of the co-developers of NLP, we had explored counter-polygraph techniques. Some worked amazingly well, including the ability to alter memories from one's past. That was not simple, but it could be done. For these experiments, I gave Cleve and Steve White, his lab assistant, permission to ask questions about some very personal matters. What we determined was that I could fool the polygraph, but not the device reading my emotional state from the oral leukocytes. The implications were huge, but not supported by any scientific theory. As far as I know, no one ever followed up on that work.

In 1986, the Army asked the National Research Council (NRC) to undertake a study of the various novel techniques for enhancing human performance that various units had been testing, including remote viewing (Star Gate), Neuro-Linguistic Programming, and sleep learning. At my suggestion, the panel also visited Cleve Backster's laboratory. While a stunning event occurred during the demonstration there, the report was almost entirely negative.[78]

The composition of the NRC board was crucial in understanding the report. The vast majority were behavioral scientists who had never been exposed to any of these topics. The one exception was University of Oregon psychologist Ray Hyman. Hyman was a founding director of the Committee for Scientific Investigation of Claims the Paranormal (CSICOP), which is now known as the Committee for Skeptical Inquiry (CSI). Despite the title, CSICOP was a debunking organization. The slanted make-up of the panel was intentional. The Army Research Institute technical contractor, George Lawrence, was very negatively disposed to all of the topics on the agenda. He had engaged in similar activity in the evaluation of other projects before.[79] This problem with the NRC board was identified before the panel met. With Congressional help, several of us attempted to have Robert Jahn, then Dean of the School of Engineering at Princeton University included on the board. But since the board was bent on skewing the report, our request was denied. In my first presentation to the panel, I mentioned the lack of physical scientists and noted that the ground-breaking work in the field was being done by physicists such as Bob Jahn and Hal Puthoff.

Trusting that Cleve's experiments could stand scrutiny, I suggested the panel visit his laboratory. That was convenient as they had a meeting scheduled for the Salk Institute in La Jolla, California just a few miles away. Cleve and I set the agenda for the visit. He would give a brief presentation in his classroom. I would follow with a very short synopsis, addressing my independent replication of his work. The presentations would be followed by a demonstration in his laboratory that was located about 200 feet in a straight-line distance from the classroom but separated by four walls.

When conducting a demonstration before members of the National

Academy of Science (NAS), it's advisable to ensure that everything is working properly, needless to say. That "the system was working yesterday" is not good enough for them; it had to work in real time. Therefore, I arrived at the lab early and donated my oral leukocytes and made a test run. All of the equipment was working perfectly. The chart reflecting the response from my cells was relatively flat with minor deviations.

The group arrived at 3:00 p.m., right on schedule. Two of them went with Steve White to donate their cells for the demonstration. After introductions and pleasantries, the remainder of the group accompanied Cleve and me to the classroom. As planned, Cleve began his presentation. Unfortunately, Cleve had a tendency toward circumlocution. In a formal setting, if you asked him what time it was, he would respond with the history of chronometers. Here, as he droned on with too much information, I could tell the panel members were getting antsy and wanted to move along.

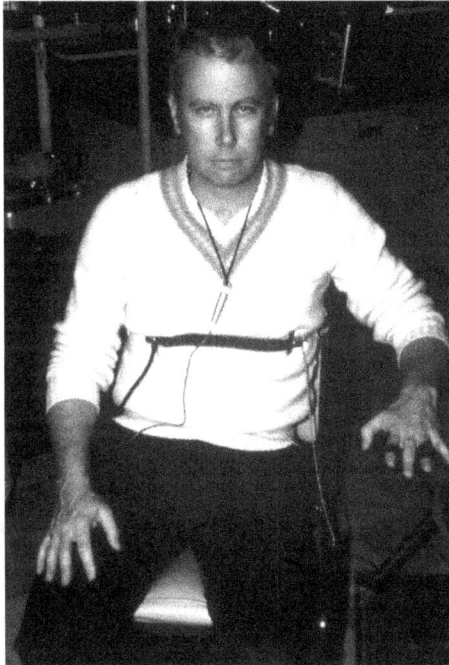

Author on polygraph while also being monitored by white cells.

Finally, it was my turn to speak. I just wanted to say that I had confirmed Cleve's results with my independent replication and get them moving to the lab. About a minute and a half into my presentation, the door flew open, and Steve burst in breathlessly asking, "What happened about 90 seconds ago?" We had never shut down the device with my oral leukocytes, and the chart had been recording for more than two hours. Just as I began to speak the charts had gone wild. Since there were limiters on the recorder, it was impossible to determine the total deviation that had occurred. It was very dramatic. The electrical signals from cells certainly reflected the emotional state of the donor. In this situation, I can attest that telling members of the National Academy of Sciences *that the universe is not built the way they think it is,* was an emotionally stimulating event.

TRACING OF NORMAL EMOTIONS WITH ORAL LEUCOCYTES

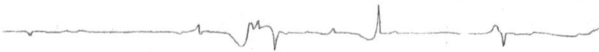

**TRACING OF EMOTIONAL RESPONSE TO THE
NATIONAL RESEARCH COUNCIL PANEL**

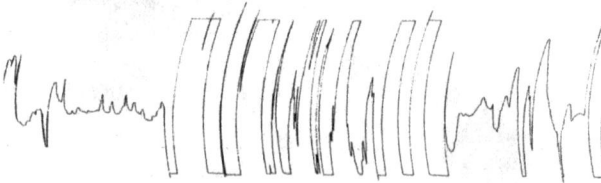

On February 10, 1986, a recording was made of responses from the author's white cells which were located in a shielded cage several hundred feet from him. These extracts are taken from that chart. The top line is representative of hours baseline that day. The bottom line is part of the responses when the author was making his presentation. Clearly they are different.

The photos show samples of tracings from the actual chart made that day. The original chart is still in my possession. It does not take a signals analyst to determine that the minor fluctuations from the prior two hours are significantly different from the period in which I was speaking before the group. When I stopped talking, the line went back to normal. It remained basically flat until I entered the lab door, when it spiked again. The rest was lost as Ray Hyman tore the chart off of the recorder.

The official report does not mention this event. It does describe going to the Backster Laboratory and remaining unconvinced that there was anything of scientific value. We did continue the experiment using the oral leukocytes from one of the panel members who volunteered to donate while the rest of the group was in the classroom. There was no remarkable change in the charts during the demonstration, but then, the donor experienced no emotional stress.

An interesting postscript to the demonstration did occur. As the group sat and discussed the experiment with Cleve, the volunteer stared intently at the Faraday cage containing the test tube with his leukocytes. Finally, he exclaimed that he had tried to mentally cause the needle to jump but had failed to do so. But as soon as he stopped trying, the needle did make a significant mark. The donor took that as proof the system did not work. However, anyone who has explored psi phenomena knows that part of the process of trying to affect a physical device involves letting go of the intention. The panel members would never know that what happened was quite predictable and in line with what we do know about the functioning of intent and psi.

That day the proverbial White Crow flew in front of an august scientific body and was totally ignored. The only report that mentioned this incident was an article I wrote for *New Realities*, called "A Challenge to the Report."[80]

CHAPTER 14
THE HUTCHISON EFFECT

The movie was impressive. Some objects seemed to levitate, others shot up into the air, accelerating as they went. The range of effects was dramatic, possibly too good to believe, especially since some of the objects were non-metallic, which would rule out a classic electromagnetic explanation for what we were seeing.

We contacted the owners of the film, Alex Pezarro and George Hathaway, both Canadians, and asked them to join us at Intelligence and Security Command (INSCOM) headquarters at Arlington Hall Station. Alex was basically the businessman, who had contact with the creator of the strange effects we saw in this film. George was an experienced electrical engineer and managed to make diagrams of the inventor's apparatus, which had produced these effects.

The inventor turned out to be John Hutchison, an iconoclast, and our worst nightmare when it came to credentials. He had none. A high school dropout, John was self-taught. He claimed to have studied photos of Nikola Tesla's workbench, then tried to figure out what Tesla was doing. How we could justify spending money on replicating the effects we saw in the film was going to be tricky at best. Still, in 1983 Defense budgets were fairly loose, and we were exploring a number of arcane technologies. Thus, we established a contract to replicate Hutchison's earlier experiments. I was the contract monitor.

What initially was called the Lift and Disruption System and has become known as The Hutchison Effect is extremely difficult to define. One problem is that there appear to be several different effects, and they are generally uncontrollable. In his book, *Mindbending*,[81] George Hathaway states: "it was a collection of phenomena lying far outside our normal experience and understanding. Its primary manifestations include causing or allowing objects of any material to lift into the air either in vertical or looping trajectory, or to hover; severely disrupting intermolecular bonds in any material resulting in catastrophic disruptive fracturing; causing plastic deformation in metals; creating unusual aurora-like lighting effects in mid-air; and inducing changes in the magnetic state and chemical composition of metals."

At issue was an elaborate collection of electronic devices, none of which could account for the documented observations. Further, our attempt to replicate those events were unsuccessful. But that does not mean they didn't happen under other circumstances.

Hutchison's initial work was done in a basement of a home in Vancouver, British Colombia. There was no intent on Hutchison's part to create some grand new scientific breakthrough. Rather, he just liked sparks. He bought discarded electronic equipment at various sales and junk shops. Of particular interest to him were Tesla Coils and Jacob's Ladders, devices that would make lots of visible electrical effects.

The story goes that Hutchison was sitting in the dark, as he often did at night, watching the sparks emanate from the apparatus in front of him when something flew out and hit him. Without thinking much about it, he picked up the object and threw it back toward the center of the contraption. To his surprise, it flew back and hit him again. Other than the electrical fields he was generating, there was no known source that would propel an object the way he had experienced. Hathaway says that Hutchison has several versions of how he discovered the effect, but this is the one he told me.

Always curious, Hutchison began to experiment further. He assembled an impressive array of electronic devices. Based purely on intuition, he designed special coils and placed them about the room. The old basement contained many exposed metal pipes, and they undoubtedly contributed to whatever fields were being generated. As Hutchison played with various designs, strange effects appeared.

Word of his experiments reached Alex Pezarro, who knew nothing about the science involved, but anticipated that a business could be derived from this work. To get a better grasp on what was happening, he contacted an accomplished electrical engineer, George Hathaway, who lived in Toronto. Hathaway wisely started taking measurements and documenting the design of Hutchison's experiments. Some elements were obvious, but others were not, such as the impact of the immediate environment in which they were operating.

Hutchison's experiments had unintended consequences as well. His proclivity for generating extremely high voltages tended to disrupt television sets in the local area. This was well before cable systems brought the signal directly into your home. As a result, nearby residents became very unhappy and Hutchison was required to dismantle his apparatus and move. The equipment had to be put in storage while Alex and George explored methods to reconstitute the experiments.

The exact path that brought Alex and George to my attention is unclear. I believe that their film came to the attention of a friend of mine, Ted Rockwell, who was an extraordinary engineer. An original nuclear scientist on the Manhattan Project, Ted had worked on creating the first nuclear materials Oak Ridge Laboratory in Tennessee (it became the Oak Ridge National Laboratory). Following World War II, Ted became the technical director for Admiral Rickover, who is famous for creating the U.S. Navy's nuclear-powered ships and submarines. Ted was extremely open-minded and we collaborated on several projects over the years.

At INSCOM, we closely examined the film and intently questioned George and Alex. In addition to the film, George brought a briefcase with numerous samples that exhibited the Hutchison Effect. There were small aluminum bars that were solid on one end and frayed like bad hair on the other. There were L-shaped bars that were twisted in manners not easily explained. More interesting were those L bars that were twisted, yet contained embedded items including wooden sticks and hardened screws. We wondered why some metals twisted, while others immediately adjacent did not. There was also a PVC pipe that retained its original structure at one end while the other was soft and frayed. According to witnesses who had seen this happen, part of the frayed end of the PVC pipe had completely vaporized.

In one sequence, the film shows a rat-tail file held between two wooden boards. Exposed to the field produced by the Hutchison Effect, the file illuminated just as a filament in an incandescent light bulb would. For a short time, the file glowed brightly, then broke in two near the middle, though the wooden boards constraining the file showed no sign of burning, as would be expected. According to a witness at that experiment, as soon as the file split, they were able to reach in and pick it up with their bare hands. That alone is inconsistent with the amount of heat that would normally be generated to cause structural disintegration of the file.

Alex showed me a drive shaft that had been exposed to the field during an experiment. It was then taken to British Colombia Hydro for metallurgical analysis. The results were astonishing. One end was case-hardened steel, as would be expected of a drive shaft. But the other end of this singular piece had the consistency of lead (i.e., relatively soft).

Through INSCOM I provided the funding (about $25,000.00) for them to attempt to reconstruct the apparatus. Unemployed at the time, Hutchison worked on the cheap which was cost effective for me. Of course, they could not guarantee the reconfiguration would work, as there were too many unknowns. For a location to experiment, Alex gained access to a vacant warehouse in Vancouver. The building remained nearly empty except for a single partitioned room in the center of the building. They used half of that room, while the other half belonged to someone else. The designated room had a flat wooden roof that we could walk on. Later this enabled us to diagram the area where the effects took place.

Alex's team reassembled the apparatus as best they could, based on Hutchison's memory and George's diagrams. I visited the project several times as the reconstruction took place. At INSCOM we were very interested in the effects that had been displayed with various materials. Working with a contact at the Night Vision Laboratory at Ft. Belvoir, Virginia, we devised a means to test the materials. Several different types of metals were selected as samples for testing. They were then cut into two pieces. One set was stored in a safe at Ft. Belvoir, and the other I delivered by hand to Hutchison and Pezarro in Vancouver. This process insured that if any changes were observed in the test samples, we had a hard baseline with which to compare them.

In addition, I had some molybdenum rods that Jack Houck had given me. These were used as test items at his metal-bending parties. Extremely strong, none of these rods was ever bent at any of our PKMB events. These, I assumed, would be an excellent test for this experiment.

Once Alex and John Hutchison reported obtaining positive results, we set a date for the review team to fly to Vancouver for the evaluation. I arrived a day ahead of the rest of the scientists. Alex met me at the airport and was very excited. He claimed that earlier that day they had experienced items levitating in the field created by their apparatus. To insure they could reproduce the effects, they had turned off the power and not touched any of the dials on the various devices. They assumed that by simply turning the power back on, the effects would return.

The protocol stated I would assemble a team of scientists to evaluate the results. From INSCOM I brought three other staff members. In addition, we obtained the services of two senior scientists from Los Alamos National Laboratory. While I knew one of them, John Rink, the other, Bob Freyman, was unknown to me. That turned out to be a huge mistake. He came with a mindset that what we reported could not possibly be real, and he was there determined to prove the point. Freyman had been with Los Alamos since the Manhattan Project days of World War II and had a very credible resume.

It was not until dinner the first evening that I recognized who he was from stories I had heard about a scientist who used to debunk any experiment that smacked of free, or alternative, energy. Suddenly, here he was on my team, and that was not a good sign.

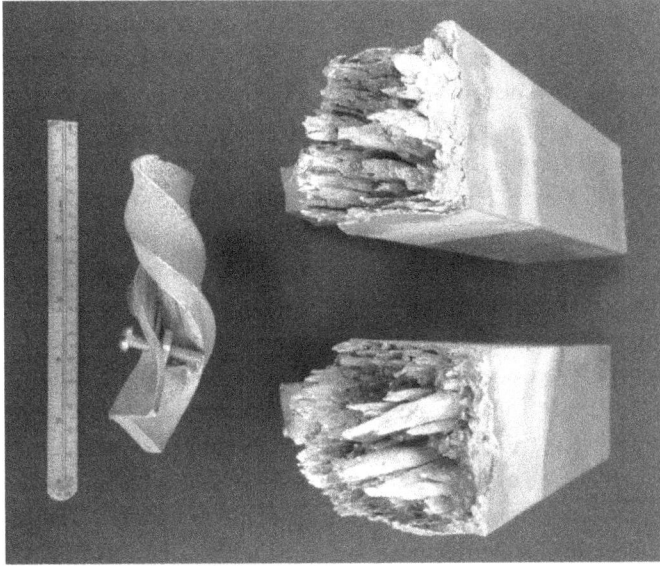

Examples of metals exposed to the Hutchison Effect. Note the twist in one metal sample while the screw remains intact. No physical force was applied to these test items. (George Hathaway)

You have probably heard the admonitions about assumptions. They are true. What occurred next was a pure disaster. A key factor in the experiment was the amount of power used to create the effect. To control for power input, everything was hooked to two electrical extension cords from 115-volt wall outlets—just like the ones you use at home. That meant there was no hidden power source pumping high energy into the device. An extension cord was plugged into a high-voltage furnace ignition transformer that controlled power to the various instruments. Almost as soon as the power was turned on, smoke arose from the transformer. It literally burned up on the spot. As this experiment was done on a very low-cost basis, there was no backup. Hathaway noted that this type of problem had plagued Hutchison's whole setup as various pieces of equipment would spontaneously burst into flames or "burn out" (cause a break in a wire) or "short out" (cause two adjacent wires to fuse together).

While Pezarro scoured Vancouver for another high-voltage transformer, the evaluation team took the day off and enjoyed the sights, including a trip to the top of the mountain which overlooks the city. The following day, after Hathaway was able to repair the original transformer, we were able to resume the demonstration. Unfortunately, nothing happened while the scientists watched. That certainly reinforced the belief of our resident skeptic.

The story of the experiment could end there. The simple response would be: we came, we saw, nothing happened. But there was more to the story. The senior LANL skeptic went back and wrote a scathing report in which he accused another controversial American scientist of slipping into Canada and orchestrating this event. That person was known to me and was in no way related to anything we were doing. It puzzled me why totally unrelated issues had been raised. Worse, they decided to classify the report "Confidential." That formal classification, though unwarranted, made it impossible for any of our Canadian colleagues to obtain copies. In fact, Hutchison, now in the U.S., has filed several Freedom of Information Act requests, but has never received the report. I suspect it was simply routinely destroyed, but that hasn't stopped conspiracy theorists from suggesting it was done to bury the technology.

There are some conflicting anecdotes regarding what might be causing these effects. Based on my experience with metal bending and other psychokinesis experiments, I wondered if what Hutchison had invented might be some form of psi amplification device. I seriously considered that possibility while pushing the envelope for an explanation. Therefore, I asked Hutchison if he was part of the device. He told me he thought so, as he could intuit when events were about to happen. He claimed he felt excited prior to those events. George and Alex, on the other hand, disagreed with him. They stated that Hutchison became excited *after* those unique events happened. The issue was never resolved, but that would explain their inconsistency and unpredictability.

Why did the events sometimes occur, albeit not when the scientists were observing? One had to accept the results as a matter of trust. Alex had shown me several new items that appeared to have been fractured or deformed. The most important object was a molybdenum rod that I had given him. He presented me with a rod that now had a distinctive shallow S-curve. Given our prior experience with these rods, we had no viable explanation. My supreme skeptic from LANL, Freyman, pontificated that the item had been heated to a high temperature and then bent in a vice. However, examination of the rod showed no sign of exposure to heat. More important, microscopic examination of both ends indicated that it had not been gripped by mechanical means. Such physical constraint would have been detected in our examination and it was not.

Since the experimenters failed to meet the predetermined standards, INSCOM's involvement was terminated. Independently, I interviewed each member of the evaluation team. I and four others stated we believed that real unexplainable events had happened. But the ranking of the senior LANL scientist insured the project's demise. What amazed me most about the LANL report pertaining to the Hutchison project was just how scathing it was. An accurate account would have stated nothing happened. Instead the report invoked rampant fraud, injected people who were not involved, and unjustly tied the project to related work. My thought about the LANL report is that it protested far too much, and for no apparent reason.

Other organizations did their own experiments on the Hutchison Effect, including McDonnell Douglas through Jack Houck. He obtained similar results as ours; that is, unusual events happened, just never when they could be observed by independent witnesses, or when instrumented. To this day, Hutchison continues his experiments with various technologies and has been the subject of numerous television programs. Alex Pezarro has died of a heart attack, but George Hathaway maintains an impressive collection of objects that defy explanation by conventional science. For those interested in the history of the Hutchison Effect, I recommend Hathaway's book, *Mindbending*, about the trials and tribulations with this work. There are some minor differences in our recollections of my involvement, but he has the far more independent history about John Hutchison and his experiments than anyone else.

PART III

SPIRITUAL EXPERIENCES

CHAPTER 15
ON BEING DEAD

Is death the final frontier? Fear of death is innate, visceral, and a driving factor in the lives of many people; but it needn't be so. For millennia, there have been tales of those who have been close to death, yet come back and relay information that suggests consciousness may continue beyond the demise of the physical body. The implications for all humanity are both enormous and mostly ignored.

Although I had heard a few stories of this kind, it was not until I met Dr. Elisabeth Kübler-Ross[82] that I learned of the pervasiveness of the phenomena. It was Elisabeth and another medical doctor, Raymond Moody, who initiated the field that would become known as near-death studies. Near-death experiences, or NDEs, have now become popularized, but in the 1970s they were not generally acknowledged. At that time, many people who experienced an NDE felt that publicity was the last thing they wanted. Rightfully, they feared ridicule, or the thought that others might think them crazy. A few of them even believed they *were* crazy, as the events they encountered did not fit either a scientific or religious model.

While finishing my dissertation, I encountered several extraordinary NDE cases that could not be easily explained. After obtaining my doctoral degree, I read *Life at Death*[83] and *Heading Toward Omega*,[84] both by Ken Ring, a professor of psychology at the University of Connecticut. While Raymond Moody's book *Life After Life*[85] had become a bestseller, Ring's books brought more scientific research to bear on the topic. I also learned that he, and a few like-minded people, had created a new organization, the International Association for Near-Death Studies (IANDS).[86] Within a short time, I was on the IANDS board of directors and getting more deeply involved in NDE studies.

Personally, I was interested in two specific types of NDEs, both of which provided hard data. One type involved cases in which veridical information was passed to the experiencer. That material was often about events that would occur in the future. The other type included cases in which spontaneous healing occurred. Both pose significant challenges for traditional science.

As mentioned, tales of NDEs have been around for a long time. One of the earliest NDEs was written in *The Republic* by Plato, when Er, a soldier, awoke on his funeral pyre. Plato wrote, "...the tale of a warrior bold, Er, the son of Armenious, by race a Pamphylian. He once upon a time was slain in battle, and when the corpses were taken up on the tenth day already decayed, he was found intact, and having been brought home, at the moment of his funeral, on the twelfth day as he lay upon the pyre, revived, and after coming to life related what, he said, he had seen in the world beyond. He said that when his soul went forth from his body he journeyed with a great company and that they came to a mysterious region where there were two openings side by side in the Earth, and above and over against them in the heaven two others, and that judges were sitting between these, and that after every judgment they bade the righteous journey to the right and upward through the heaven with tokens attached to them in front of the judgment passed upon them, and the unjust to take the road to the left and downward, they too wearing behind signs of all that had befallen them, and that when he himself drew near they told him that he must be the messenger to humanity to tell them of that other world, and they charged him to give ear and to observe everything in the place."

Many readers will have read some of the ever-increasing body of literature on NDEs. This being autobiographical, it is appropriate to present cases that I encountered and have not previously been written about.

Don

Not surprisingly, combat-related NDE cases would come to me while I was in the military. One in particular stands out in my mind as it had unique components to it. Don, a pseudonym, was an Apache helicopter gunship pilot in Vietnam. Thin and sleek in design, the Apache was a two-seat aircraft in which the two pilots sat in tandem. Don was in the front seat that afternoon as they flew across miles of lush forest. Normally gunships were deployed in pairs, but on this occasion Don and his copilot were flying alone across disputed territory. Suddenly, they came under intense fire from an enemy .51 caliber, heavy machine gun. The Apache was struck several times and the controls between the front seat and back seat were severed. Despite having armor plating protecting his lower body, the impact of the bullets was sufficient to break his left leg above the knee. The helicopter immediately caught fire, causing Don's face to be burned severely.

According to the pilot seated behind him, Don slumped forward over the controls when they were hit and physically did not move. But Don's perspective was quite different. He remembers slipping out of his body and hovering just above it for a while. He then "saw" a small clearing in the densely wooded jungle, but unfortunately it was not large enough in which to land the burning Apache. Though out of his body, Don believes he crash landed their craft, as the controls for the back seat were shot away. Since there was insufficient room in which to set the Apache down, Don remembers he pulled the nose upward so that they would contact the ground boom first. While that technique would destroy the helicopter, it would mitigate that impact of the crash. At best, this was a very bad day.

With blades still spinning, the Apache beat itself to death on the surrounding trees. That is an important feature of the story as it means that until the thrashing stopped, the final orientation of the craft could not have been known. Don then reports moving further away from his body, to a position high enough that he could see the wreckage and surrounding territory. From this vantage point, he noticed a friendly fire-support base located about a mile away, and that the nose of the Apache was pointed in the direction of that base. That information could not have been obtained at any time they were in the air. It was only after the helicopter finally came to rest, that the relationship between the Apache and the fire base could have been known.

Don indicates that he then encountered a hooded figure with a bright light behind him. He believes this was a male figure who asked him, "What are you doing here?" Don responded that he wanted "to get help for them." Interestingly, he did not identify the body in the burning ship to be his. Allegedly, the figure then said, "Don't you know?"

"Know what?" Don answered. The hooded figure then said, "You're not dead yet." With that, Don instantly found himself back in his physical body. Recovering, he sat up. The pilot who was running from the burning helicopter, spotted the movement, returned, and pulled Don free from the wreckage. He stated that he thought Don was dead as he had not moved since they were strafed and Don had collapsed.

Don tried to run, but couldn't because of his broken leg. Instead, he hid behind the giant ant hills that dotted the terrain. His companion told Don there was a friendly fire-support base nearby, and he was going to get help. Don informed him the base was in the direction directly off the nose of the destroyed Apache. The copilot insisted it was in another direction at about right angles to the base's actual location. With Don's face burned off and leg broken, pain was setting in and he was no longer in a position to debate the issue. Unfortunately, the copilot chose to head in the wrong direction, toward the uncharted jungle.

Soon after the copilot departed, the Viet Cong came to the site of the crash and swept the area looking for Americans to take prisoner. Taking prisoners was a high priority for them. Ho Chi Minh knew the war would end with negotiations. Knowing our value system, he understood that American prisoners would make excellent bargaining chips. But the enemy soldiers did not find Don, who had managed to conceal himself. Shortly after that, a friendly patrol made their way to the crash site, and Don was rescued.

It is at this point that Don's NDE story becomes unique. An evacuation helicopter was dispatched to the scene. Unable to land, they lowered a stretcher and then hoisted Don up into the hovering bird. While being lifted, Don now had the same vantage point that he had when he was out of his body a short time before. Looking down he could see that the fire support base was in fact aligned off the nose of the damaged Apache gunship. That meant the other pilot had gone off in the wrong direction. Before passing out, Don was able to tell the crew where his comrade had gone. Thanks to Don's observation and reporting, the other pilot was rescued a short time later.

Many people who have NDEs report perceptually being out of their physical body. What makes this case unique is that it is the only one I know of in which the person physically replicated the event immediately following the NDE. There are a few cases in which data was obtained that verified the external observation reported in the NDE, but I have never heard of a situation in which the NDE was physically replicated.

Don and I later worked together for a period of time. One day we went to a meeting at Walter Reed Army Medical Center located in Bethesda, Maryland. The discussion centered around these usual events. Among the officers present was the staff psychologist who served as the medical adviser to the Army's remote viewing program. A skeptic, and not accepting of the concept that one could be out of body, he attempted to convince Don that what he experienced was simply a dissociative state, a condition that involves disruptions or breakdowns of memory, awareness, identity, or perception. According to the medical definition, people with dissociative disorders use dissociation, a defense mechanism, pathologically and involuntarily. Dissociative disorders are thought to primarily be caused by psychological trauma. Don just looked at him and said, "You can believe whatever you want. I was dead!"

It is worth mentioning that Don was the recipient of some of the finest reconstructive surgery available anywhere in the world. If there is any positive side to combat, it may be the medical advances that are made. The U.S. Army has been at the forefront of burn injuries, and the Army Institute for Surgical Research at Brook Army Medical Center in Texas is absolutely world class. In addition to military casualties, they also provide support in civilian disasters.

Tom

Special Forces Command Sergeant Major Tom Holloway (a pseudonym) provided another interesting NDE case. Seriously wounded by a mine explosion in Vietnam, Holloway was stabilized and then medically evacuated back to the United States for further treatment. As a matter of course, he had consultations with his doctors to determine the best options for treatment. It was decided he would undergo surgery in an attempt to restore the function of his severely damaged leg.

On the day of the scheduled operation, Holloway was anesthetized and taken into the operating suite. While there, things took a bizarre twist. Suddenly and unexpectedly, he was out of his body. Observing the scene from near the ceiling, he saw the doctors and nurses as they prepared to surgically repair his lower leg. Then, surprisingly, the doctors abruptly left the operating room and retreated to another room that had no direct connection with the operating room. A discussion then ensued between the surgeons as to whether or not they should amputate the leg rather than try to save it. Unbeknownst to the doctors, in his out-of-body state, Holloway had followed them into this secluded room and overheard the entire conversation. He states he became really upset, as there had never been any prior discussion of a possible amputation. Holloway would never have consented to amputation unless there was no other viable solution.

The decision was made to proceed with the surgery that would save his leg. However, after regaining consciousness, Holloway confronted the surgeon about the conversation he had overheard in the second room. The doctors initially denied the incident, and pointed out it would have been impossible for Holloway, who was under anesthesia in the other room, to have heard the conversation. In response, he provided sufficient detail about the incident that the doctor was forced to admit it had happened. That the surgeon was perplexed would be an understatement. For Holloway to have heard the discussion was impossible—yet it happened.

George

Called the Chinese Claymore, the command detonated Chinese Communist (Chicom) Dh10 directional type mine can be a fearsome weapon. In Vietnam, they were employed in areas where the Viet Cong or NVA thought helicopters might attempt to land. Captain George Weinstein (a pseudonym) was an experienced combat pilot who flew CH-47 Chinook helicopters. Assigned to the 1st Calvary Division (Airmobile), the twin-engine Chinook was a workhorse for troop transport and heavy lifting of supplies into dangerous combat landing sites. Of the 750 CH-47s used in Vietnam, 200 were shot down or crashed, including Captain Weinstein's.

Operations in the mountainous Central Highlands of Vietnam were particularly hazardous. To support troops on the ground, these large helicopters would often hover a few feet above the terrain while troops jumped off or supplies were delivered. On the fateful day, Captain Weinstein was on an operation to resupply a small camp located on top of a mountain. Since there was no room to land, he hovered with the ramp at the tail end of the helicopter facing the camp. Suddenly, there was a horrific explosion directly below the doomed Chinook and the bird came crashing down. Due to the relative altitude difference between the rear and front of the helicopter, where the pilots were seated, had farther to fall before impact. The front engine, located directly above the pilots, came crashing downward, essentially crushing both crew members.

Miraculously, Weinstein survived and was later pulled unconscious from the crumpled wreckage. When he awoke in the medical evacuation hospital, he had a tale to tell, but was puzzled by the information he had been given during his NDE. George reported that he had been given an option to stay on the other side, or to return to his badly injured body and continue his life. There was, however, more to the offer. He was informed that should he return to the living, he would become a single parent and would be needed to raise his boys as they reached adolescence. At the time, this information made no sense. At the time, he had been happily married for a few years, so obviously he chose to return. But three years later, without warning, his wife filed for divorce and left him to raise the children on his own. The prophecy from his NDE turned out to be accurate, though George had no way of knowing about these future events at the time of his crash.

Marilyn

This next case is an example of spontaneous healing related to an NDE. Marilyn Hoffa (a pseudonym) was a medical basket case. That is not a scientifically acceptable diagnosis, but although only in her 30s, she suffered from multiple illnesses and afflictions. Therefore, when she died in a New York City hospital, the nurses and doctors in attendance were not surprised. As was the routine when patients die in most hospitals, they placed her body on a gurney and sent her to the morgue to await an autopsy and disposition.

Unlike many NDE cases, Marilyn did not report being out of her body in an autoscopic position, in a tunnel, or bathed in light. Rather, she just woke up. Spontaneously regaining consciousness, she found herself alone in the refrigerated morgue. Her response was quite unique, and probably not what one would expect under those conditions. She simply got off the gurney and began to do ballet, just as she had when she was a young girl. What makes this case so special, is that prior to her death, she was a paraplegic. For several years, she had been paralyzed from the waist down. Yet, with no medical intervention, Marilyn near-instantaneously regained the use of her legs. When I met her, Marilyn was completely mobile and in modestly good health.

Other Incredible Cases

While Marilyn's case may stretch the imagination, there are other similar cases reported with even more astounding results. One such case is that of Mary Neal, an orthopedic surgeon who was the victim of a kayaking accident in northern Chile. Her story is covered in her book, *To Heaven and Back.*[87] The multiple miracles that surrounded her survival defy all scientific explanation. Neal was trapped in her kayak upside down underwater for a minimum of 15 minutes, and most likely for more than half an hour. It is impossible that she could have held her breath that long. Because of the manner in which the kayak was wedged under rocks, the raging current forced her knees to bend backwards. She was aware of the ligaments tearing and her legs breaking. While physically devastating, that eventually allowed her to extricate herself. In a separate miracle, assistance arrived at the remote area where none exists.

Also significant is what transpired while she was incapacitated. She describes an interaction with a spiritual being. Like George, Neal was given information about a future event. In her case, it was the kind of news no mother would ever want to hear. She was advised that her son would die when he reached 18 years of age. She says she did not tell anyone about the disturbing information during her lengthy recovery. Then, as her son approached his eighteenth year, she told her husband. And true to the prediction, her son was struck and killed by a car while skateboarding.

There are a number of other credible NDE cases that challenge the basic scientific or medical notion of what constitutes death. It is generally agreed that most NDE reports are simply the personal anecdotes of the patient's perception at a time of severe stress or trauma. Many come from accident scenes, others from illnesses when there is no independent means of verification. That does not negate their reality, or their significance, especially to the individual involved. (In addition, there are other circumstances that simulate the NDE, but in which the person is not close to death. As the president of IANDS, I answered several letters in which the writer stated they had experienced an out-of-body state, possibly received information about future events, and yet was in good health at the time of the incident. While not classified as an NDE, those cases are equally challenging to science.)

Studies have been conducted on the effects of NDEs. The intensity of the memory is one characteristic that stands out in NDE reports. It is usually similar to a critical emotional event, one in which the memory does not fade. A classic example for those older readers may be what they were doing at the time when they heard President John F. Kennedy had been shot, or possibly the events of the 9/11 attack. Unlike regular memories that generally fade with time, these stay with us and details that normally diminish remain vivid. For most experiencers, that is what they report an NDE is like.

Over the decades, I have been privileged to meet many people who have shared their NDE stories, as well as many of the researchers in the field, and I consider many of them to be personal friends. While far from having all of the answers, these extreme cases provide evidence pointing to the complexity of the topic.

One involves Anita Moorjani who had an NDE accompanied by healing that was certainly miraculous, as mentioned previously. In February, 2006, Moorjani was at the end stage of cancer, Hodgkin's Lymphoma, and had been given less than 36 hours to live. Many of her internal organs had ceased to function, and her body was shutting down. While physically unconscious and in an out-of-body state, she, like Tom, observed and overheard a conversation between the doctors and her husband that took place some distance away. Like George, she was given a choice to return to life or stay. Obviously, she chose to return in order to support her family and provide testimony to millions of people. Physical healing that should have taken months was accomplished in days. Anita Moorjani's complete story can be found in her book, *Dying to be Me*,[88] on her website (anitamoorjani.com), and on several television interviews available on the internet.

Another extraordinary case is that of neurosurgeon Eben Alexander. In November 2008, Eben suddenly developed a very rare form of spontaneous E. coli meningitis, a disease with a 90 percent mortality rate. Within four hours, he was in a coma. He was hospitalized comatose for seven days. There are several unique aspects to this extraordinary case. As a neurosurgeon with nearly 30 years of experience, including teaching at Harvard Medical School, he understood that the condition of his brain during that period was such that there could be no cognitive processing of information. Yet Eben did report having encounters with discarnate spirits, and access to a comprehensive understanding of what underlies our reality. Infinite in nature, his story can be found in his books, *Proof of Heaven*[89] and *Map of Heaven*.[90]

What makes Eben's NDE so significant is that he is one of very few people who had an in-depth knowledge of brain functioning, and yet had an experience that defies what he knew was possible. As could be expected, his books have received scathing criticism by such luminaries as professor of neurology Oliver Sachs. Their basic argument is it can't be, therefore he is mistaken. These skeptics simply refuse to even look at the data. They also discount the fact that Eben, like many other people who had an NDE, also received information he did not previously know and later proved to be accurate. While Eben was adopted as a young child and we share the same last name, there is no relationship between us other than a personal friendship.

Pam

One argument against the NDE hypothesis is that in none of the aforementioned cases can the person be proven to be clinically dead at the time of the incident. But the Pam Reynolds case is different, as she was in an operating room and completely instrumented at the time of her experience. A young mother, Reynolds had a large aneurism deep in her brain, so deep that traditional brain surgery was impossible. Though extremely risky—both because of her age and the fact that she had young children—the rarely performed surgical procedure, known as hypothermic cardiac arrest, was authorized. Without it, there was no chance of survival if the aneurism burst.

In order to operate, all involuntary bodily functions were halted. This included the hazardous procedure of draining and cooling the blood from her brain. Under anesthesia, her breathing, heart, and even cortical brain activity were stopped. This was monitored by both an electrocardiogram (ECG) and electroencephalogram (EEG). By medical definition, a lack of breathing, a lack of heart functioning, and lack of brain activity is called death.

During her NDE, Reynolds described an autoscopic view from above herself and the activity in the operating suite. She accurately remembered the location of the staff members and their activities. As she returned to her body, she even remembered that they played the song "Hotel California," which she took to be quite inappropriate. The words of the last line include, "You can check out any time you like, but you can never leave!" An interesting detail about that observation is that Reynolds had molded plugs in her ears at the time that should have made it impossible for her to hear any external noises such as the saw, the conversations, or the background music.

Reynolds described her NDE to Michael Sabom, a cardiologist who became interested in the topic and began conducting his own research. While most NDEs are reported sometime after the fact, Sabom, as a heart specialist, was often present when patients were resuscitated. To his surprise, the reports he received confirmed the initial studies. Thus, when Reynolds told him about the operation, he followed up on it. Reynolds had mentioned they opened her head with a tool that looked like an electric toothbrush and made an awful screeching sound (like fingernails on an old blackboard). Sabom learned she was correct, but the instrument was a circular saw that could be mistaken for an electric toothbrush. In addition, he noted that everyone who has done brain surgery is aware of the hair-raising sound produced as the skull is opened. The initial report on the Pam Reynolds case can be found in Michael Sabom's book, *Light and Death.*[91]

Although about as good as NDE cases come, this one is not without controversy. An anesthesiologist named Gerald Woerlee has vociferously claimed that Reynolds' memories were of events when she was under general anesthesia, not flatlined, so her brain was still functional. Even if true, that does not explain many aspects of the case. She was clinically dead for some period of time, and accurately described activities that occurred while she had no access to the information via her physical senses. Like others, she was given a choice to stay or return, but she told the disincarnate entities that she should return to life to care for her children. Years later, in 2010, she transitioned permanently.

For years, the Pam Reynolds case was considered the Gold Standard of NDEs. It was suspected that similar cases existed but no patients or doctors came forward. In 2016 a very experienced anesthesiologist named Ravi Parti reported on another NDE case involving "hypothermic cardiopulmonary bypass and circulatory arrest." Again, the patient had no heartbeat, no respiration, and no brain function, as monitored on an EEG. Dr. Parti describes him as being in a state of *suspended animation* with all bodily functions stopped and his internal temperature dropped to about 50° F from the normal around 98.6° F, (37.0° C).

After resuscitation and regaining consciousness, the man accurately described observing the operation from an out-of-body perspective. But Dr. Parti did nothing. Based on his materialist worldview, Parti knew it could not be true, yet it happened. Rather than investigating the event or discussing it with others, he simply chose to ignore it. During his training, he had learned that cases involving such "hallucinations" should be referred to psychiatrists. Of course, that is one of the things people who have had an NDE fear most. It wasn't until December 2010, when Parti had his own, very dramatic NDE, that he again thought about what he termed "The Frozen Man."[92]

While NDE cases in which the person is totally instrumented are exceeding rare, they do exist. Importantly, they support the more anecdotal reports of incidents in which we rely solely on the information provided by the patient.

Blind people have NDEs, too

One unique study conducted by Ken Ring and Sharon Cooper involved NDEs in people who were congenitally blind. That means they were blind from birth and had never experienced sight, as opposed to sighted people who become blind due to accident or illness. While they did study some people who had lost their vision, it is the study of the congenitally blind group that is most perplexing from a scientific perspective.

It turns out that these congenitally blind patients reported the same characteristics of NDEs as sighted people, even though they previously had no frame of reference for vision. Various patients indicated they had been in an out-of-body state, had a tunnel-like experience, saw clearly their physical surroundings, heard music, and had transcendent experiences of other, non-physical realms.

Beyond just the NDE issues, these cases also address the concept of out-of-body states. As an article by Ring and Cooper in the *Journal of Near-Death Studies* stated, "they speak to the long-standing controversy in parapsychology over whether the OBE represents some kind of true extrasomatic state, or only a retrospective reconstruction based on sensory cues and imaginal processes."

At least anecdotally, there is evidence that some of the blind people who report having acute vision during an NDE may be truthful. If so, it challenges the traditional premise about how vision is created. There is no doubt that our eyes play a most important role in sight, but there is also processing in the brain that is less well understood, especially if the blind can see, even if under extremely limited circumstances.

A somewhat confounding issue is that many who undergo an NDE allege interactions with other forms of realities, including spiritual beings, and other dimensional aspects that do not conform to consensus reality. Still, the confirmation of sight of objects in our reality by blind subjects during an NDE is very significant.

Children and NDEs

My friend Melvin Morse has studied the subject and written some of the most important books about NDEs. I consider his first book, *Closer to the Light: Learning from the Near-Death Experiences of Children*,[93] to be one of the most significant as it counters some of the skeptical statements about survival stories.

A pediatrician who flew with medical evacuation aircraft in the Northwest, Dr. Morse initially was not particularly interested in NDEs. A least not until one young patient described her remarkable experience, which turned out to be quite accurate. Crystal had been found floating lifeless in a swimming pool. She had been underwater for an undetermined period of time. Melvin was one of the doctors in the emergency room and had been the one to resuscitate her. Although Crystal had other severe medical problems and had been given less than a ten percent chance of survival, she made an unusually quick recovery. Her family attributed this to their bedside prayers, even after the supervising doctors had recommended taking her off life support.

After spending three days in a coma, she was released from the Primary Children's Hospital in Salt Lake City, and flown back to Pocatello where Melvin came to visit her. As he was introduced, Crystal correctly identified Melvin as the doctor who had revived her. She knew there was another tall, clean-shaven doctor present. But she was aware that it was Melvin, the one with the beard, who had brought her back. Asked if she knew him, she stated, "Oh, yes, I do. You are the doctor who put a tube in my nose." According to Melvin, she was profoundly comatose when that happened. There is much more to Crystal's story, but what is important is that this was the case that convinced Melvin to research NDEs more thoroughly. ("Katie" in Melvin's book has self-identified as Crystal Merzlock and has appeared on television. No medical confidences are being betrayed by revealing this.)

While it is true that there are now many movies and television programs that depict NDEs, that has not always been the case. The argument that these children have been influenced by popular culture does not stand up in the older cases. In addition, Melvin found cases of NDEs in very young children. Some were only a few months old and pre-verbal. Not until they acquired adequate language skills were they able to relate their profound experiences.

Certainly, they had not been unduly influenced via the media.

As Melvin studied more and more pediatric NDE cases, he catalogued the same characteristics in their experiences as adults had experienced. Like Crystal, some had an autoscopic observation of their event; some reported traveling through a tunnel and seeing bright lights, and a few had encounters with discarnate entities or spiritual beings.

Shared NDEs

While the observations of children bring a scientifically challenging aspect to the corroboration of near-death experiences, there is another area that is even more problematic: shared NDEs. Those are events in which people other than the patient observe the NDE. These are covered in detail in Raymond Moody's book *Glimpses of Eternity: Sharing A Loved One's Passage From This Life to the Next.*[94] In the book, Raymond describes numerous veridical cases in which at least part of the transition process was witnessed by one or more other people.

One compelling encounter was Raymond's own experience when his mother died. While I have known Raymond for many years, this took place while we were both working for the same sponsor in Las Vegas, Nevada. Raymond held the Bigelow Chair of Consciousness Studies at the University of Nevada-Las Vegas (UNLV), and I worked at the National Institute for Discovery Science for Bob Bigelow. Because of our periodic meetings, I had the opportunity to learn about his experience firsthand.

When Raymond first learned of his mother's terminal diagnosis and imminent death from non-Hodgkin's lymphoma, he immediately flew to her bedside in Macon, Georgia. The family gathered and held hands as the moment drew near. He later wrote that four of the six people present felt as if they had lifted off the ground as the room changed shape. The group's perception of the lighting in the room was also altered. It seemed to soften and looked more like "a swimming pool at night."

Raymond tells of others who have shared a transition experience. Some people had their own out-of-body experience and observed the transition from that vantage point. A few said they saw a mist or haze rising from the body; that has been described in folklore for many years. Still other observers have indicated the presence of discarnate spirits, sometimes of a deceased relative who returns to assist in the transition process. Known as deathbed visions, such incidents are far more common than is generally acknowledged. Before we relegated death to sterile hospital environments, it was a norm for people to die at home in a more peaceful setting. The number of deathbed vision reports may have decreased because of the heroic treatments that are used in hospitals to prolong life at any cost.

Still, it should be noted that many hospice nurses have found patients talking to dead relatives or other unseen entities. Of course, it is easy to pass these experiences off as hallucinations, and some of them may well be. Yet there is a consistency to the reports that lends credibility. Then, too, there are stories in which the patient gets information not previously available to them, including in a few cases learning of deceased close relatives that the patient never knew existed.

Elisabeth Kübler-Ross told of an encounter in which a man was driving across the desert and came upon a serious accident. There the driver met a man who was dying. The victim asked the driver to inform his family that even though he had passed, he was all right and was with a close relative. So impressed was the driver, that he drove several hundred miles out of the way to inform the family. What was most shocking about this case was that the relative the victim described as being with him had also just died. That relative had died a considerable distance away, and the victim found in the desert had not been notified of that incident.

The Aftermath

When we first began discussing NDEs at IANDS, we thought they were short events that occurred over a discreet period of time. In most cases, they lasted seconds to minutes, though there were cases that involved longer periods of time. What we soon discovered is that the effects of NDEs could continue without let up after the NDE experience itself. Many experiencers reported psychic episodes, often beyond their control, including enhanced precognitive abilities. Some people reported having trouble with electrical watches after their NDE, but not mechanical ones. This is significant, as it is a physical manifestation of an event that most people believe is a purely cognitive experience or psychological aberration.

Many experiencers reported profound shifts in their worldview. Sometime these would have negative impact on their families. As one woman told me, her children didn't understand what had happened and why she behaved differently. From her perspective, she had met God, but they just wanted mommy back.

Beyond anecdotes, research was conducted into how NDEs changed perceptions and the behavior of that person. A Life Changes Questionnaire (LQC) was developed and administered to people who reported having an

NDE. In summary, the findings indicated they had a new appreciation for life and how precious it was, a greater concern for other people and an ability to love them, a less materialistic worldview, and a tendency to be more spiritually oriented as opposed to a specific religion. Not all people having NDEs have the same reaction, and we must be careful not to extrapolate from these general trends to any individual. For more details, I recommend Ken Ring's book *Heading Toward Omega* where these studies were first reported.

Spiritual versus Religious

The concept of a spiritual versus religious orientation was of specific interest to me as it fit directly with the work I had done on my doctoral dissertation. I had evaluated the changes that took place in people who attended Elisabeth Kübler-Ross's workshop, Life, Death, and Transition. For my dissertation, she insisted I change one word, from changes in *religiousness* to changes in *spirituality*. That simple alteration made a giant difference in the results.

In the workshop, Elisabeth introduced the concept of NDEs to many people who previously had never heard about them. Life, Death, and Transition was an extremely powerful workshop, as about a quarter of the attendees were terminally ill, and half were in the medical profession. There were questions about their changes in religious beliefs. Quite a number of respondents specifically crossed out the word religious. There was a very significant shift towards changes in spirituality. Respondents wrote things like, "I reject the dogma of the church, but am more spiritual now." Testing was done pre-workshop and at the end of the workshop. The results indicated an anticipated shift known as a euphoric artifact. That just means that people generally feel good after a workshop and is not indicative of real change. What was most impressive was that when I conducted a post-post instrument, the change had not disappeared, and in many instances, it was stronger in their reports of being more spiritually oriented. Post-post means that it was done after leaving the workshop and up to 18 months following their attendance. The results confirmed that the exposure to the intense environment in coordination with hearing firsthand accounts of NDEs had a profound effect on them.

Mary Schwartz

An incident that reportedly happened with Elisabeth Kübler-Ross takes a step well beyond even what is reported in NDE literature. It is one event that she personally told me about. I also heard public versions of it as well. The details have remained constant over time. It occurred while she was teaching at the Pritzker School of Medicine at the University of Chicago. The topic of death and dying was not often discussed at the time. It was Elisabeth who first broached the hospice concept in America, though it was already emerging in Europe.

She and a hospital chaplain, Renford Gains (who was known as "Renny" and later took the name Mwalimu Imara), began bringing terminally ill patients into the classroom and allowing medical students to question them. This was an innovative approach to the subject. Her premise was that if you wanted to know what these patients were thinking or worried about, it was best to just ask them. For many practitioners in the medical community, death was, and in too many cases still is, considered to be the enemy. Doctors, more than nurses, appear to have a greater fear of discussions with patients surrounding their mortality. These classes brought considerable focus on the topic, and Elisabeth's book *On Death and Dying* was pioneering. It has become a classic in the field.

After the courses had continued for many months, Elisabeth thought it was time to move on. She envisioned that other instructors would pick up where she had left off and continue exploring how the medical community would evolve in its treatment of the subject. Therefore, she made the decision to quit teaching that course but wanted to tell Renny about it. After what she expected to be her last class, she went to tell Renny. He was busy and talking about other matters. Elisabeth was a very small woman, the runt of triplets as she described herself, and could not get his attention. She decided to reach up and grab him by the back of his collar when an amazing event happened.

There, standing down the hall was a woman beckoning to her. Elisabeth couldn't quite place who she was but thought she recognized her. The woman then escorted Elisabeth to her office and opened the door. Elisabeth took this to be very strange behavior for a guest, and began reality checking herself. Once in the office, the woman stated she was there to tell Elisabeth it was not yet time to give up the classes. She was told she must continue her ground-breaking efforts on death and dying.

Eventually Elisabeth came to realize how she knew this person. The woman had been a hospice patient and had died 10 months earlier after participating in one of her seminars. Thinking she needed proof that this was not a hallucination, she asked the woman for a note with her autograph to pass on to Renny. That, she told the woman, would be needed to convince Renny to stay the course. In reality, it was her own sanity check. The woman smiled knowingly and wrote a note. She obligingly signed it *Mary Schwartz*. The name, indeed, was that of her former hospice patient. Thanking Elisabeth, Mary got up and exited the room. Within seconds, Elisabeth gathered her wits and ran to the door. Opening it, she found the long hallway totally deserted. Mary could not have walked out of sight; she had simply vanished.

As a further attempt at verification, Elisabeth had the note analyzed by a handwriting expert and compared with a file copy of Mary Schwartz's signature. They matched. This incident, and other similar accounts, while very rare, are extreme challenges for most scientists, as well as many religious officials.

Elisabeth's story about being visited by a spirit, or person known to be dead, is far from unique and follows in a line of similar stories that transcend history. Of course, Christianity is based on that premise, albeit with some twists, and other religions accept avatars and immortal entities. Her story stands out as she was able to obtain physical evidence from the entity. However, I have heard of similar encounters from many friends. One estimate is that about one-third of surviving spouses, or people with close personal relationships, believe that they have had some form of communication with their departed loved ones. That ranges from simply sensing their presence to having a physical interaction, such as Elisabeth had with Mary Schwartz.

Obviously, there is an inclination to assume these encounters are simply psychological aberrations or hallucinations on the part of the living person. And many may be just that. Still there are many instances in which the person has received information or warnings of impending danger that cannot be accounted for via traditional mechanisms.

My friend Tom Clancy relayed an intriguing story regarding afterlife visitations to me. Tom and I had discussed these phenomena many times. When first we had these talks at his apartment on the Baltimore Harbor, he said, "Alexander, if you weren't from Los Alamos, I'd throw your ass out of here." As years went on, his position softened considerably. Few people knew that Tom was actually a Beefeater, one of the very few outsiders formally accepted as a ceremonial guard for the Tower of London.

The story he told me was that one evening a guard had taken a bouquet to the Tower. It was on the anniversary of the celebration of the birthday of Anne Boleyn, who had been beheaded there on May 19, 1536. After the flowers were placed on a mantle, a woman appeared and told him, "So nice of you to remember." The woman then abruptly disappeared. An interesting anecdote as the Tower of London has long had a reputation for being haunted. For a couple years before his untimely death, Tom would catch me on occasion and say, "Tell me about…" Some of this he wrote about in novels that were never published. His wife, Alex, later told me the publisher demanded he stay in his genre.

Raymond Moody has collected many reports regarding human interaction with deceased persons. His book *Reunions: Visionary Encounters with Departed Loved Ones*[95] addresses the topic at considerable length. Based on extensive research into scrying,[96] he came to develop a means of eliciting interactions through a chamber called a psychomanteum. When accompanied by physical evidence or producing information not available through traditional communication channels, these encounters pose a serious challenge to the materialistic paradigm.

Skeptical arguments about NDEs

There are several arguments raised by skeptics in efforts to debunk NDEs. But in my view, they fail as they often ignore the data, or address only part of the experience. At the top of their list is that NDEs are hallucinations. With the premise that anything unseen must not be real, it is easy to dismiss the observations that are reported, often with a high degree of consistency. There being variations to the stories, skeptics often point to the differences as indications of prevarication.

In all likelihood, some of these cases are hallucinations. But that does not eliminate the reality of all NDEs. There are just too many situations in which the person obtained veridical information not available through their physical senses. When that information can be independently verified, by definition that is not a hallucination.

Another favorite skeptical explanation is that what is reported is the result of drugs. Elsewhere in this book, I address the use of dimethyltryptamine (DMT) and how psychopharmacology does not explain the effects observed. With regard to terminal patients, it is true that palliative care often includes the use of pain-killers, opioids in particular. We also know that they are over-prescribed, a situation that has led to an epidemic of abuse. For those patients, it may be reasonable to conclude that drugs did have something to do with that patient's state. But the problem with the drug argument is that there are many other incidents in which the patient is not under the influence of drugs of any kind. This is certainly true for NDEs that come as a result of accidents that are of no fault of the victim.

Anoxia, or oxygen deprivation, is also suggested as contributing to reports of NDEs. This argument suggests that there is an innate response to the lack of oxygen being delivered to the brain, and that it triggers a response, such as an endorphin release. The argument is that an NDE is a mechanism that has evolved and is designed to help ease us out of physical existence with minimum pain. To be sure, most people having an NDE indicate they entered a place of great peace and tranquility, but that is also true for patients who are not experiencing anoxia. Therefore, the causal relationship of this argument fails.

Electromagnetic stimulation of the brain has produced some of the effects observed in NDEs. The work of Michael Persinger at Laurentian University does show that the brain can be stimulated intentionally with very weak electromagnetic fields. The effect produces visions that approximate out-of-body and other mystical experiences. Persinger even worked with Ingo Swann to create a device he calls the *God Helmet*. While Persinger's work is absolutely fascinating, the notion that a patient or victim recalling an NDE was somehow exposed to electromagnetic stimulation is specious, nor does he claim they were.

Of course, the ultimate skeptical argument is that the brain does not function as detailed in some of the extreme NDE cases. Skeptics usually attribute the observations as happening at some other time while brain functioning was possible. In the Reynold's case, they suggest that her recollections came at a period before she flat-lined but still had limited awareness. This is countered by her correct identification of the music that was playing when she claims to have returned to her body, a time at which she was known to be flat-lined on the EEG.

The fundamental question raised here is whether the brain and the mind are the same or separate. If they are the same and the mind is a product of the brain, then it is assumed that the mind dies with the demise of the physical body. However, if the mind functions outside the brain, as many consciousness researchers believe, then it is separate from the brain. Under that hypothesis, the brain is still important as it modulates perception. An analogy often used is that of a television set. If you take it apart, you cannot find the pictures as the TV only receives the signals that are externally generated and projects them onto the screen. If you accept mind and brain as being separate and distinct, as do I, then NDEs can exist as a window into complex realms we cannot yet fathom.

Even after considering all of the possible arguments to the contrary, I find none that are not lacking. Rarely do skeptics include all of the data, nor can they provide theories that are sufficiently inclusive to explain how, for example, Don saw a complete scenario that was not generated before the crash of his Apache helicopter. They do not explain Tom listening to a conversation taking place in another room. They do not explain Marilyn getting off a gurney and doing ballet. There are just thousands of similar veridical incidents that challenge mainstream science.

It is important for anyone who has had an NDE to know they are not alone. Even today, many experiencers believe they are unique. The estimates on the number of people who have had an NDE vary considerably. But if we take the most conservative number, five percent as found by Gallop, then there are over 13 million in the U.S. alone, and the phenomenon is global. Based on those statistics, some 774 NDEs occur every day in America.

Chapter 16
The Mediums

Throughout human history there have been tales of encounters between living humans and entities believed to have passed on. In most societies, there are people who claim special skills at communicating with discarnate spirits. There are various titles for these talented folks: shamans, curanderos, sangomas, babalawo, budian, and mediums, as they are called in Western countries. Science is not kind to this field, and almost all traditional scientists reject their information out of hand. If consciousness ceases with the death of the body, especially the brain, then further communication must be impossible. End of discussion.

But these same scientists refuse to examine the evidence that supports these claims. Societies that generally accept spirit communication with ancestors are considered by these scientists to be primitive and uneducated. It may be that it is the scientists who are uneducated.

Before describing my personal encounters with the legitimate mediums that I have met and known, I must acknowledge that there are many frauds as well. These unscrupulous charlatans have plied their trade for centuries, often targeting the most vulnerable among us, especially those in grief. There is a well-known technique called a cold reading which may seem valid but is really so general as to be meaningless. Tricks include obtaining prior knowledge of the victim, which with the internet is far easier than in the past. They also elicit information from the visitor looking for instant feedback from both spoken responses to questions, or nonverbal clues that are hard for the person to hide. Questions might be "does the name Tom mean something to you?" The name is one that is prevalent, and in the U.S. almost everybody knows a Tom, or Mary, or pick your common name. As the skeptics correctly point out, the fake seer can be very skillful, if pretending to talk with the dead is their livelihood

My experience has been that the biggest flag is when the intermediary asks for large amounts of money or expensive gifts. Anytime the reader starts by suggesting that you, or an object, is cursed and you must divest yourself of it, run, don't walk for the nearest exit. While legitimate mediums are entitled to a fair living for their work, your antennae needs to be up when the requests seem extravagant.

When stationed in Hawaii, I witnessed this firsthand and was flabbergasted at the success fraudulent mediums had in conning the audience. One individual claimed he was in contact with St. Germaine who was passing messages through him. Using billet reading to engage the audience, his basic move was known as *one ahead*. One ahead is a gimmick in which he would answer requests that appeared to be sealed. It seemed as if he could access material written privately by the applicant and seemed to provide accurate information, including their name, before opening the envelope. In reality, he was reading the information about what people believe will be the next sealed envelope. Johnny Carson frequently made an entire act out of Carnac answering questions from a sealed envelope. The audience in Honolulu seemed captivated, and this fraud passed a collection plate several times during the multi-hour service, usually for different causes. In addition, he sold special crystals and apports that he claimed had magical powers. (Apports are objects that appear out of nowhere from an unknown source.) If purchased for a hefty sum, they would turn on that evening at midnight. But those gimmicks paled before what I saw him pull off in real estate. Honolulu had some of the most expensive property in the country. This guy stated he wished someone would buy him an apartment so that he could spend more time near us. Damned if he didn't get his wish.

While James Randi and I have had disagreements, I think his work in exposing televangelist Peter Popoff was commendable. In the 1980s German born Popoff was making a huge profit using similar techniques at his services. In front of huge audiences, he would call out individuals in the crowd by name and provide very specific information about them, even about their afflictions at times. He attributed this knowledge as coming from God, and he would tell them what they needed to do. That included, of course, making large contributions to Popoff himself as a reward for acting as a direct intermediary between them and the supreme power.

Again, the reality was quite different. On arrival at the service, audience members would fill out cards providing personal information and the specific reason for attendance. These were collected and taken backstage where Peter Popoff's wife, Elizabeth, would open them and select the most interesting ones. Popoff himself had a tiny receiver located in his ear so that his wife could transmit information to him in real time. Suspecting this, Randi in 1986 hired a crime scene analyst and electronics expert, Alexander Jason, to sweep the frequencies until he located the one that the Popoffs were operating on. Their transmissions were recorded, and included some cute personal commentary along with rather derogatory remarks about their victims from Elizabeth.[97]

There is more to that story. After exposure in 1987, the Popoffs declared bankruptcy. But that did not keep them down. They have re-emerged and can be seen on television today. To check them out, I sent in a prayer request last year. The response was a small vile of blessed water followed by many requests to send them love offerings. Employing a concept called *seed-faith giving,* they promise that if you send them a specific amount, often hundreds of dollars, then through divine intervention, they claim, you will receive ten-fold that amount. The gullible pay, and the Popoffs are raking in millions of dollars per year. *ABC News* did a special on fake healers in 2007. They estimated that Popoff took in over 23 million dollars in 2005. Worth noting is that this type of fraud can be far more damaging that just embezzlement.[98] To their detriment, there are people who actually believe in the process and forego traditional medical treatment.

Of course, over the years many of these charlatans have been exposed. Unfortunately, the media tends to place more emphasis on exposing frauds than on confirming legitimate mediums. The other issue with television programming is the emphasis on entertainment, often at the expense of reality. Television is driven by ratings. But if researchers are correct about mediumship, and I believe they are, then we are dealing with a spiritual realm, one that transcends the physical world and certainly has no use for ratings.

People tend to expect perfection, but even the best mediums get things wrong. A good way to look at the topic is an analogy to basketball put forth by Gary Schwartz at the University of Arizona in Tucson. Gary has one of the few funded research centers located in a traditional academic setting that studies mediums and related phenomena. Gary, a Harvard trained psychologist, was a professor of psychiatry and psychology at Yale for many years before coming to his current positions in Arizona. Now he is the Director of the Laboratory for Advances in Consciousness and Health (LACH, formerly the Human Energy Systems Laboratory) in the Department of Psychology. The center focuses on the study of mediums and alternative energy healing.

As a result of his unique position, Gary was able to assemble his Dream Team of mediums and test them in a laboratory under controlled conditions. While there has been some controversy about his research protocols, he has produced some dramatic results. One of the key issues is accuracy. The analogy Gary employs he calls the Michael Jordan Model. He points out that Michael Jordan is revered in basketball because of his scoring prowess. At his best, Jordan made about 45 percent of his shots. He was acclaimed, not because he made all of his shots, but because he was so much better than everybody else in the NBA. So too, Gary's Dream Team members do not score 100 percent, but he studies them because they are better than most others.

Anne Gehman

My friend Anne Gehman appears in several chapters in this book because of the success that she has demonstrated over time. In 2010 *HBO* ran a special called *No One Dies at Lily Dale*,[99] which featured several mediums, including Anne. The title comes from the spiritualist community called Lily Dale, which is located on Upper Cassadaga Lake in upstate New York. Since the late 1800s, spiritualists have been gathering at this location. In the summer, it becomes a mecca for those seeking to have a reading with the mediums who live there. The setting is idyllic. Forested with a large variety of trees, including hemlock, ash, poplar, and birch, Lily Dale is chock full of homes that are up to a century old and adorned with well-cared-for gardens dating from the beginning of the settlement. When warmer weather takes hold, the area attracts visitors from all over the world. While many arrive with appointments, others just meander through the village and stop when a medium's sign beckons them.

No One Dies at Lily Dale provides a pretty good look at mediumship as practiced today. Watch it and you will see examples of both good and bad readings. One of the latter was a male medium who provided such generic information that it could applied to anyone and would be totally useless. Anne, however, was most impressive. Her reading was given to a man who had recently lost his young son. As a way of providing evidence of authenticity, she gave him information that only he could have known, and which she could not have accessed in any traditional way. In this case, she told the father about toys he surreptitiously had slipped into his son's coffin, just before it was closed for the last time. The message she provided was far more comforting once he knew that the communication was likely valid.

Several of my friends have had readings with Anne and believe the information is both valid and useful. At Lily Dale, Victoria and I waited while a friend sat with Anne for more than two hours. At the time, he was experiencing a spiritual transformation himself, and exposure to professional mediumship was something relatively new for him. As he confided in us late that afternoon, he was certain that he had received useful and illuminating guidance. Contact had been made with deceased relatives, ones that Anne could not have had prior knowledge of.

Suzanne Giesemann

One of the most unusual mediums I ever met was Suzanne Giesemann.[100] While many, if not most, mediums have a lifelong history of mystical experiences and contacts with discarnate entities, Giesemann did not. In fact, she had a career in the U.S. Navy and retired as a commander before unintentionally becoming a medium. Her meteoric rise in the Navy was remarkable. One of only a few female ship commanders, she also served as special assistant to the Chief of Naval Operations, and was Aide to the Chairman of the Joint Chiefs of Staff, General Hugh Shelton, on the day of the 9/11 terrorist attacks.

I mention General Shelton as he and I worked together as majors in the 25th Infantry Division in Hawaii; we both had come from Special Forces assignments in Vietnam. Obviously, he did a lot better with his career than I did with mine. While Susan's mediumship did not begin until well after her retirement, Shelton plays down any association because of the possible negative connotation to any association with the field. While I can't fault him, it is indicative of just how much needs to be overcome if we are to advance the study of this important topic.

Being unaware of her book *The Priest and the Medium*,[101] I asked Suzanne if she knew Anne Gehman. The occasion was the 2015 IANDS conference in San Antonio, where we were both speakers. Looking at my name tag, she responded, "I've heard of you." That book was a biography of Anne, and in researching it, Suzanne had heard about the metal bending incident.

While engaging in a career in writing, she continued her practice of meditation. Eventually she began having her own mystical or intuitive experiences. To explore the subject further, she took some classes on mediumship. That culminated with an intensive at the well-established Arthur Findlay College of Psychic Sciences in Stansted, England.[102] The college was an endowment to the Spiritualist movement and has residential programs where students can study "Spiritualist philosophy and religious practice, Spiritualist healing and awareness, spiritual and psychic unfolding and kindred disciplines."

According to Suzanne, her eye-opening experiences there allowed her to develop her contact with the unseen world. As often is the case of rapid unfoldment, her venture was predicated on a most unfortunate circumstance. On June 6, 2006, her pregnant step-daughter, Susan Babich, a U.S. Marine sergeant, was struck and killed by lightening while walking across the tarmac at Cherry Point Naval Air Station. Along with burgeoning mystical experiences, this tragedy gave Suzanne the impetuous to attempt to make post-mortem contact. On becoming successful, she found that she could contact others as well.

Suzanne has now written quite a few books. Some of the material provided through her comes in a uniquely dictated form of rhyming poetry. With her remarkable background, word of her capabilities quickly spread. Among those who tested her capabilities was my friend Gary Schwartz, who gave her glowing reviews and rates Suzanne as one of the best mediums he has ever investigated. She also received high marks from Dr. Wayne Dyer, the recently departed motivational speaker and consciousness explorer. While backlogged with requests for personal readings, Suzanne does produce near-daily channelings from *Sanaya*, guides which Suzanne says appear to be a collection of higher consciousness beings that provide much needed wisdom for those who will listen. Sanaya, we are told, means "Eminent, and of the Gods" in Sanskrit.

John Edward

While visiting Gary Schwartz in Tucson, we had a chance to interact with several of his Dream Team. One of the best known was John Edward, who is very personable and tends to be conservative with his readings. Gary has published several of the experiments he conducted with Edward in his book *The Afterlife Experiments: Breakthrough Scientific Evidence of Life After Death.*[103] He is very popular, and readers may be familiar with his television program, *Crossing Over*. I go along with Gary's analysis when he says, "The probability is that John is the real thing—engaged in something honest and spiritual..."

To be sure, the skeptics do not agree. One of the most vocal is Ray Hyman. He and I have crossed paths on several occasions, not all of which have been friendly. Hyman claims Edward and others are all conducting cold readings. The skeptics focus on the misses while ignoring the hits, even when the probability of the exact information being a lucky shot is astronomical.

George Anderson

George Anderson is a well-known American medium who impressed me during a presentation in Ham Hall, at the University of Nevada, Las Vegas (UNLV). Anderson claims that after a serious illness when he was young, he began to communicate with the spirits of deceased people. His website states he has conducted over 35,000 sessions and has appeared on many television programs. Anderson has written a number of books suggesting that life continues beyond bodily death, most of them designed to assist in bereavement counseling.

Aware of the public acclaim for his work, I had an opportunity to attend his event at UNLV. As I recall, it was free to the public and probably sponsored by the Bigelow Chair of Consciousness that was then active at the university. Ham Hall is quite large and holds just over 1,800 people. Though there was not a lot of publicity about Anderson's appearance, it was standing room only.

After brief introductions, Anderson began his session. When connecting with spirits he employs a distraction technique using pencil and paper. You can watch as he scribbles back and forth, not really writing anything down. At first, he began giving out messages to people in the audience, which would be underwhelming and hard to confirm. The recipients seemed impressed, but as a researcher I found it too general to be of significance.

What got my attention took place about half an hour into the session. Most of the audience seemed riveted on Anderson's presentation, when a young couple, probably in their twenties, who were sitting a few rows behind me, quietly got up and began to make their way out. The seating in Ham Hall is such that to leave you must step over several people to get to the side aisles. Anderson froze and shouted out, "Don't Leave!" He then went on to deliver a message of such a high degree of specificity, that there was little doubt of the accuracy. While young people all have older relatives who have passed on, only a few have lost children. In this case, he correctly identified that their very young daughter had drowned in a home pool, and that they felt extreme guilt about the incident. Excluding using a plant, and I have no reason to suspect that, the probability that Anderson would blindly guess so many features of that event is highly improbable. Anderson went on to provide a message of hope, and told them their daughter did not blame them for the accident. To say the audience was touched would be an understatement. I fully recognize that was a one-off incident, but one that was certainly notable.

Today, Anderson continues to conduct readings, albeit at significant expense. Even by phone he asks $1,500 for a session. For some people, the information provides comfort. What clients should be aware of is that even the best medium does not get everything right all the time. But since many approach a medium while in a state of grief, there is a strong tendency to believe what they are told. My best advice in all situations is caveat emptor, let the buyer beware.

Adele Tinning

The table weighed at least 40 lbs., yet the elderly medium, Adele Tinning, managed to make the table rise on its own, a feat for which I could find no rational explanation. This experience proved to be another entry into a realm that most people have never heard about, let alone experienced.

Though still stationed with INSCOM in Northern Virginia, my job on occasion took me to the West Coast. This trip involved research I was doing in coordination with Cleve Backster who ran a polygraph school in San Diego, and whose work I have detailed previously. Over the weekend, I had visited my mentor, Dr. Elisabeth Kübler-Ross at her estate near Escondido. There was a serious controversy swirling around two of her assistants, and I wanted to learn the details about it personally from her. It was a sad chapter in what was otherwise an amazing career that over time would benefit millions of people as they transitioned through the dying process.

It was Saturday, January 29, 1983, and as I was driving south on I-15 I had time to contemplate the meeting that was scheduled with the well-known medium, but was not sure what to expect. Approaching the University Avenue exit, I turned off, crossed the 805, and entered into a quiet residential area of San Diego called North Park. The aging historic township was noted for craftsman cottages, cafes, and diners.

It was early evening but still light when I pulled my rental car up in front of her home. It was a very modest bungalow, but from it she had entertained thousands of seekers such as me. Being relatively close to Los Angeles, as her reputation grew, she ended up seeing many many people, most of whom were looking for contact with departed relatives.

Graciously Adele, and her husband, a retired San Diego fireman, greeted me at their front door. She had penetrating blue eyes and had an infectious smile that would put anyone at ease. (Unbeknownst to any of us at the time, he would be transitioning to another plane of existence within a few months.) After brief introductions, Adele and I were seated in a small room where she had held her sessions. Before departing for another room in the rear, her husband jokingly suggested I look carefully for the hidden wires by which the table could move. Of course, there were none, but they were well aware of the criticism raised by skeptics who assumed all séances and mediums were frauds. They were used to the criticism and took it all in stride.

Because of the accuracy of the messages she provided, Adele Tinning had slowly become known throughout the Southern California area, and beyond. Unlike many mediums who attain a degree of fame, Adele never charged anyone for her remarkable services. In fact, she would refuse money if offered. It may be that she was aware of the degradation that followed some psychics when a profit motive crept into their practices. There is the now famous case of Edgar Casey, who was known as The Sleeping Prophet[104] and who experienced terrible losses when he attempted to use his intuitive skills for personal financial gain.

To encapsulate her message, Adele wrote a book entitled *God's Way of Life*,[105] and she gave away copies to those who came to her. Adele believed she was in contact with ascended masters who could assist those of us remaining on the Earth plane. She had been psychic her entire life, as her mother had been before her. She told some people the story that when she was six years old she saw an angel floating in her backyard, which was taken to mean that she had specials gifts. As she grew older, other psychic events occurred and she learned table rapping as a means of communication with the spirit world.

There is an unconfirmed report that Adele was involved with a NASA investigation following one of their fatal accidents. The first message she received was spontaneous and did not mean much to her. But after she mailed the information to NASA, scientists from that agency contacted her in an attempt to learn more about what had actually happened to the astronauts.

Adele's fame was catapulted forward when actress and psychic adventurer Shirley MacLaine wrote about her in the 1987 book *It's All in the Playing*.[106] MacLaine stated, "Then I remembered that I had visited a spiritual medium who contacted disembodied spiritual guides through a table that tipped and leaned and moved…. She lives in San Diego, is about 79 years old, is as kindly as anyone I've ever known, and quite simply has incredible mediumistic talent."

As many before me had done, I assumed a seat at Adele's white kitchen table. There was nothing overtly remarkable about this small, yet sturdy, table. Unlike most séances I had attended, the room was well illuminated so any attempt at shenanigans could be easily caught. Unfortunately, I was not inclined to take notes, and I have long forgotten the exact contents of the messages Adele provided. None, however, were related to my departed mother or any other deceased relative. As I recall, the information was generic in nature about how guides from another plane of existence were concerned about mankind and what we were doing to the biosphere.

What is more germane from a scientific perspective was the process by which that message was derived. Adele and I placed our hands on top of the table in a manner seemingly devoid of any significant pressure. During the information transmissions, the table would tap out the individual letters. One tap represented the letter a, two taps, a b, three taps the letter c, and so on up to 26 taps for the letter z. Her method was, at best, cumbersome. One had to pay close attention and count accurately to insure the message was transcribed correctly. Obviously, great patience was required as the spirits often produced rather lengthy missives.

In addition to the tapping routine, the table on occasion would have a leg rise several inches of the floor. To be sure, never did I observe, or even hear of, Adele's table totally levitate so that it had no contact with the ground. Prior to our actual session beginning, she showed me photos that had been taken during such levitations. Inexplicably there were white columns of light appearing in the photos that were not visible during the filming.

There are several challenges for science in evaluating mediumship. Generic messages of gloom and doom and the need to change our ways cannot be qualitatively evaluated. Similarly, many of the messages of hope and well-being regarding loved ones that have passed would not meet an acceptable level of standard of proof for continuation of consciousness. It is well recognized that grieving relatives are prone to interpreting messages in a favorable light. But there were, on occasion, messages that were so specific to both the deceased individual and the recipient that the evidence is at least supportive of the life-after-death hypothesis.

Physics is another matter. There is no room for psychological misinterpretation or wanting to hear how lovely things are on the other side. The physics I refer to here are those of the energy requirements to move the table in the manner that I personally observed. As with many such incidents, I have consulted magicians who are familiar with the range of tricks employed by charlatans, of which there are too many. They have shown me methods by which tables can appear to levitate, often by using their thumbs to move the table. Lighter tables are easier to manipulate. Yet, Adele's kitchen table was about 40 lbs., and at all times her hands were on top of the table. Her knees were never in contact to push the table from below. The probability that any physical force was employed to cause an illusion is vanishingly small.

That session with Adele Tinning was quite remarkable although at the time I failed to recognize the significance of the event. And to be honest, I should have been more cognizant of the full measure of the privilege that had been bestowed on me in meeting that advanced soul.

Chico Xavier

There was a Brazilian medium who stood out and is worth mentioning; his name was Chico Xavier. I was not fortunate enough to meet him before he died in 2002, but I believe he is unique among all other mediums in the world because of his prolific psychographic publications. Born in Minas Gerais province in 1910, he was orphaned at an early age and subjected to abusive relatives during his upbringing. Shortly after his mother's death, he began having visitations from her in spirit form. Later he acquired a guide who went by Emmanuel and who Xavier claimed to have been a Roman senator, Catholic priest, and professor at the Sorbonne in prior incarnations.

Xavier published nearly 500 books, all allegedly channeled by deceased entities. Always modest about those works, Xavier never took credit for being the author. Of interest from the perspective of verification is the fact that many of those deceased entities were of known origin. Furthermore, many of them had written material when they were alive, so a comparison of styles could be accomplished. In addition, a number of documents were physically signed by Xavier but attributed to the discarnate entity. These too could be verified when compared to previously existing autographs made on letters and receipts during their recent incarnations.

In 2014, a study was published in a peer reviewed medical journal by a group of professors from the University of Sao Paulo, in which Chico Xavier's writings were compared to the deceased author. The research consisted of analyzing 13 letters known to be from an author by the name of J.P. in both his physical incarnation and Xavier's psychographs. From these documents, the researchers identified 99 items that could be tested for comparison between J.P.'s documents, both when he was living and dead. They also contacted the deceased entities former friends and relatives for validation. Their findings were astonishing. The researchers concluded that 98 percent of the compared items were accurate (rated a clear and precise fit). The remaining two percent could not be determined, but none were found to be false or inaccurate statements (no fit).[107]

While barely known in North America, Chico Xavier was extremely popular in Brazil. He appeared on several television programs, so there are still records of his public efforts. Interestingly, there was a lawsuit brought against Xavier by the widow of Humberto de Campos, a well-known writer who had transitioned. She claimed, unsuccessfully, that the psychograph material was from her deceased husband, and therefore the copyright should belong to her. Based on viewer popularity, an *SBT* network television program that aired in 2012 named Xavier, "the greatest Brazilian of all time." In addition, there were roads, stamps, and statues erected to him. That is unheard of for any other medium anywhere else. An excellent movie of his life, titled simply *Chico Xavier,* is available on the internet.[108]

Scientifically, even in cases as extraordinary as Chico Xavier, the origin of the communications via mediums cannot be confirmed. While preponderance of evidence would suggest the sources can be identified, what cannot be positively eliminated is that some form of collective consciousness has not generated the material and emulated a previously incarnate source. That still would be extremely interesting and pose a challenge for modern science.

It must be stated that placing reliance in any medium's statements, versus, what is known to be true, is foolish. There is no doubt that the information can be helpful for many people. But one must be aware that even the best mediums are not always correct. At best, they are dealing with imperfect communication from sources that we do not fully comprehend. Testing the information against ground truth should be preeminent. But a paradox exists, as what is believed to be ground truth, may also be inaccurate.

I am concerned when mediums engage in entertainment, especially public performances and television programs. We know the phenomena are elusive, so for any medium to have to produce accurate information on a continuous basis is challenging. The reality is that sometimes they will be wrong. On TV that is not good. Also, perennially waiting in the wings are the skeptics/debunkers, who will pounce an any mistake as proof of fraud.

Remember that as a spiritual being in a physical experience, you have the skills necessary to obtain all of the guidance needed to conduct your life. Legitimate mediums may assist you, but you must be aware of their limitations. Their job is not to lay out your life for you. Mediums are not fortune tellers; they communicate with those who passed over into another plane of existence.

One of the cute lectures I once attended at a psychic seminar was titled, "Just Because You're Dead, Doesn't Make You Smart." That is a great premise. That sentiment was echoed by a former Special Forces commander of mine, then-Major Stan Olchovik. Like many members of the early Special Forces, Stan lived in Eastern Europe during World War II. Originally from Czechoslovakia, he was among the millions who were displaced and left homeless as the war ended. As such, he was sent to a Displaced Person's (DP) camp where he stayed for many months. Like similar camps today, the occupants have little to do and are confined to the premises. Stan was aware of my interests in phenomena, and he confided that while in the DP camp they often passed time by attempting to contact discarnate entities. While they appeared to be successful in making contact with something or someone, Stan believed that "Many of them were dumb fuckers." Far too many people who seek out mediums for advice come with an expectation that their deceased relative has become omniscient. There are people I know who ask the departed for help with lottery numbers. So far, they have not been successful.

From a scientific perspective, mediumship may be one of the hardest phenomena to test. There are a vast number of variables, and we do not have an agreed upon common ground of understanding what continuation of consciousness might consist of. A number of post-mortem paradigm models have been proposed. None has gained universal acceptance and probably never will. The search for truth will continue to be complicated by formal religions, which for various reasons, including economic ones, will maintain their brands even in the face of evidence that contradicts some of their tenets.

CHAPTER 17
"MOMMY, WHY IS HE KILLING THOSE PEOPLE?"

Somewhat timidly, the little girl stepped into the aisle. She was no more than six years old. Her short blond hair bobbed slightly as the priest took her hands. She had spoken quietly to her mother, but the priest had heard her comment and bid her to join him. Then, ever-so-lightly, she touched the grown man, a complete stranger, standing in front of them. In an instant, the man was lying on the floor, seemingly unconscious, but in a state known as "slain in the spirit."

I witnessed this remarkable event thanks to Ann Armstrong-Dailey who is an extraordinary woman. We first met through our common friend and head of my doctoral committee, Elisabeth Kübler-Ross, MD., soon after I arrived for an assignment as an inspector general at the Pentagon. As many people know, it was Kübler-Ross who was largely responsible for bringing the hospice concept from Europe to America. At that time, Ann was working at the National Hospice Organization (NHO) and attempting to enlighten the staff to the need for service to pediatric patients.

But her efforts were unsuccessful with NHO. Admittedly, pediatric patients and their families have very different requirements than older adults. There is a qualitative difference in emotional involvement for hospice workers between working with adults and children. Though it's one thing to accept the fact that old people die (and even some younger adults), children aren't supposed to die. But each year in the U.S. there are about 8,000 deaths of children ages 14 and under. The leading cause of those deaths are accidents; however, the reality is that there are a substantial number of terminally ill children, ones who desperately need support. Equally important are the needs of their parents and siblings. Studies have shown that many parents divorce following the death of a child. Guilt and incrimination, though often unwarranted, tend to destroy families.

Based on that evidence, Ann recognized the need for an organization designed specifically to support pediatric hospice care. Thus, Children's Hospice International (CHI) was born with Ann serving as the Founding Director, a position she still holds today. I was privileged to serve on the initial board of directors along with my mentor, Kübler-Ross, and other luminaries of the hospice movement. Uniquely, CHI generated comprehensive programs designed to treat the entire family unit, including care beyond the life of the child.

The development of CHI took some time. During that period, I met with Ann on several occasions, and she became aware of my interest in near-death experiences and other psychic phenomena. She was present at our apartment the night of Jack Houck's metal bending party and experienced some effects herself. She also observed the critical event that caused Major General Stubblebine and me to take the process very seriously.

A devout Catholic, Ann was a close friend of a local priest. Following a traffic accident in which her car was hit from the rear, she was diagnosed with multiple sclerosis. I don't intend to suggest a causal relationship between these two events, but it did bring to light a number of symptoms. Under the priest's guidance, she also was involved seeking spiritual healing.

One day, Ann called to inform me that a priest from the Boston area would be coming to Northern Virginia where we lived. This priest, Father Angelo Rizzo, was well known as a healer in the Catholic community. As such, the diocese was issuing tickets to prevent overcrowding at the service. Ann's friend from the priesthood was able to obtain two tickets, and she offered to take me along. What I did not know until years later was that Ann had previously been in attendance at another ceremony with Father Rizzo and had experienced significant improvement in her eyesight.

It was mid-afternoon on a Friday when we entered St. Anthony's Church (pseudonym) in Falls Church, Virginia. Through Ann's contacts within the church we had learned that the presiding bishop of the diocese was not happy with the presence of this charismatic priest. There had been a private service for the local priests the previous day, and tensions between the philosophical factions was apparent. In my opinion, it was the bishop who seemed threatened by the appearance of Father Rizzo. But they had to proceed as hundreds of tickets had been dispersed, and parishioner interest and expectations were high.

Entering the rapidly filling sanctuary of the traditional Romanesque-style church, we found seats in the nave about ten rows back. Light oak wooden pews bifurcated the assembly. Ann chose to sit next to the aisle on the left side; I sat next to her. We were well located to observe the service that was about to unfold. Not being Catholic myself, I was not sure what to expect, except that it would probably be rather stiff and formal. Never in my wildest dreams would I have contemplated what was about to happen.

The church filled to capacity, and then some. Soft organ music was playing and people spoke in hushed tones as they jockeyed for the remaining seats. A change in the music indicated the arrival of the bishop and an entourage of about a dozen priests. They all took up their assigned places on the dais and the service began. The bishop made a few obligatory remarks, and then introduced the main attraction, Father Rizzo.

Then in his late forties, Father Rizzo had already spent decades as a missionary in Brazil, which I was not aware of at the time. While in Brazil, he learned the charismatic arts of spiritual healing and wrote a book about his experiences.[109]

On stage, he looked much younger than his age. He was dressed in the traditional black cassock with the near-ubiquitous white collar. Clean shaven with short brown hair, he looked just like the television model of the local Catholic priest. Knowing that the audience had come for the healing aspects, he kept his preliminary comments short. I have long forgotten the specifics, but he emphasized body-mind connections. Sometimes, he opined, the body develops symptoms that are physical metaphors indicating that healing is needed on another level.

Completing his remarks, Father Rizzo told everyone to be patient. He would bless everyone; there was no need to rush the dais. True to his word, he came down among the throng and administered to every single person who wanted his touch. Because there were hundreds who so desired, the service would last for more than an hour.

Instantly, as he touched the first parishioner, she collapsed and fell backwards. In anticipation of that response, the falling woman was caught and lowered safely to the floor where she remained immobile for several minutes "slain in the spirit."

The term "slain in the spirit" is defined as "A phenomenon of Pentecostalism and the charismatic movement, where a person is believed to be overcome by the Holy Spirit. The experience is temporary, during which the individual collapses in a faint, although the faculties of thought and volition remain intact. The 'slaying' takes place when a charismatic person, already possessed by the Spirit, lays his or her hands on the head of another person. It is considered one of the external signs of a special outpouring of divine grace."[110]

Father Rizzo continued down the line, blessing and lightly touching each person on the forehead. It had the same effect on men and women alike. Most of them dropped, though a very few seemed to stagger to the pew. Each contact took but a couple of seconds, and within a few minutes bodies were strewn along all open spaces on the floor.

As Father Rizzo progressed up the aisle, we could clearly observe the process. He was within two rows in front of us when I heard the little girl turn to her mother and ask, "Mommy, why is he killing those people?" While she did not speak loudly, Father Rizzo had heard the comment as well. He turned to her and said, "Oh no, I'm not killing them." He then asked the shy little girl to join him, and obligingly she stepped into the aisle. Once there, he took her hands and touched the next person. Just as the others before him, he too was slain in the spirit and collapsed, then gently lowered to the floor. The girl then touched another person, and another, each responding the same to her gentle touch.

Somehow, Father Rizzo had transferred the power to cause a significant change in their state of consciousness to this unassuming little girl. I heard him wisely tell her, "Look, you cannot play with this." As she continued through the crowd, the phrase "dropping like flies" came to mind. The little girl continued for many minutes, and each contact had the same effect.

Since I know nothing about that little girl, other than my observations that day, it is impossible to comment on how it affected her, or if she had any prior experiences. Of greater interest would be to know whether or not she continued to have these experiences after she left the church that day.

It should be noted that such experiences are not exclusively Roman Catholic, but are quite common in some Christian evangelical denominations as well. Exactly what is occurring is not well understood, even though numerous explanations have been offered. One hypothesis is that the crowds are hypnotized and thus made susceptible to the suggestions of the minister. In some evangelical theatrics, such elements are incorporated into the performance. Repetitive music, with themes such as the song "He touched me," bombard the audience. Then, there are psychological maneuvers; we must consider that those attending have a predisposition to be influenced, otherwise they would not be in attendance.

There are religious divisions about the efficacy of invoking these spirits. Some believe that while the effects are real, they are not of God, but rather from a source of evil, such as Satan. Those ministers warn that people should not engage in these activities for fear of possession. There are also debates about whether or not Biblical scripture accommodates, or authorizes, such events.

Decades later, we invited the lone Jesuit priest in Las Vegas to lunch to discuss the church's position on the effects of being slain in the spirit. While he was not aware of Father Rizzo, he did inform us that during the 1980s, when that event had taken place, the Catholic church did have several priests involved in healing activities of this kind. Father Rizzo, who died in 2012, was not alone in demonstrating those capabilities. There were others, such as Father Ralph DiOrio, who continued that work until he retired in January, 2017.

A popular movement in the 20th Century was the ministry of the American healing evangelist Kathryn Kuhlman. Though having no theological training, she garnered a large following. She began her healing crusades in 1933, and as television came along she created the series, *I Believe in Miracles*.[111] Controversial, and unsubstantiated, the ministry claimed to have healed more than two million people. In reviewing films of her events, there are times when she also seems to cause people to be slain in the spirit. In each case I reviewed, she addressed the patient directly, usually pushing on their forehead.

One of her disciples, Toufik Benedictus Hinn, better known simply as Benny Hinn, took the art form to a new level. At his events people in the audience are frequently dropped to the floor. As anticipation grows, Hinn becomes increasingly animated. At times, he can be seen taking off his coat and waving it at attendees who then collapse. Even more impressive, he is seen on stage, sweeping his hand towards the audience, who then fall by the tens or even hundreds.[112]

Skeptics generally dismiss the whole process. Some will point to the possible danger of seriously ill patients rejecting competent medical attention in favor of faith healing. That is always a danger and should be avoided. Some claim there is a physical explanation; that the healer knows where cranial nerves are located and thereby causes a bodily response through direct pressure.

While there is some truth to these hypotheses, they do not explain what I observed in Falls Church, Virginia, three decades ago. Even allowing for psychological predisposition by some parishioners does not clarify what that very young girl did. Also mystifying is how Father Rizzo was able to transfer his capability to her. No discussion or instructions were provided. He simply took the girl's hands, and with her touch, people fell, slain in spirit.

CHAPTER 18
GO TO HELL

Across the Chattahoochee River from Ft. Benning and Columbus, Georgia, lies Phenix City, Alabama. It is a quaint, small southern town where some claim the last battle of the Civil War took place. Later, in the 1940s and 1950s, the city gained a reputation as a haven for organized crime and corruption. That may have led to my personal anomalous experience there: my physical encounter with a ghost. Just how that came about was the culmination of a number of improbable circumstances.

In the academic year 1971 to 1972, I was sent to the Infantry Officer's Advanced Course at Ft. Benning, Georgia. The instructors had a hard time getting much attention from the students. Almost exclusively, we were captains who recently had come from combat in Vietnam, and we would most likely be going back to Southeast Asia at the end of the nine-month course. It turned out that ours was the first class in several years that would have a broader range of assignments. Still the attitude was, "What are you going to do, send me to Vietnam?" The program was not academically challenging, and most of us sought other activities.

One diversion I found was a not-for-credit night course in parapsychology taught by Professor Charles Logue at Columbus College.[113] During the course, I struck up a friendship with a local woman named Janet (a pseudonym). She and a few friends had a small group that conducted sessions akin to séances, though they probably would not have identified their efforts as such.

As it turned out, Janet was an emerging medium who could easily slip into a trance state under hypnosis. She appeared to access past-lives and other unique sources of data. One instrument the group used that got my attention was a planchette. The planchette was like the moving piece on a Ouija board except that the front contained a pen that would write out the messages.[114] This was much quicker than the painstaking Ouija approach of spelling each letter one at a time. This planchette not only had a pen on the front end but two rear pens, each on a small roller, as well. That made the speed at which messages could be written extremely fast. Much of what was received was very generic and similar to other New Age writings. With Janet, there were often messages about ancient Egypt and Nefertiti. On at least one occasion, she suddenly began speaking in French, addressing old events in southern France. These sessions routinely were tape-recorded for posterity. In one session, there was not much new information and a translator did indicate the voice had a heavy American accent.

When in light trance, Janet could make the planchette fly as messages were produced on butcher paper that would be pulled aside by one of the other participants. When I joined them, the group had been active for years and had established their own protocols. For the most part, the messages were of a generic nature, indicating the human needed to play nice, worry about the environment, and not cause the end of civilization. While the messages may have seemed interesting at the time, there was nothing verifiable in the text. That said, on occasion I did observe Janet produce pages that seemed to be nothing but random scribbling. Then suddenly, with a few final deft lines, an entire picture would come clearly into focus. It still seems highly unlikely that she had a unique artistic ability or was faking these psychographs.

Classes with Logue were mildly interesting but very mundane for parapsychology. One skill I managed to learn from him was the art of mental cloud-busting. This is depicted by George Clooney, a composite of several real-life characters, in *The Men Who Stare at Goats*. The movie was based on an unfortunate book of the same name, that took a minimal amount of truth and expanded it several-fold—and then they made the movie.[115] One can find real names used throughout the book, though the basic premise on goats dying from staring is nonsense. And for those who saw the movie, the general who was my boss, Major General Albert Stubblebine, in real-life never tried to run through a solid wall.[116]

Still, there is some truth to manipulating clouds with your mind, though it is extremely hard to prove scientifically. The process Logue taught us involved selecting the cloud to be dissipated, then mentally instructing that cloud to disintegrate. I found pointing at the cloud and exhaling worked, at least some of the time. If this seems inexact, it is. I never quite got an understanding of what I was doing. Sort of like riding a bicycle, when it happens you know it, and it becomes effortless. For Clooney, paying attention to the cloud meant wrecking his car.

Several months after I joined the Columbus group, we learned of a haunted house in Phenix City. The current occupant was having problems with noises and at times reported seeing discarnate entities. Their presence was not pleasant, and the occupant wished to have them stop. The occupant wondered if the man who had died in the house under mysterious circumstances was related to the current haunting.

Without making any promises, the group agreed to visit the house. Thus, on an appointed evening, three of us ventured across the river and drove to the site of the alleged haunting. The house was two-stories high and several decades old. The brown wooden building, with its open front porch and screened-in backyard porch, had seen better days. The internal architecture was a bit odd as it had rooms that did not have access to any windows or external doors.

The owner was there to greet us and bid us enter. The initial response by Janet was clear and disturbing. She immediately sensed that a woman had died in the living room, a painful and lingering process due to cancer. As the bedrooms were all located on the second floor, the living room had been converted temporarily for the woman. We had not been told about the woman and her illness prior to our arrival. Janet's instant and correct assessment of that situation impressed the owner.

While that was not what we had been asked to evaluate, Janet believed that some of the ongoing events were tied to the deceased woman. Some visiting children had reported seeing gruesome-looking heads floating about that room at night. Those sights had frightened the children who refused to stay there anymore.

We were then taken upstairs to one of the second-floor bedrooms where the man had died. We were told that he had sustained a severe beating while on the back-porch downstairs. Since that incident, the house had been remodeled. One very strange aspect was that one of the old bedrooms was now completely sealed off. As there was no connecting door, the only access to it was to enter the attic via a ceiling entrance, crawl on hands and knees to a similar entrance atop that now sealed-in room, and then literally drop in.

The owner indicated he had done that only once. Using a candle for light, he had struggled his way into the attic. He told us that as he crawled he pushed the candle along. However, before he entered the room, the flame suddenly increased, then arched downward, and burned the back of his hand which was holding the base of the candle. He had no explanation for how the flame could have acted in such a manner. Despite the injury, he continued on and did manage to enter the sealed room. He reported that except for a few papers dated a couple of decades earlier, there was nothing remarkable about the room save the lack of a door or windows.

Other parts of the second floor had also been altered. As I stood with my back to a wall, I suddenly felt a distinct push on my back. Janet indicated she could see a large dark entity looming directly behind me. The owner indicated that I was now standing precisely where the door to the room had previously been located.

The experience was very unpleasant, and Janet stated she was being physically hit by an invisible entity who was very upset by out intrusion. Capitulating, we decided to go back downstairs and hold a brief séance. The room we chose was in the center of the house and had no external doors or windows. That fact would become extremely important a few minutes later.

Using the planchette, Janet began receiving extensive messages that she believed came from the male victim. From a discarnate state, he informed us about what had happened that fateful day. While everyone knew that the beating that had taken place on the back porch, he indicated that there had been a second beating, this one from a different assailant. This second beating was the fatal one. The perpetrator was never arrested, primarily because nobody was aware that there had been multiple attacks.

While little of the information could be verified, what happened next does defy explanation, and we were all firsthand witnesses. Suddenly, the inner door to the room we were in vigorously swung open. The handwriting on the planchette changed dramatically. In swift, bold letters, the message **"Go to Hell"** appeared on the page. The handwriting was intensely different from all previous transmissions I had seen. Then the door slammed shut. It did not just swing shut; it was clearly slammed shut, as if by a very angry person. Yet there was no other physical person present.

Having worked with Janet for several months, I had become very familiar with the automatic writing she produced. This was unlike anything we had seen previously. I am personally convinced it was not volitional on her part. In fact, she appeared frightened by this spontaneous, temperamental intrusion. The message was taken as a threat and an indication that we were now dealing with a different kind of entity.

What made this episode different from psychographs or more common automatic writing were the physical interactions that took place with the door. As mentioned earlier, this room had no external exits or windows. The adjacent rooms were searched and all orifices found to be closed. Neither wind nor gravity could account for the multiple movements of the door. Even if a draft had swung the door open, it would not explain its violent closure.

Allowing for the legitimate controversy regarding the existence of discarnate entities, how can science explain the physical actions of the door swinging both ways, which was directly related to the writing of the message? And the following day Janet reported that bruises had appeared on her body at places she said she had been struck by the entity. She was not seen by a doctor for these bruises.

This was firsthand experience with a spirit. Never before, or since, have I been aware of being physically pushed by a ghost.

Chapter 19
Entering the Spirit World

Belief in spirits and extradimensional worlds is actually quite widespread. Unfortunately, most scientists educated at Western universities deny the physical existence of anything nonmaterial. They simply disregard the observations, and even hard data, that proves we are more than physical bodies on a singular trip transiting consensus reality.

This chapter addresses a variety of personal experiences that strongly support the concept of a multidimensional universe. Just as astronomers keep finding more stars, planets, and other celestial bodies, so too are researchers finding more and more evidence pointing to the reality of undiscovered dimensions. Prior to the Hubble Space Telescope, a majority of the new discoveries were unseen. That was because we did not have the sensor systems capable of detecting their existence.

In October 2018, an Ariane 5 rocket belonging to the European Space Agency is scheduled to lift the James Webb Space Telescope into orbit. When that happens, it is certain that we will discover even more about the unknown reaches of the universe. What we will discover already exists, or in some cases, due to the immense distances involved, will have existed but have been extinguished, before we actually make the observation.

On the other end of the physical spectrum we now make observation at nanoscales that previously were impossible. The Department of Energy's Lawrence Berkeley National Labs recently activated an electron microscope with the capability to make images at a resolution of half the width of a hydrogen atom. At this time, it is the most powerful microscope in the world, yet another will one day come along with even better resolution. With the Large Hadron Collider,[117] searches are conducted for the God Particle.[118] We once thought that to be the Higgs Boson, but before long we were informed that pentaquarks had been discovered that are even smaller. Yes, those particles were always there, they were just unseen, as we lacked the instrumentation necessary to make the observations.

Here I will argue there are solid indications that one or more spirit worlds do exist. They are generally unseen because the Western world has embraced a materialistic belief system, one that does not allow for the possibility of other dimensions. I will provide a small part of the evidence that supports not only the existence of spirit worlds, but indications that they can, and sometimes do, interact with our version of consensus reality, the one we live in every day. The problem is that most scientists refuse to even entertain the possibility or consider the data.

The Goddess/Mother Ayahuasca

The sun sets at about 6 p.m. every night near the equator. In 2000, security was lax, and the airport in Iquitos, Peru, was simply chaotic. It didn't help that we did not know who we were looking for. Fortunately, one gringo, Howard Lawler, who was well over six feet tall, stood out. The natives living near the Amazon River tend to be much smaller and, of course, darker in complexion.

This would be our first venture into the Amazonian forest to explore the fabled visions that are attributed to ayahuasca. The transportation, a dilapidated blue Volkswagen van with a badly cracked windshield, did not exude confidence. At that time, there were few flights between Lima and Iquitos, so the eight participants for the ceremonies arrived at once. There were quick introductions, and we headed off over the bumpy roads leading to the river. Traffic was heavy, mostly with tuk tuks, those three-wheeled contraptions that are the main source of local conveyance in many developing countries. Within an hour our gear was thrown onto two shallow draft river boats. Shortly, we pushed off into the darkness that promised an almost mystical transformation. The outboard engines chugged away while a young assistant shined a handheld spotlight as we maneuvered into the current.

Near Iquitos, the mighty Amazon is a murky mess, with all kinds of debris flowing towards the Atlantic Ocean, nearly 2,300 miles downstream. Watercraft must dodge large tree limbs and other items that could do significant damage. Soon the channel narrowed as we entered a tributary, the Rio Nanay. Here, the spotlight revealed reflection from eyes that peered just above the surface. We were not sure what animals they were, but we were certainly not interested in joining them.

A half hour later, we approached a steep muddy bank. Perched at least 30 feet above us and set back more than 100 feet was the entrance to our camp. Sans electricity, the main building, resting on stilts, was illuminated with small flickering oil lamps. The scene, which was decorated with blowguns and feathered jungle paraphernalia, was truly transformational. It was more exotic than any Hollywood production and heralded numinous experiences yet to come.

While ayahuasca is an inner experience, this introduction convinced me that the setting does make a difference.

Howard was an attentive host, but he was the only one with English as his native tongue. He also spoke Spanish fluently. Holding dual citizenship, he was married to a Peruvian, and had a comfortable home in the city. As sole translator, there were constant demands for his attention and a thousand questions to answer. This experience was so far from our Western reality that it would take a bit of time to fully integrate into our consciousness.

No electricity meant no refrigeration. At times, there was a little ice, but as temperatures hovered around 90° F, day and night, it quickly melted. Cooking was done outside on the ground within a circle of stones more reminiscent of a campfire than a kitchen. The food was very simple, as the ayahuasca diet was generally enforced. Victoria had started the diet a month before our arrival, but she is used to an extremely restrictive regime.[119] The prescribed diet eliminates salt, sugar, and almost everything we think of as tasting good. There was a fair amount of fish, bananas, and papaya. Rice was imported, but a staple as well. Alcohol was verboten. While not culinary, Mother Ayahuasca also demands no sex during the ayahuasca period.

The first night was magical. Arriving in the dark, we could only imagine what the surroundings were like. Walking up from the boat, I was surprised at the lack of insects. Later, I learned that the incessant mosquitos of the area come out in droves near sundown but then soon dissipate. Sleep would come easily as we had travelled continuously for more than a day, with only a short layover in the capital, Lima. We were now immersed in a world of new sounds. The area was truly alive and adventures awaited.

Regarding ayahuasca, Victoria was the inquisitive one and willing to take a leap of faith. Because I was holding high-level security clearances, I chose to be an observer, a role that has served us well in our many trips since then. On rare occasions, I have ingested just enough to understand the experience. Many films have vainly attempted to capture the vivid visions that come with ayahuasca. The closest depiction I have seen was James Cameron's blockbuster movie *Avatar*; there is a lot of speculation that he may have used ayahuasca at some point.[120]

Ayahuasca is a medicine that has been around for millennia. It is brewed from the mixing of specific plants, but there are many variations. As we observed, the main ingredient was the native plant, Banisteriopsis caapi, which is also called "the vine of the soul." Based on their training and the intended outcome, shamans then add other substances as well; the leaves of Psychotria

Viridis is a common addition. When mixed together, a psychotropic drug is produced. The process may take more than a day. At our camp, we watch our shamans, Hermana Mari and Don Romolo, as they conscientiously stirred the bubbling caldron. As the kettle boiled, they added another traditional element: they sang their icaros as they worked. Icaros are sacred songs that are given to each shaman as they advance in training. They may sound similar but are usually unique to each person.

It is known that the psychoactive substance in ayahuasca is dimethyltryptamine, or DMT as it is commonly known. Most scientists believe that the reactions are based on drug interactions that stimulate the brain. Personally, I do not believe that psychopharmacology alone explains the experiences derived from ayahuasca. I have seen people ingest copious amounts of the brew with little or no effect, while others partook of a very mild dose that produced transformational experiences.

Dinner was very light on the night of our first ceremony, and wisely so, as ayahuasca induces an intense purging process. A few minutes after drinking from the cup, one's stomach begins to feel uncomfortable. Soon cramps begin, usually followed by regurgitation. While that is unpleasant, it is not uncommon for the participant to start running at the other end as well. Most authentic shamans have attendants that assist those in need to the conveniently adjacent outhouse. Purging is an important part of the cleansing process in preparation to receive the visions. It is also one reason I am convinced that ayahuasca will never become a recreational drug.

Our initial ceremony began well after nightfall. Although it took place indoors, the encroaching forest ensured a cloaking form of darkness, one that expelled all vestiges of the world beyond. Dimly lit by the lanterns, we sat in a semicircle facing Don Romolo and Hermana Mari. Large, loosely packed cigars of indigenous tobacco were lit. With an invocation similar to a Roman Catholic service, the shamans offered prayers. Moving about the entire room, they blew a considerable amount of smoke to both cleanse the venue and offer spiritual protection for what was to follow. As an inveterate non-smoker, I found this to be the most distasteful part of the program.

Next, each person quietly went forward and accepted the cup presented to them. It was filled by Don Romolo from a plastic three-liter soda bottle that now contained the concentrated brew. The amount provided varied based on what the shaman intuited was the appropriate quantity for that individual. The recipient then offered a silent prayer, or otherwise invoked their intention for the trip they were about to embark on. Downing the vile tasting medicine was an extreme challenge. Most gulped to get it over as quickly as possible. Gaging was a common reaction.

No amount of discussion or education could prepare you for the events that followed. Once the last person had been served, the kerosene lamps were extinguished and we sat in silence not knowing what to expect. Before long there were the recognizable sounds of participants beginning their cleansing process as they vomited into the plastic bowls that had been provided. The shamans then began their melodic chants, singing the icaros. This would continue uninterrupted for the next several hours.

Though sitting in total darkness, we began to mentally notice brief flashes of extraordinarily colored lights, including hues not yet imagined by artists. The experience was beginning and Mother Ayahuasca was in charge. It continued for the next six to eight hours, then slowly dissipated. While the visions were intense, the participants still had active control of their mind and, when necessary, could move about. Some young tribal members were assigned to assist those that needed it to get to the restroom. I noted that several members of the local Bora tribe were invited to participate in the ceremony. Having had ayahuasca many times before, they sat still, though some purged like the rest of the foreigners. Obviously, repetition does not necessarily alleviate the cleansing process.

Around 3 a.m. everyone was coming out of the experience and moved softly off to their quarters to sleep. By 9 a.m. the next morning everyone was up and moving about. There were absolutely no residual effects of any kind. There was, however, another part of the ceremony. Each individual was taken by the shaman to a secluded area. Once there, Hermana Mari poured flowered water over the participant who sat naked. Again, she was chanting her icaros. The day was then spent in introspection, each contemplating the unique experience they had encountered. We later experienced more ayahausca ceremonies, but the first is usually the most memorable and indescribable.

As a devotee, Victoria has explored ayahuasca in several venues, and with various shamans. Her experiences have been very powerful and often ineffable. It often takes her time to integrate into the consciousness of the consensus reality; the world that we all live in. It was long after her first ceremonies that that she confided what attracted her to repeat the ayahausca experience. With considerable deliberation, she finally mentioned that there was an episode in which she had an encounter with a supreme deity, or what is traditionally called God. As indicated, it was such a powerful experience that the meaning is almost incomprehensible to mortals.

It usually takes several sessions before one learns how to control the mental events induced by ayahuasca. Initially overwhelming, the participants usually just go along for the ride. Curiously, while you are likely to experience brilliant visions, you can open your eyes and move about freely. There is no reason to fear loss of physical or cognitive control of your senses. However, the visions will continue until they wane and are finally extinguished. I have never heard of anyone having aftereffects or flashbacks, as may happen with LSD.

While I very rarely ever drank ayahuasca again, I have attended many more ceremonies and spoken at several International Amazonian Shaman's Conferences. Victoria and I have met many shamans in Peru, Ecuador, and Brazil. She believes, as do many, that when the time is right, the Goddess Ayahuasca will call. It takes several sessions to learn how to work with the medicine. The first encounters are usually so wild that it is hard to focus your intent. In Victoria's case, she now travels mentally to another planet that she believes she can access. On arrival, she is now recognized by the inhabitants.

While that may sound far-fetched, it is consistent with the findings of Richard Strassman, M.D., one of the few people to have gained permission to study DMT in a clinical setting. While working at the University of New Mexico Medical School in Albuquerque, Rick obtain legal authorization to administer DMT to human subjects. In one of the most amazing passages in his book *DMT: The Spirit Molecule*,[121] Rick states, "We enter into invisible realms, ones we cannot normally sense, and whose presence we can scarcely imagine. Even more surprising, these realms seem to be inhabited."

Ayahuasca is a very powerful tool and should not be used without an experienced guide. The participant tends to get what they need, but it may not be what they expect or want. I have seen several people flip out, screaming, shouting, and sometimes running wildly about. But the following morning they are perfectly fine and thankful for the gift they received. Under guidance ayahuasca seems to work effectively and offers hope for treatment of PTSD,[122] though additional study needs to be done.

As the drug has become more widely known, more and more people are seeking it. DMT is generally a controlled substance in the U.S. and in most Western countries. In Peru, not only is it legal, it has formally been adopted as part of their national heritage. Still, finding the right shaman and quality product can be challenging. Unfortunately, as the popularity of ayahuasca increased, so have expenses.

For any Americans wishing to try it, I recommend Ron Wheelock, aka The Gringo Shaman.[123] Ron has been featured in television programs such as

Lisa Ling's CNN series called *This is Life*.[124] From our experience, we know he has a quality product; in fact, some indigenous shamans buy their supplies from him. In addition, he has kept his prices quite reasonable. Trained under one of the grand masters, Don Agustin Rivas Vasquez, Ron has been functioning as a shaman and curandero for two decades. An American by birth, he holds permanent resident status in Peru. Ron has built a relatively new center just a few kilometers outside the city of Iquitos. Still, it is secluded from the bustle of the city and is a great place for a retreat.

Since Victoria and I have worked with Ron for several years, I can say we trust him to provide the services needed. His background is unconventional, including a short stint in prison. He was a marijuana distributor when it was not legal, raises fighting roosters, and is a motorcycle enthusiast. But make no doubt about it, his heart is in the right place, and he has helped many people who have come to him with severe problems. In his healing role as curandero, we have seen him treat patients and achieve dramatic positive results. A significant advantage for English speakers is that, being an American, he can understand and answer your questions. Note that he may be quite blunt in his responses, but what he says is what he means.

The art work induced by ayahuasca visions is amazing and worth commentary. While not an artist himself, Ron did train with Don Jose Coral Mori, who was the teacher of the renowned painters Pablo Amaringo and Eduardo Luna. Together they were the authors of *Ayahuasca Visions*,[125] which is probably the most famous books depicting the iconography associated with the medicine. In July 2009, we were fortunate to meet Pablo Amaringo in Iquitos. He seemed in good health so we were saddened to learn of his death only a few months later. At another conference in Curitiba, Brazil, we had the opportunity to meet the legendary illustrator, Eduardo Luna. Luna is Brazilian and has a well-known studio in Florianopolis, where he holds ceremonies and conducts classes.

At the 2014 International Amazonian Shamans conference,[126] we also met Mauro Reategui Perez. From Pucallpa, Peru, he is one of the students of the late Pablo Amaringo. The paintings he displayed were extraordinary. The images appeared to come off the canvas. Using 3-D glasses one could actually envision jaguars and other beasts emerging from the jungle with a discernable depth. To obtain a 3-D effect requires that a double image be made. That is usually accomplished by computers that determine exactly how the overlap must occur. When I asked Mauro how he accomplished this task, he stated he didn't know. According to Mauro, he could feel his mentor, Pablo, take over his hands and complete the painting. He believes it was Amaringo, operating from the spirit world, who could determine exactly where the oils should be administered to add a living dimension to the images.

Of course, the artwork embraces the spirit of ayahuasca, especially the connection to vegetation. I once asked Hermana Mari what possessed the original indigenous shamans to put the critical elements together and boil them in order to produce ayahuasca. Her answer was simple but hard for most Westerners to understand. She lucidly said, "The plants told us what to do." We discussed further the concept of using plants to heal. She believed that if we could just bring the problems of disease to them, the plants would tell us what was needed for a cure.

That response was from a native healer, who was uneducated in the Western sense. But her comments were supported by statements made by Dennis McKenna, Ph.D. Dennis was the brother to the better-known consciousness explorer Terrance McKenna, an American ethnobotanist who died in 2000 of glioblastoma multiforme, a highly aggressive form of brain cancer. While Terence was concerned about a possible connection between his extensive use of cannabis or psychedelic drugs, and his brain cancer, there was none.[127] Dennis is an ethnopharmacologist and has extensive personal experience with those plants. His doctoral dissertation was titled "Monoamine oxidase inhibitors in Amazonian hallucinogenic plants: ethnobotanical, phytochemical, and pharmacological investigations." He continued to do post-doctoral work at both the National Institute of Mental Health and the Department of Neurology at Stanford Medical School.

We were together in Iquitos when I heard him make a most interesting suggestion: "What if plants have consciousness?" That was exactly the same concept that Hermana Mari had told me while out in the forest several years before. Plant consciousness is a repeated theme in ayahuasca art as well. It is a common leitmotif in the experiences of many people who attend the ceremonies. The message seems to be, "The plants are talking to us." In a previous chapter, I addressed the work of Cleve Backster, the polygrapher who found that plants responded to human emotions. These disparate elements lead me to believe that there are communication channels between plants and humans. If true, it is unfortunate that we don't listen very well. Mostly we seem to be tone deaf.

Santo Daime

Santo Daime is one of the world's fastest growing religions. Its services are more formalized than those of the shamans, but they also employ ayahuasca in the form of a tea, albeit a very powerful one.[128] We have attended Santo Daime services in both Maua and Curitiba, Brazil. Visiting Maua, with its hippies and tie-dyed clothing, is akin to traveling back in time to the 1960s. Our first encounter was deep in the forest and attended by only a few people. Most Santo Daime events last for several hours. There is always music as there are prescribed hymns to be sung. The fact that they are sung in Portuguese mattered little to our understanding of the event. The ayahuasca tea is much weaker than what was provided by the shamans. However, one needs to be able to sing and dance for hours. But there are quiet periods as well when the participant engages in their inner experience.

Attending the ceremony with us in Maua was our interpreter, Rinaldo (pseudonym), a Jesuit priest who had left the order several years before. As expected, Victoria found the brew to be very mild compared to her intense encounters in Peru and Ecuador. But for Rinaldo, the experience was transformational, clearly unlike anything he had ever experienced before. That observation is another reason I suspect there is more than a psychopharmacological reaction going on with ayahuasca.

The service we experienced in Curitiba was very different and far more formal than the one in Peru. Geographically, Curitiba is located much further south in Brazil. While the public thinks of the Amazon straddling the Equator and the warm temperatures of Rio de Janeiro, Brazil is a huge country with many different climates. Near Curitiba that June night, the thermometer read just above freezing. There was a small fire outside, but inside the temple blankets were in order. Men and women sat on opposite sides of the octagon. Next to me on wooden folding chairs was the venerable Stanley Krippner and a Russian acolyte of his.

They told us this would be the short version of the ceremony. Still the 21 songs prescribed by Santo Daime ritual took more than three hours to complete. Again, because of the linguistic issues, we tended to just hum along. The ceremony was a mix of standing, sitting, and quiet introspection. While there were periods of darkness, for the most part the room was well illuminated. That afforded me the opportunity to closely observe the participants.

The vast majority of the attendees were members of the church who attended these services twice a month. That is fortitude, as the foul-tasting tea never gets any easier to swallow. As this service coincided with a seminar, about 15 of us gringos were bused to the relatively remote location. As the service progressed, I became fascinated with a few of the Brazilian women and their reactions as the evening wore on. It seemed to me that a few of them actually entered a state of ecstasy. While most were experiencing visions, they were clearly in a different state of consciousness, albeit one that could be witnessed externally. We could not guess what they were experiencing, but you could tell that something unique was happening.

At one point Victoria found it necessary to go outside to purge. Her perception upon reentering the hall was interesting. I noticed she remained near the wall rather than going back to her original seat. Later, Victoria explained that she had become aware of a very strong circle of energy that encompassed the group. In her mind, it was impenetrable and only accessible to those who had created it. Once one went outside, for whatever purpose, the invisible ring tightened and intensified.

Whether or not there was a swirling ring of physical energy cannot be determined by our current scientific instruments. There are very few scientists who would even contemplate such an experiment. Still, the existence of group energy has been speculated for a long time, and I have experienced it in more mundane settings. In the military, we ran. We ran a lot. When we ran in formation, we could feel changes in energy. As a young instructor at the 101st Airborne Jump School, it was often my assignment to take the students on daily runs of up to five miles. With one person out of cadence, the group would physically struggle. But there were times when everything fell into place and the team or platoon moved smoothly and almost effortlessly. When that happened the need for physical energy seemed to disappear, and the unit could run distances that would normally seem impossible. It was like the sports analogy of "being in the zone."[129] I have seen academic articles questioning whether or not a zone, or flow state, can exist. Clearly, they are written by people who have not experienced it.

The question for science then becomes: does such energy exist? The experiential evidence suggests it does. But what are the components? In military running, or sports zone or flow state, there is a physical activity that triggers it. In Santo Daime, a chemical as well as intentional mental activity has been introduced to the mixture. It is one thing for an individual to be part of a flow state, but another for it to be perceived as an external observer. How this is possible is a question that is unanswerable at this point in time.

In the institution of Santo Daime, integration with the plant world is imperative. There is more to it than just the ingestion of ayahuasca tea, but on a larger scale it involves protection for the forest. There is a reason that the Amazon is known as "the lungs of the Earth." Deforestation is a huge problem both in Brazil and Central Africa. There is a relationship between being an adherent of Santo Daime and the protection the rainforest. Scientifically, it would be difficult to prove a causal connection, but anecdotally the empirical data seems to suggest that Hermana Mari and Dennis McKenna were right. That would mean plants do have consciousness, and they may be trying to save us from ourselves.

A Dark Side

Not all is love and lightness when it comes to how shamans behave. Thus far I have discussed the positive aspects of ayahuasqueros. But there is a dark side as well. Some shamans work on both sides of the fence, meaning good and evil, according to the desires of their clients. There often are economic interests involved. Shamans usually are paid for their services. The indigenous cultures are steeped in a belief in the power of curses. Jealousy is a universal attribute. There are shamans who can be retained to psychically damage an adversary. The same shaman may be asked to remove that curse and will do so for the right price. It is an attractive business model. Second to healing, the most common request of shamans is to employ love curses. These may be used against a departed lover, or to target a man or woman who is believed to have seduced one's partner. That business is very brisk.

The artist Pablo Amaringo was once a practicing shaman but left the profession because of the endemic infighting among them. Operating ayahuasca retreats is competitive business. As ayahuasca tourism has expanded, so has the rivalry among indigenous shamans, as well as the foreigners who employ that title.

While most Western-oriented people would reject the concept of psychic conflict out-of-hand, that might be premature. The example I have comes from Don Howard. Many gringos attempting to do business in Peru have encountered significant problems with local business partners. By Peruvian law, Westerners who do business there are required to have Peruvians as business partners.

Howard had more than one encounter with disgruntled partners who sought revenge via shamanic methods. He has also experienced malaria, which is prevalent in the Iquitos area of the Amazon.[130] Malaria is a painful disease that kills many people each year, especially children. But the issue being discussed is about curses. Howard explained that after an intense argument with a partner, he was attacked with psychic darts. Called *tsentsak* by the Shuar, these are invisible pathogenic projectiles. They are very effective. These tsentsak can be removed by another shaman. Importantly, Don Howard could both feel and see them being extracted. He compared the pain caused by the psychic dart attack as far greater than that inflicted by malaria or any of the other tropical diseases he has endured.

A UFO Connection

When visiting in Las Vegas, our friend John Mack, the Harvard medical doctor who famously began studying UFO abduction cases, discussed his experiences with ayahuasca. We also had many conversations with him about the nature of these phenomena. I am certain most readers of his works do not understand the complexity and the multidimensional aspects which he associated with his research. The topic of ayahuasca came up as a means to explore these relationships. John told us that he had participated in ceremonies on four occasions. Like many other people who have tried the medicine, he told me that he was not ready to try it again, primarily because he was still working on mentally integrating his prior experiences. That process took years for him. He believed the experiences to be very powerful and a way to explore consciousness.[131]

During my travels with Amazonian shamans I have conducted many interviews. They are always interesting but sometimes hard to follow for one primary reason: our worldviews deviate so widely. In fact, I have found this to be a critical issue, one we can learn from. In Western culture, we think of *the spirit world* as being separate and distinct from *the real world*, or consensus reality. That is, if one believes in the spirit world at all. Most scientists reject this notion as non-sustainable, which I believe is a serious mistake. Many of the shamans I spoke with appear to *move seamlessly between those worlds,* as if there were no clear and defining barrier.

Therefore, during interviews it became necessary to ask the shaman to define which world they are talking about. Many of them talked of discarnate entities as if they were humans in their current form. I often asked them about UFOs. Their responses sometimes suggested physical craft, and at other times mystical encounters. Some shamans stated they can call UFOs from another dimension and have seen them materialize in our physical world. A few also professed to seeing them rise out of the Amazon itself, which is consistent with many reports of unidentified submerged objects that have been described as coming from the depths of the ocean. Tales of such craft are not uncommon and are depicted in some of the ayahuasca inspired art. Of course, most shamans claim to communicate directly with vegetation of all varieties.

The Role of the Serpent

In both visions and folklore, serpents play an important role. After ceremonies participants often report having encountered large snakes that sometimes stare directly into their eyes. The snakes are the protectors of the forest, and this is taken as a very positive omen. People suffering from ophidiophobia, an abnormal fear of snakes, may have problems with such imagery but had best be prepared for such encounters.

Central to the creation myths is Sachamama, or the mother of forests. Some shamans told me that Sachamama was so big that the forest grows on her head. In some legends, you could tell when Sachamama was around because you could find the bones of large animals she had devoured. These legends seem to emanate from the native experiences with the giant anaconda that are prevalent in the upper regions of the Amazon. Some versions of the myth say that Sachamama is large enough to be mistaken for a tree and may crush and consume unwary hunters.

While not growing a forest on their skin, anacondas have been captured that approach 30 feet in length and a girth of 44 inches.[132] There are several credible reports of anacondas two to three times that length. In archives, I have seen undocumented aerial film that would support those claims. On rare occasions, they actually have eaten humans, so it is easy to imagine how the myths originated.

Remember, parts of this area of the Amazon region have never been explored, and there still are uncontacted tribes in the area. Just a few years ago, while we were engaged in ayahuasca ceremonies with Don Luis near Tena, Ecuador, several miles north of us members of a white missionary family were found speared to death by one such group. The area we were in was quite remote and in the headwaters of the Amazon. Apparently, members of the unidentified tribe were upset with the petroleum industry that has ruined parts of their habitat. In addition to killing most of the family, they kidnapped their baby. She was later recovered. This is a region populated by the Shuar, some of whom we met. Formerly known as the Jivaro, this group is famous for shrinking human heads, a practice they claim they gave up several decades ago.

Kambo – Frog Poison

While at the 2015 shaman's conference in Iquitos, we had an opportunity to observe *Kambo* administrations. This is the use of frog poison from *Phyllom-*

edusa bicolor to induce non-hallucinogenic altered states. In my view, when uncontrolled, this has the potential for considerable physical danger to the participant. In this instance, the demonstration was conducted by Peter Gorman, a well-known American journalist who leads expeditions into the jungle on ethnobiological adventures. Several volunteers came forward to try the Kambo, which is introduced subcutaneously on the end of a sharp wooden stick. The onset of effects was very fast and dramatic. The pulse raced, and people became flushed and vomited profusely. There was no way to tell what happened with their blood pressure, but my educated guess is that it skyrocketed, though some claim that their blood pressure fell dramatically. No one has taken measurements during these rather dangerous ceremonies.

A simple Google search for "frog poison" will net several sites with extravagant claims. Some literally announce it is effective in treating cancer, AIDS, Parkinson's, Alzheimer's, fertility problems, and nearly anything else you can imagine. If frog poison was anywhere close to as effective as claimed, Big Pharma would have been all over it long ago. You would only need to raise a sufficient quantity of the brightly colored amphibians, from the *Dendrobatidae* family, also known as poison-dart frogs. These creatures secrete the poison as a natural protection mechanism. The name "poison dart frogs" is appropriate as the Amazonian tribes for centuries have been dipping their blowgun darts in the exudate in order to paralyze their prey. That should tell you something about the potency of the substance used in Kambo ceremonies. The frogs are not harmed in the extraction process and therefore can be reused, or as the indigenous people do, released back into the forest.

There is, however, a story I received from Bill Bassett, or Wild Bill as he was known at The Yellow Rose of Texas, a popular hangout for gringos visiting Iquitos. Bill grew up across the street from me in La Crosse, Wisconsin, and I knew him extremely well. In 2003, Victoria and I were planning to go to Peru, but I was sent off to Afghanistan instead. Bill and Victoria decided go to the retreat near Iquitos. On their departure, Bill was suffering from Parkinson's and had braces on his legs. After two weeks, he returned to the U.S. without the need for the braces. Enamored with the area, he married the retreat's cook and spent about half of his remaining life in Peru.

While traveling deep into the forest Bill would experiment with various drugs and plant medicines. One incident he described to me is particularly noteworthy. It is an event that can't happen, yet seems to have occurred. One midafternoon in March, Bill allowed the frog poison to be put into his skin. The bamboo stick barely had been withdrawn, whereupon he collapsed onto the forest floor, a short distance from the hut in which he was staying. A few hours later he regained consciousness. There is a reason they call this area a rainforest. As happens most every day during the rainy season, a downpour had taken place. Bill found the ground a short distance from him was drenched, yet a circular area a few feet around him was not touched. He could not explain how it happened: despite being exposed to the thunderstorm, he remained completely dry. Impressed by the experience, Bill continued to take Kambo every time he was in Peru.

Bill's experiences with ayahuasca actually brings more to the table than interesting visions. It is worthy of serious research. Not only was he able to walk without his leg braces after a few ceremonies. He also found that ayahuasca helped reduce the tremors that Parkinson's patients often have. He indicated to me that if he drank ayahuasca at least once every three months, the shaking was far more manageable. That remained true for several years before finally succumbing to the disease in 2009. For him, ayahuasca was not a cure but did make the symptoms far more manageable, and life more pleasant.

Field Effect

Our experiences with ayahuasca are strongly indicative of interactions between a physical world as we know it and one or more alternative dimensions, including spirit worlds that few humans perceive. Several religions acknowledge that all things are interconnected. Ayahuasca ceremonies are supportive of that concept.

One additional observation I have experienced lends credence to interaction between those worlds, that can, on occasion, be perceived. Attending many ceremonies, I have generally remained the external observer. However, I suspect there is actually a field effect that is generated by the participants. While sitting in the dark in the malocas, I have often been aware of changes in state, even though I did not ingest anything. Visions have come, though they were not as intense as in those who did ingest a medicine. Clearly, the chanting of the icaros was an audible input, but there seems to be more to it. Unfortunately, we are at a state of research, or lack thereof, that I would not know where to start looking.

What is certain is that there is a need to conduct serious research into the effects of ayahuasca, especially in relationship to PTSD. It is by no means a panacea, and should only be used by those who are ready to face the consequences. The epidemic of PTSD, brought on by incessant wars, demands we explore all alternatives that offer hope. Ayahuasca is one of those.

CHAPTER 20
SPIRITS OF BRAZIL

Our experiences with the spirit world, facilitated by our Brazilian hosts, have been amazing. While Western traditions are prevalent in the large cities, there lies an undercurrent of mysticism that today still plays an essential role throughout their society. We have been privileged to participate in a small part of that subculture.

Brazil is an emerging nation with vast resources and a convoluted history cloudily enmeshed with the slave trade from Africa. The majority of North Americans are unaware that the U.S. is approximately the same size geographically as Brazil, or that it spans several climatic zones. Most, but not all of the Amazon basin, lies within its borders, but there are huge areas of rich farm land, pampas, and even mountains in the east.

To avoid war, in 1494 Pope Alexander VI, the author of the Treaty of Tordesillas, dictated that the land 370 leagues west of Cape Verde be given to the Portuguese. Known as the Spanish Pope, Alexander VI wanted to protect the interests of his native country. The purpose was to establish a dividing line between the Portuguese and Spanish domains. The treaty ceded Africa to the Portuguese, but that was already under their control. In the Western Hemisphere, it split the South American continent, but gave primacy for exploration to the Spanish. Thus, all countries there speak Spanish as the formal language, except for Brazil which relies on Portuguese.

Although the U.S. continues to struggle with the discreditable history of slavery, it should be acknowledged that the majority of African slaves went to South America. As in North America, the indigenous people of South America were also pushed aside by the Europeans. Their numbers are unknown even today. Recent archeological findings, however, suggest that there may have been some very large, quite advanced, societies. While there long have been rumors of sites, like the lost city of Z in the Matta Grosso, there is now increasing evidence to support those claims.[133] More recently, ancient craved megaliths have been discovered in Amapá, a state in northern Brazil just above the Equator. As with

England's Stonehenge, it indicates that someone there was taking astronomical measurements more than 1,000 years ago.[134] Who they were is yet unknown, but estimates now place the pre-Columbian population in that area at over ten million. Clearly, the indigenous population was far different from the isolated nomadic groups that anthropologists previously recognized as living on the South American continent.

As with Peru and Ecuador, the western Amazon regions of Brazil are also the home of a number of uncontacted tribes.[135] Deforestation, via the logging industry, has encroached on their lands. Laws prohibit anthropologists, missionaries, and other groups from attempting to make contact. However well-meaning these groups may be, it never seems to end well for these tribes. Unfortunately, illegal miners and loggers who do encounter these people usually just wipe them out, either by shooting them or by the introduction of diseases for which they have no immunity.

Brazil has taken steps to protect indigenous groups. Founded about a century ago, the National Indian Foundation, or FUNAI, is the Brazilian government's body that establishes and carries out policies relating to indigenous peoples.[136] The results of their efforts have been mixed. In 2014, I was invited to Vitoria, Espirito Santo, to give a non-lethal weapons presentation. Knowing of our interests in native cultures, our sponsor arranged for Victoria and me to visit Reserva Indígena de Aracruz. It is an area ruled by the Guarani tribe, an indigenous group whose home spans more than a thousand miles to Paraguay and Argentina. In discussion with the elected chief, he indicated some dissatisfaction with FUNAI. He found that Europeans and North Americans were more sympathetic to the plight of their indigenous tribes than many Brazilians.

Martial arts also played a role in the cultural development of Brazil. Like slave-masters everywhere, the owners tended to be ruthless and totally focused on production. The slaves, on the other hand, were always looking for ways to escape or overthrow their masters. The owners kept close tabs on all activities of their slaves. Any hint of rebellion brought harsh punishment.

In Brazil, the slaves invented an ingenious method of training, one that could be practiced in the open without raising suspicion. It was called Capoeira. Although the slaves outnumbered the owners, traditional weapons stayed in the hands of the overseers. Therefore, alternative means of fighting would be required. What emerged was a form of music and dance that could be performed openly. These movements also could be used in unarmed defense.

Today there are schools that teach Capoeira, which looks more like competitive dancing than a martial art. I have observed a form of Capoeira in Brasilia, Brazil. The choreography is amazing to behold since the street demonstrations are often spontaneous. Worth noting is that after slavery was abolished in Brazil, some practitioners of Capoeira became bodyguards and hitmen. That led to the prohibition of all Capoeira for several decades. It has now expanded into a global enterprise. Like other martial arts, advanced forms incorporate an understanding and application of chi or ki energy. While science debates the existence of that kind of energy, Capoeira puts it to use.

With the importation of African slaves came their animist and spiritist religions. Catholic missionaries, especially the Jesuits, worked hard at converting as many people as possible to Christianity. For many of the displaced Africans, Christianity did not have the same visceral impact as did the ceremonies they had previously practiced. Today, one can still see the integration of the various religions, including African animism, Islam, and Christianity.

Umbanda and Candomblé are religions that were imported from African traditional Yoruba, Fon, and Bantu beliefs, and have taken root in Brazil. Initially formed in Bahia, the spiritist religions have spread throughout much of South America, mostly in communities comprised of the descendants of the slave trade. Candomblé is an oral tradition that does not have scriptures. Practitioners believe that each person has an orisha, or protector, that guides them throughout life. That is similar to the concept of spirit guides found in many other religions, including some subsets of Christianity. Unlike Santo Daime, there are no drugs or medicines involved in the rituals. Instead the catalyst for their services is music.

Similarly, Umbanda represents an amalgamation of beliefs, including Catholicism. There is a strong belief in spirits, and their ceremonies incorporate possession in which some practitioners are believed to allow external entities to enter and use their bodies temporarily for a period of time. That concept would be easy for me to dismiss had I not observed it personally. More significantly, the possessed person in this case was Victoria.

Curitiba

The 54th Annual Parapsychological Association (PA) Conference, held in 2011, had a most unusual structure. Running contiguously prior was the 7th Psi Meeting: Psi Research and Anomalistic Psychology hosted by Faculdades Integradas Espírita, a group that studies Spiritism. They were, however, the same local people who helped organize the PA conference. In addition, a third meeting was held that spanned days before and after these conferences. Administratively it was a lot of work, but the venue remained constant. The third meeting was called the 6th Journey to Altered States and run by the Integrated Centre of Experimental Research. This was indeed experiential and included the Santo Daime ceremony (covered in the Goddess Ayahuasca chapter), an Umbanda ceremony, and an Aty Guarini ceremony, each one held at night at various sites.

While lecturing at a parapsychology conference in Curitiba, Brazil, a small group of foreigners was offered the opportunity to attend an Umbanda service on Saturday evening. The setting was a quite formal with hundreds of parishioners in attendance. It was very chilly that night, near freezing, and we needed heavy clothes at first. The Umbanda temple was brightly illuminated and quite ornate, with many statues of deities, 12-15 inches in height, all lined up along the gleaming stone and glass brick wall. There were also lots of swords, usually displayed in a crossed fashion. It was clear that a hierarchical order was maintained among priests, initiates, and curious attendees. Most people were dressed all in white, and many were adorned with bright sashes of red and blue. A few others, presumably officials, sported lavish robes. Across the room was an area for musicians. Most prominent were six large atabaque, conga drums, their sides draped in white cloth with a brilliant red fabric tied with a bow. They would infuse the room with their pulsating, hypnotic, and soul-embracing rhythms throughout the ceremony.

Soon the audience broke into small groups as key members of the church read fortunes or answered personal inquiries. Obviously, they made allowances for the Westerners, who were able to get very close to the action. The predictive comments and personal responses all were made openly for anyone within earshot to hear. Selected by the High Priest, Victoria received some personal information via a translator. While she was well covered, the High Priest stated Victoria was a lover of jewelry. At his insistence, she took off her coat, revealing that her arms were adorned with many bracelets. Happy with his correct evaluation, he asked Victoria to show the crowd her arms as a means of confirmation.

As the ceremony became more organized, most of the attendees moved to the elevated benches that formed a semicircle facing the altars and musicians. Selected again, Victoria was asked to choose a few beans. They were then deftly sliced to reveal divined information regarding her spiritual journey. While that reading was only mildly interesting, what was to follow was mind-boggling.

A young woman, by her dress and manner obviously an intermediate level priestess, asked if anyone wanted to experience a healing. As expected, Victoria was one of the dozen or so people who obediently formed a line on the main floor. The healing priestess stepped in front of each person, said a prayer, and used her hands in a cascading motion from the head towards the floor. Victoria was near the end of the line, and I stood off to the side taking photographs.

The priestess was probably in her 30s, thin, and dressed all in white. Around her neck were strings of colored beads, and her waist was wrapped a cyan silk sash. Victoria stood in front of her, head slightly bowed, a blanket draped around her shoulders. As the priestess hands descended past Victoria's head, something totally indescribable happened. In an instant, she was in an altered state of consciousness. A mystical smile appeared on her face. This was not the Victoria I knew. Normally a bit withdrawn with strangers, she became the focal point of attention. Quickly removing the blanket and her coat, within seconds she spun out to the middle of the floor.

*Victoria in trance, possessed by discarnate spirit at an Umbanda ceremony in Curitiba, Brazil
About 300 people just stopped and stared even though they often witness spirit possession.*

She was possessed by the spirit of some unknown entity. I mean that she was literally possessed at that time. This woman who, except on rare occasions, is normally quiet and sedate in public gatherings, became the center of attention as 300 people instantly came to a standstill and stared at what was unfolding before them. The Brazilian audience was used to seeing possession occur as it is a part of the Umbanda religion. But never before had they seen an American woman, barefoot, arms outstretched, as she pivoted intensely in the middle of the floor to the rising tone of the atabaques. This was a showstopper in the most literal sense of the world.

As I was busily taking pictures, an attendant approached me and asked rather impetuously if I was a reporter. Fortunately, he spoke fluent English, and I explained that I was not a reporter. Gesturing toward Victoria, I told him I was her husband. His tone changed considerably, and he went to great lengths to assure me that everything would be okay. After a few minutes, the music slowed, and Victoria was escorted to the side and seated in front of the high priest. While Victoria was still unaware of her surroundings or performance, the priest made movements similar to what is observed in energy healing. After several minutes, Victoria went off to sit alone while the experience of possession wore off.

After another 20 minutes, she rejoined me, and we briefly discussed what had happened. She was totally unaware of the spirit that had entered her. Victoria was cognizant that when the priestess stood in front of her, she felt something leap inside her body. The entity knew she was open to the experience and not frightened. Who or what that spirit was remains a mystery. Victoria believes the entity accepted her invitation and chose to spend some time experiencing life through her senses.

This is one of those events that defies explanation. Had I not seen the possession take place firsthand—and known Victoria so well—I would probably have discounted it, or suggested that she just made it all up and wanted to attract attention. Such public displays are completely antithetical for Victoria. We have an unspoken agreement concerning these events. She can be brave, knowing that I'm watching over her, and I record objectively and approach each situation from a scientific perspective. Therefore, she is always open and ready for any spiritual experience and is never afraid. She also says she is protected by a large snake that came to her during a previous ayahuasca ceremony near Iquitos, Peru. What happened that night in Curitiba defies conventional explanation.

The Umbanda ceremony continued for at least another hour. Part of the service included a time for attendees, who may not have been part of the normal congregation, to ask for divined information. For that, about 30 or 40 initiates, known as *filhos-de-santo*, set up areas in which to address the questions. Each had a board, candles, and small sharp knives. As questions were asked, the priestess would throw knives into the board. I'm not sure what that did, but a conversation would then take place. Without a personal translator, all I can say is that it was interesting to watch.

Later there was more drumming and healing. At that point, many in the congregation gave the appearance of being possessed. I watched it all very closely, but saw nothing that approached what Victoria had done. With red capes flaring as they spun about, the participants usually would stomp off as if possessed by an angry male spirit. They would then approach each other and do a cross-armed salute that seemed to be recognized by all members. They all made it a point to salute the high priest and priestess.

Frankly, that demonstration did not impress me. Each person knew the persona of the spirit who they claimed possessed them and reacted accordingly. It is not what we observed in later Umbanda ceremonies. As a final gesture, I was taken to the center of the floor. The high priest took his ornate royal blue cape and threw it over me. That was an interesting salutation, but I was not aware of any effect it might have had. They said it was healing, which everyone can use, sick or not.

Aty Guarani

The release forms we were required to sign in order to attend the ceremonies that involved ingestion of various drugs were onerous. They warned of terrible things that could happen, and if they did, we had to agree to hold the organizers harmless.

Aty Guarani was an unknown for us. Umbanda and Santo Daime we had studied and understood the basic premises. We did know that Aty Guarani included the use of some very powerful drugs. The shaman we met, Awaju Poty, described a concept of spirituality of the Guarani people that incorporates all of nature, including a universe with multiple spirit worlds. There is a life force that permeates everything. And there is *Ñemi'Guaxu,* or the great mystery, that cannot be resolved in this life. Much like the Hindu tradition, they see death as a transition and final integration into an ultimate understanding of the cosmos.

We were familiar with the Guarani people and knew that their indigenous culture has struggled to survive. They transcend international borders in the southern part of the continent, but they have not been treated well by any of the national governments. Awaju Poty is a most unusual man.[137] A shaman, he also is an accomplished musician with advanced degrees. He plays the harp exquisitely, even in the forest.

The August evening when we visited him was about as cold as it gets in the state of Paraná. His remote site is at a higher elevation than Curitiba, further depressing the temperature. We travelled on a small bus but eventually ran out of road, and had to traverse the muddy path on foot. Because it was dark and uphill, there was considerable slipping and sliding. Within a few minutes, we sighted a circular building constructed of upright wooden poles, each two to three inches in diameter, and a thatched roof. The design reminded me of some of the kraals we had seen in southern Africa.

We entered and found a small fire delineated by rocks in the center of the room. A metal pot was on the fire brewing something. According to Aty Guarani tradition, everything in the world goes counterclockwise. Therefore, we stooped through the small doorway and moved to our left. Each person secured a spot next to the outer wall and made a miniature nest. We knew we would be there for several hours and needed to get as warm as possible

Soon, Poty and his female assistant, a woman of about 40 with very short hair and a faint smile, extinguished the lanterns, leaving only the slight glow from the fire by which to see. He retreated to the far wall and began playing one of the many musical instruments he would employ in the ceremony. Beating a drum loudly, Poty then circumnavigated the fire counterclockwise several times. Next, his assistant handed him a long, thin pipe filled with tobacco. Pipe in hand and puffing profusely, he continued his circling. Then he stopped and handed the pipe to the nearest person in our group. Then, in turn, we each made three trips around the fire, moving always with it to our right. Hating smoke, I quickly found that by blowing into the pipe it would appear as if I was actually inhaling it.

After completing the pipe ritual, the assistant rose from the fire, carefully turning to her left, and approached each person with a globe-like metal bowl containing a bubbling liquid concoction. I was invited to suck on the attached straw but declined. The others of our group all took part. We don't know what the liquid substance consisted of, or how it was made. Obviously, the psychoactive component was an extremely powerful DMT derivative.

Poty continued to play his musical instruments and periodically circled the small fire. Victoria said the music helped make the forest spirits visible. What was reported by the participants did not match what I can confirm in consensus reality. David, who quite familiar with psychedelics, stated he saw an old woman kneeling next to the fire. Several people reported strange animals cavorting wildly about the room. Obviously, each person, while remaining relatively still in their nest, embarked on their own inner journey.

The ceremony ended around midnight. The first trick was to navigate back down the dark, slippery trail. That was more difficult than before, as most of the group was still heavily under the influence of the medicine. Unlike ayahuasca, the effects did not dissipate quickly. After arriving at our hotel, we entered the elevator and went to our room on the sixth floor. Putting Victoria to bed, I decided to go to the lobby and observe what was taking place. Entering the elevator again, I was surprised to find a young woman who initially had gone up with us. Unable to figure out where her room was, she just kept riding up and down the elevator.

Vitoria

On the east coast, an hour's flight north Rio de Janeiro, in the state of Espirito Santo, lies the bustling city of Vitoria. In preparation for the upcoming World Cup and Olympics, the Policia Militar[138] decided to conduct a course on the use of non-lethal weapons, and I was honored to be invited as the opening speaker. Doing her homework, Victoria set about finding the local Umbanda organizations. Using the internet, she found two such local groups and their addresses.

We asked our hosts if we could have a couple of extra days and they agreed. I wanted a day to recover as travel time was going to exceed 24 hours, including an overnight flight from Atlanta to Rio. Arriving mid-morning, we were greeted by my host, Major Marsuel Riani, and a driver, Private Mario Magalhães, who turned out to also be my interpreter for the presentation. Having lived in Canada for a while, he spoke fluent English and had remarkable linguistic skills, which allowed him to translate in real-time. His knowledge of international affairs was extraordinary for a private. Soon we learned that despite his rank, he also served as an advisor to the governor of Espirito Santo.

There was one additional unique aspect to Mario: he possessed eidetic memory. He was not born with this skill; that should be of interest to neuroscientists. He had been involved in a serious automobile accident, and when he came out of a coma, he could remember everything he saw or heard. This proved useful later during our visit, as he was able to identify one of individuals who attended the services when we found him in a totally different setting.

We told our hosts we were interested in finding Umbanda ceremonies. We intended to get a taxi from the hotel to the sites. That, it turned out, was very naive on our part. The places Victoria had identified were located in the local favelas (slums). As Riani told me, "Taxis will not take you there." The drivers deemed these areas too dangerous and considered them off-limits.

Most of Vitoria is Catholic, but there is a small subset that practice Spiritism. Now traveling with armed guards, we ventured to the first church. It was located in an area that Mario previously had patrolled in uniform. "Daily gunfights were not uncommon," Mario informed us. We did hear a few gunshots while we were there.

The temple, called the Spiritual Center of Grandpa Antonio Aruanda, was located in a multi-story building that sat back off the road. There were no signs indicating the church existed. Mario mentioned that local gang members were afraid of Umbanda, as they believe it evokes spirits. The service was underway when we arrived. We clearly stood out. Though Riani and Mario were in civilian clothes, the people knew immediately they were police. That was not always considered to be a good thing. And then, there were two Americans.

After answering a few questions about why we were there, we followed protocol and lit candles outside the church. Then we were invited to join the service. Riani is a Catholic and Mario is a Buddhist, so Umbanda was new to both of our Brazilian friends as well. While they had heard of Umbanda, they had never attended a service before.

The setting at this spiritual center was very different from what we had experienced in Curitiba. The group was much smaller, about 40 participants, and the venue more like a living room than church. Everything was far less formal. We later learned that Umbanda was a generational religion and that many of these participants were related. With our escorts standing in the rear, the initiates moved us to the front of the seating area, placing Victoria on the left with the women, and seating me with the males on the right.

It is common for females to lead, and this service was headed by a high priestess. Most attendees were dressed all in white. The colors in the house were bright, but the setting not ornate. The walls were white, except one in sapphire blue which faced the congregation. In front of that wall was an altar adorned with a scarlet red covering. Placed carefully on the altar were several vases containing flowers, a few small statues of their orisha, or spirits, and some beaded necklaces. A painting of an Umbanda saint hung between two narrow, open windows.

Uninterrupted by our entry, the priestess continued the service. Drawn on the floor were chalk symbols, similar to ones I had seen at voodoo ceremonies. Symbolism is very meaningful in these religions. Ones such as these, made with chalk, are temporary and erased when the service is over. A number of initiates assisted the priestess. As singing increased, the parishioners went forward and proceeded to dance, generally in a counterclockwise circle.

Unbeknownst to me, Victoria had set the intention to allow possession to take place as we had entered the temple. Although not understanding a word of what was being said, Victoria soon got up and was dancing among the group. She said that she had intuited a message to participate. Although unlike her previous possession experience, it was powerful and convincing just the same. Recognizing that Victoria was having some inner strife, a woman took her to the altar and had her bow three times

Three hours passed swiftly. It was now dark, time for a break in the service. While nothing was said to me, the high priestess went over to our hosts and insisted they recognized Victoria. They were quite insistent that she must not leave. Some kind of acknowledgement had taken place between these women, even though they had never met before. From my perspective, this meeting seemed more than mere coincidence.

Due to a prior engagement, our escorts left, promising to return. We were left alone in the favela. The Umbanda group seemed to become protective of us, and we found a few who spoke English moderately well. They invited us to join in refreshments provided from a small adjacent kitchen. The friendly conversations were typical of new acquaintances and offered us an opportunity to ask about their participation in Umbanda. One stand-out conversation was with a man who spoke very good English. This gentleman informed me that he had been an American sailor in a past life, and that had helped with his linguistic skills. It's important to know that the belief in reincarnation is a core tenet of Umbanda.

As if on cue, the service began again. The high priestess, now joined by a male leader and supported by music, called on the gods and goddesses to come and participate with the humans. Soon a healing session took place with Victoria and a few other people in the center, surrounded by the initiate healers. Open to the process, Victoria felt light-headed and began to sway. At some point, a female orisha entered Victoria's body. In her mind, she then clearly heard the orisha saying to her, "Why are you in the inner circle?" The orisha insisted that Victoria should be part of the outer circle assisting others.

At this service also, there was a period for parishioners to ask for personal guidance from the spirits, albeit through the initiates. A number of the initiates took on different personalities, many of which seemed cross-gender and distinctly male. That led to participants drinking some beer and wine. Smoking was also prevalent. Frankly, it was difficult to for me to determine if any real possession took place, or if this is just a convenient way to break with traditional role norms.

Other events were more convincing. Late in the ceremony, without warning, the high priestess was possessed by a rather violent male personality. It took several parishioners to calm that spirit down so that the priestess could continue as the leader. The reclamation of personality was carried out, apparently with no adverse effects.

Shortly after 9 p.m., Mario returned just as the service ended. One woman, still possessed by an orisha, cornered Victoria with the help of an initiate who spoke English, and offered Victoria a small bouquet of white and red carnations. She was told that she must return at least twice more. With an exchange of pleasantries that included email addresses and phone numbers, we headed off with a lot to think about.

Mario and Riani went home and related the evening's events to their families, who were not familiar with Umbanda. When they agreed to take us to another Umbanda church, their wives and children decided to join us. That adventure began three days later, when together, we attended another Umbanda ceremony in a different favela. The most significant aspect of this meeting was finding the location. Our escorts had arranged to be in cellphone contact with a person who supposedly knew the area. Even so, we wandered around quite a bit. With great difficulty, Riani finally narrowed the search down. This was more complicated, as we were accompanied by Mario's wife, a certified therapist, Riani's wife, a police sergeant, and their three children, including a teenage daughter. None of them had ever attended an Umbanda ceremony, and this was mostly a welcomed curiosity for them.

It was dark when we parked the cars in an open area and decided to walk to the location. Without armed protection, I never would have ventured into the area where the service was ongoing. Walking past a huge pile of trash, we located a tunnel illuminated by a single light bulb. Insane as it was, we continued through the concrete orifice and emerged into the Casa Do Senhor Ogom, a concrete building with a tin roof and bars that served as windows. There was a single room, which was divided, with benches for observers. At the front was another high priestess wearing a blue dress and smoking a cigar. She stood before a long altar, draped with a white cloth on which were dozens of small statues of various orishas. Some Christian symbols were included as well.

Having young children along complicated matters, and we only stayed about one hour. Here again Victoria went forward for a blessing, and she was joined by Nilma, Mario's wife. Again we saw several parishioners who appeared to be a mild states of possession. The general behavioral characteristics seem to transfer from one spiritual center to another. Whether this is expectation and programming, or real possession, is difficult to determine but certainly worth further research.

Rio de Janeiro

During the past two decades, I have made several trips to Rio, primarily related to non-lethal weapons issues. However, our hosts were well aware of our interests in both phenomena and indigenous religions, and coordinated our Santo Daime trip to Maua. They do get a little nervous when my profile in these areas gets too high. Being businessmen, the company is concerned about their image. That occurred in an interview that included both non-lethal weapons and UFOs. It appeared in *O Globo*, the leading newspaper in Brazil in April 2016.[139]

As we would expect to find in the U.S., business people often have both a public and private position on controversial matters. While staying at their mountain retreat near Itaipava, about an hour's drive north of Rio, we discussed personal incidents that are hard to explain. In one, the company president, Carlos, a considerably overweight gentleman, was leaning against a handrail that, without warning, gave way. It was a drop of about eight feet to the next turn in the path. He told me that as he was falling completely out of control, it was if a large hand reached out under him, broke his fall, and gently lowered him to the ground. I have used this path many times and know that the potential for severe physical injury from such a fall is very high. Yet, the description of this event defies what is conventionally believed about the laws of gravity. He attributes the incident to divine intervention, and to honor this "divine help," Carlos erected a statue of the Blessed Virgin Mary at the top of the path. While very private about this personal experience, he did show Victoria and me the altar he had created.

Two religious services we attended in Rio stand out but took place years apart. The first was a visit to Tempo Espirita Tuvara. It was early one Friday afternoon and the large concrete temple was packed with hundreds of people. I immediately wondered, don't any of these people have day jobs? Our guide was my friend, Edson Pereira, a retired colonel from the Brazilian Army. Edson has served as an interpreter for me on several trips to Brazil and is known and respected throughout the country. Also with us was Edson's wife, Mary, who is central to this discussion.

The Spiritism religions in Brazil are generally based on the work of Allan Kardec, a French educator who lived during the mid-19th century. Actually, Allan Kardec was the pen name of Hippolyte Léon Denizard Rivai, who wrote several books that defined Spiritism. While there are a few Spiritism churches in North America today, the religion is better known and more popular in South America. It is important to know that Kardec was strongly in favor of scientific research into the phenomena he posited.[140]

The Spiritism religion is supported by Kardec's writings and philosophy that detail establishing connections with disincarnate entities. Parishioners also embrace the concept of reincarnation. Their practices run counter to conservative Christian religions that often warn their congregations to steer away from contact with unknown spirits as they may try to deceive them. These groups are very concerned about the possibility of possession by evil, or mischievous, spirits.

At Tempo Espirita Tuvara there was no head priest. Rather, there were many initiates, about equally divided between men and women. For the service we attended, the left side of the seating area was reserved for females and the right for males. They did inform us that there are other services in which mixed seating is the norm. In preparation for the service, we had obtained glass bottles and filled them with water. These we placed alongside the dozens of other bottles brought by members of the congregation. The hypothesis was that the water would become charged with positive energy during the service and could be used for healing at a later date. The biggest trick for us would be getting them through security at the airport, but we did manage to get them back to Las Vegas.

After singing for a while, it was time for the healing aspects of the service. The initiates, dressed all in white, formed two lines at the front. Everyone wanting to be blessed or healed then proceeded to the front. The process was long but orderly. As each person stood in front of the priest, he or she would use their hands to convey psychic energy as they said prayers for each person.

The reason that Mary is central to this story is that she is a medical miracle who was healed at this temple. Suffering from severe back pain, she had been seen by many traditional medical doctors, each of whom wrote her off as incurable. Edson had stood by her, watching hopelessly as conventional medicine failed. Mary was bedridden and given little chance of ever recovering. But after attending Spiritism healing services, she regained full use of her body. She is the young lady in the center of this picture taken of us at the temple. There is no traditional medical explanation for her total recovery.

Left to right: translator Andrea Levy, Mary Pereira, Victoria Alexander, and the author.

As of this writing, the most recent Umbanda ceremony we attended was in April 2016. I was invited to Rio de Janeiro to receive an award regarding non-lethal weapons work, and again we took advantage of the location. This time it was Edson Pereira, Jr., a brilliant young graduate student, who escorted us. Physically much larger than his father, Edson Jr. can be an imposing figure. His knowledge of world affairs is stellar. He is a practicing Catholic and had never been to an Umbanda ceremony. Once again, we introduced Brazilian friends to one of their country's indigenous, vitally important religions.

We arrived at the temple Caminheiros da Verdade ("Those who walk the path of Truth") just before 5 p.m. While we expected the service to begin at that hour, we found it had been underway for some time, and the door was locked. When I rang the buzzer at the exterior black iron metal fence, I was confronted by a man who seemed none too pleased at my appearance. This was not a place frequented by foreigners. With the help of Edson Jr., who can be quite persuasive, the attendant was convinced to allow us to enter. Seeing the blue Cannon PowerShot digital camera in my hand, he informed us that no pictures would be allowed.

Quietly we entered and found seats on the bench along the back wall. This was a modest sized temple with azure blue walls and the familiar statuettes. A low divider with swinging gate in the center separated the priestess and initiates from the observers. I asked, but was told that Victoria could not join with those dancing in this part of the service. Nonetheless, within a short time, she managed to move near the front, while Edson Jr. and I continued our vigil from the rear. Victoria had whispered to me that if directed (by the spirits), she would disregard any attempt to stop her from joining the ceremony.

The service was typical of the other Umbanda rituals we had attended. Men and women dressed almost exclusively in white clothing and moved in rhythm to the music. Again, they appeared to be in light trance and behaved in the anticipated manner. The main priestess seemed to be in charge and directing the activities. About 100 people, mostly waiting for the second part of the service, observed the activities from old wooden benches.

Soon, there was a break as the initiates needed to rehydrate after their long period of activity. Several in the audience looked questioningly at us, the two lone Americans. Still, they seemed to be warming up to our presence. After about half an hour, the consultations began. We were told that we could now join in. Quickly, Victoria again took her place near the front, while Edson Jr. and I continued to warm the bench. Fortuitously, a young man who spoke English lined up right behind Victoria. He said this was his first Umbanda encounter and had been encouraged to attend by a close friend. Still, he did not know what to expect. The priestess and initiates entered and presumed to take on the identities of their orisha or guides. They situated themselves around the room so that they could engage in private conversations with those seeking consultation. At the gate stood a stern woman whose job was directing traffic. As Victoria approached, she indicated that Victoria should be seen by the main priestess. Her new male friend accompanied her to act as a translator.

Abruptly the priestess asked, "Why are you here?" Victoria's response was that she was seeking grace. Whatever Victoria said, or otherwise conveyed, seemed to strike a chord with the high priestess. She proceeded to conduct a long healing session, which included energy transfer via her hands and lots of smoke for cleansing Victoria's spirit. This became so touching that, as the session continued, Victoria began crying. In recognition, the orisha gave Victoria her name: Cabocla Jureminha da Cachoeira. Then the orisha said to her, "If you ever need me, just call my name." It was a very powerful personal message.

As her session ended, Victoria approached the bench where we were sitting. From her demeanor, I knew she was visibly shaken. Edson Jr. did not pick up on that and suggested we leave immediately. I told him we needed to wait for a while longer. I signaled to him to watch her: she was physically vibrating and close to tears. About ten minutes later, we slipped out into the night and drove off to dinner at one of the famous Brazilian churriscarias.

Such emotional engagements are hard to characterize scientifically. For the participant, it is clear these are meaningful experiences. From a Spiritism standpoint, these are believed to be valid transfers of information where at times physical as well as mental healing takes place. The main point of contention is that the experience needs to be evaluated from two divergent worldviews and belief systems.

One point I should reiterate: at none of the religious services we attended in Brazil was there a request for money. There were no offering plates or baskets passed around, as is so common in American Christian churches. There was not even a box along the wall where parishioners could leave donations. Early on I asked Edson Sr. about this. After all, there were some real overhead expenses for these temples, including upkeep and utilities. He said he didn't know and had wondered how the organizations got support. One of my red flags with psychic healers is when they ask for large donations. In Brazil, we found the opposite to be true. Never did we see any attempt at fundraising.

Abadiânia

Located about 60 miles southwest of Brasilia, the gently rolling countryside near Abadiânia reminds U.S. visitors of the farmlands of middle America. There, down a dusty side road from BR 060, lies the Casa de Dom Inácio (the house of St Ignatius Loyola). This is the operational headquarters of João de Deus, or John of God, as he is known in English.[141] Born João Teixeira da Faria, he is one of the most famous psychic healers in the world. Having twice visited him, I am personally convinced he is the real deal.

When first we visited him in 2005, there were about 300 people seeking his help. Returning in 2014, we saw thousands gathered at the casa, many of them arriving on tour buses. There are several things that may account for the increase in attendance. In years past, João de Deus has operated from multiple sites in Brazil. Now he functions exclusively from Abadiânia, except on the few occasions he travels aboard. The second reason is Oprah. The American superstar Oprah Winfrey did a series of shows from the casa, thereby increasing awareness of João de Deus by at least an order of magnitude. The motivational speaker Dr. Wayne Dyer was not only a supporter but a recipient of one of the most dramatic spiritual healings I have ever heard of. As João de Deus's fame has spread, people have come from all over the world. There are quite a few Americans and many Europeans, along with a sprinkling of Asians and Africans.

Flying from Foz de Iguaçu, we landed in the evening in the capital, Brasília. It was early May of 2005, and due to drug trafficking in the area we were advised to not travel the country roads at night. The hired car arranged for us arrived an hour late the next morning, so we did not leave until 7 a.m. for the hour and a half drive to Abadiânia. We were concerned about being late as the first service was scheduled to start at 8 a.m. As it turned out, we got to our destination with time to spare. Through discussions with locals we learned the scheduled times at the casa were very approximate.

The true blue and gleaming white casa sat near the end of the newly developed area of the city. There were dozens of cars in the parking lot directly across the street. The high blue metal gates were open, and people, all dressed in white, were milling around. Upon arrival, we were checked in by assistants. Everyone received a ticket indicating whether it was your first visit, a return trip, or for scheduled surgery. Everything was well organized.

An open auditorium stood before the sanctuary. Along the walls were paintings of saints. Television screens played a video showing João de Deus engaged in surgery, depicting several types of procedures. One involved a knife and making a physical incision in the patient. Surprisingly, the bleeding was minimal and considerably less than I would have expected. There was no doubt about the authenticity of the cut, and no fake material was produced. Another video showed João de Deus inserting long forceps far up a patient's nose. On still another he took a knife and scraped the patient's eyeballs. This technique, we were told, was indirect, as the eyes are considered the window to the soul. Throughout these procedures there was no indication of pain or discomfort displayed by any of the patients. It appeared that João de Deus was in deep trance and seemed not to even pay attention to the physical actions he was taking.

Then the service began. João de Deus came out from the sanctuary and stood on the small, low stage in front of the audience. He spoke for a short time and an assistant translated into English. In a few minutes, he started doing surgery in front of the group. We saw him do the forceps technique. (See the photo I took of this procedure.) The man involved bent forward slightly as the forceps were twisted in his nasal cavity. A tiny drop of blood emerged and the procedure was over. With little fanfare, the entourage reentered the sanctuary and lines were formed. Those in wheelchairs—and there were several—were taken in first. As first-time attendees, we were in the last group to be seen that morning. Despite the size of the crowd, everyone was polite and patient, and I saw no jockeying for position. People seemed to believe the attendants who told us that everyone would be seen.

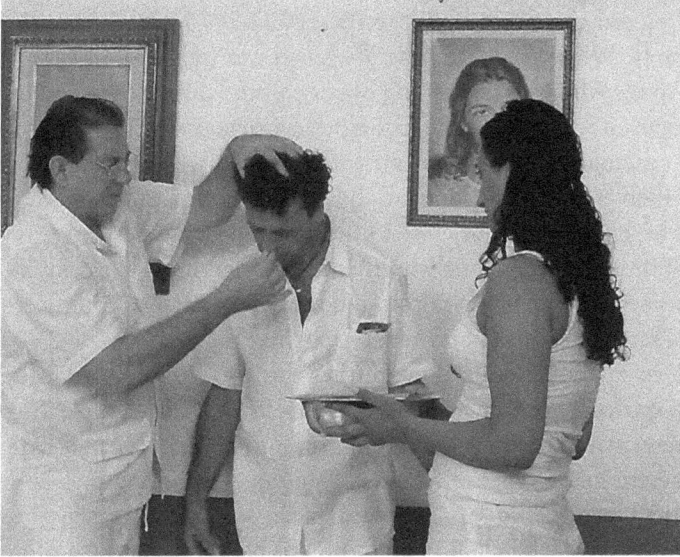

John of God doing surgery with forceps well into the patient's brain. At most a drop of blood. Patient seems impervious to any pain.

It was quiet as we entered the sanctuary. João de Deus was seated at the far end of the room. To our surprise, both sides of this room were lined two deep with seated mediums who prayerfully assisted him. There were at least 60 in that group. Situated close to him were several additional mediums, those who were apparently considered to be quite powerful. Large quartz crystals were prominently displayed.

During our first encounter, we met one-on-one with João de Deus several times. Each session was very brief, a few seconds, but personal. He does not speak English, but there were two assistants who translated for us. In trance, he would respond and hand each person a scribbled prescription that could be filled for a very nominal fee (just a few dollars). Importantly, he saw every person who came, no matter how long the lines.

After the blessing, we were directed to take seats in an adjacent room immediately to his right. There we remained with closed eyes in meditation for about 20 minutes. The purpose, we were told, was to add our healing energy to that of the assembled collection of mediums. Assistants quietly then led groups to the door that exited into the gardens. Located close by was the kitchen. The casa feeds everyone who comes. It was a homemade vegetable soup, which was provided at no cost.

During our more recent visit to the casa in 2014, the encounter changed considerably. While the same general agenda was followed, it was almost impossible to see what was happening because of the throngs. Instead of the personal attention we received the first time, participants were moved in groups into the sanctuary. There we sat on wooden pews with our eyes closed. Joao de Deus then entered the room and did a general blessing. He did touch a few people who happened to sit close to the aisle. Sneaking peeks, I was caught a couple of times by attendants who silently signaled me to close my eyes.

This time, instead of staying around the casa grounds, people were advised to go back to their hotels and remain in their room alone for 24-48 hours. We were to take our meals alone during this time and focus on healing, or whatever spiritual need we had come for. Victoria followed these instructions, while I returned to the casa several times just to observe the proceedings.

There are many types of healings going on. According to João de Deus, he is assisted by hundreds of discarnate spirits, some of whom had been in the medical profession when in human form. It is believed that the healing process begins taking place as soon as you arrive and may continue well after you have returned home. There are restrictions, based on age, regarding who is eligible for physical surgery versus purely psychic healing. It is claimed that there has never been a case of sepsis from the incision. Since no sterilization or antiseptic is used, that is pretty amazing.

In addition to the sanctuary, there are blessed places around the casa where symbolic triangles are posted. The sites are always filled with pictures of patients requesting healing. On this trip, I participated in the remote healing process. Some of the readers will know Whitley and Anne Strieber. Whitley has written many books, but he is best known for *Communion*. We have been friends for many years, and at that time Anne was seriously ill with cancer. I had suggested they go to Abadiânia, but they believed her physical condition would make the travel impossible. Since we were going, they provided me a good photograph of Anne. I took the picture and placed it in one of the sacred spots, then prayed over it asking for help with her condition.

The next day I sent Whitley an email, telling him what I had done and when it took place. In response, he sent me a reply noting that Anne had shown substantial improvement that lasted for a few days. Importantly, from a research perspective, Anne did not know either the date or time I initiated the prayer for her recovery. Yet, it was before I contacted Whitley via email that he had noticed an improvement.[142] Unfortunately, the healing was temporary and she succumbed a year later.

As I mentioned, Wayne Dyer, after being diagnosed with leukemia two years prior, received a most remarkable and documented healing. It was done remotely, as according to Dyer's own blog, he was at a hotel room in Carlsbad, California, while João was at the casa in Abadiânia. Due to his writing schedule, Dyer turned down the opportunity to travel to the casa in Brazil. Instead, arrangements were made for him to have remote spiritual surgery at 10 p.m. on April 21, 2011. He was instructed to wear white, drink blessed water, and stay in bed for a full day. The following morning, he awoke, and not noticing any difference went for his usual walk. In a few hundred yards he collapsed, just as if he had received physical surgery the night before. He was helped back to bed where he remained exhausted for several days going through a detoxification process. A week after the initial surgery, the entities allegedly returned and removed the psychic sutures. A short time later he was pronounced free of cancer. Dyer noted that surgery is not a traditional treatment for leukemia, let alone having the procedure done by spiritual entities.[143]

Wayne Dyer died in 2015, four years after his treatment by João de Deus. The obituaries made it clear that the cause of his death was a heart attack and had nothing to do with his earlier bout with cancer.

Another remarkable case was posted by Heather Cumming, a Brazilian shaman who became a key assistant to João de Deus. In her book, *John of God: The Brazilian Healer Who's Touched the Lives of Millions,* she included the case of a relatively young doctor by the name of Roger.[144] Obese, he had a heart attack at age 49 and died in the emergency room of the hospital where he worked in Brasilia. His death certificate indicted he was deceased at 10:15 a.m. That was mid-morning and the staff was quite busy. Being bad for business to have dead bodies in the Intensive Care Unit, they wanted to move the doctor's body out to the morgue as quickly as possible.

The doctor's wife contacted João de Deus. His wife then told the hospital staff not to move her husband's body before 3 p.m. that afternoon, and that a nurse should stay with the body. That was both against policy and inconvenient, but because Dr. Roger was one of their own, the staff agreed to abide by the wife's wishes, knowing that she was relaying instructions from João de Deus. Shortly before 3 p.m., Dr. Roger suddenly took a deep breath and regained consciousness. He then asked for a glass of water. According to Cumming's account, although he had visited the casa, Dr. Roger was not a believer in spirits and had previously refused assistance from them. In fact, he had ridiculed the treatments given there. Two days after the incident he was released from the hospital. Despite being clinically dead for nearly five hours, he showed no sign of brain damage. According to Cumming, Dr. Roger was a changed man who lost weight and became a supporter of the spiritual healing at the casa.

Skeptics have claimed that no one has been healed after visiting Joao de Deus. They are wrong! An American case was referred to me by a local Jesuit priest. Twelve years ago (2005), a nine-year-old boy was diagnosed with terminal brain cancer. His father, a physician, accepted the consequences. However, another doctor suggested seeing John of God. A few months later, family members took him to Abadiânia. According to the grandmother I interviewed, the spirit entities worked on him, and he showed some improvement, but the healing was not instantaneous. He was not subjected to chemotherapy or radiation treatments. Family members made repeated trips, escorting him to the casa. They also believed that the entities made visits to treat him at his home three or four times a year. At the time of this writing, he is alive and well and a senior in high school. He does have a psychological burden of wondering why he was saved and for what purpose.

Several medical research studies have been done on the healing work of João de Deus. The renowned, internationally respected materials scientist, Rustum Roy, was helpful in facilitating those efforts. Rusty and I had an opportunity to discuss the research. Though firmly established in the physical sciences, he had broad interests, including the subject of the interaction of consciousness and healing. There was no doubt that, in some instances, long-term cures did take place.

There is a plethora of testimonials to João de Deus' healing powers. He is very careful to note that he does not heal, but rather he is a conduit for the Holy Spirit, which does the healing. As a believer in reincarnation and karmic debts, there are times when he has recommended that healing not be done. He indicates that for some patients, if they are healed in this life, they will need to endure the same affliction in another.

The question that looms large is: why is it that some people are healed and others not? How are the choices made? In observing the busloads of people who came while I was there in 2014, I noted that everyone who came in a wheelchair, left in a wheelchair. From a traditional Western medical point of view, none of the healings make sense unless you assume some subset are strictly psychosomatic. That, however, does not meet the known facts. People with very real physical ailments have been cured. Cases, such as Dr. Dyer's, done remotely, add another order of complexity.

The casa waiting area. The casa itself contained many crutches, braces, and wheelchairs of people claiming to have been healed.

Joao de Deus believes that discarnate entities assist in the healing process. He says that one discarnate entity recently added deserves special mention. Chico Xavier (see chapter "The Mediums") has allegedly has joined the spiritual staff. While he was relatively unknown the North America, he became legendary in Brazil. Chico and João did overlap in life and had met. It was reported that shortly after his death in June 2002, Chico began assisting in the spiritual healings at Casa de Dom Inácio.

Overview

Our spiritual experiences in Brazil were both real and counterintuitive from medical or scientific perspectives. We also had other encounters in places like

233

Brasilia, Belo Horizonte, Recife, and Salvador. While many of the shamans come from descendants of the slaves, they have adherents in all sectors of the population. As in the U.S., there are many skeptics in Brazil. There are also those who are a bit fearful of rituals that incorporate discarnate entities. However, what I have found in Brazil are people who are highly educated in Western traditions, yet still are willing to explore the spirit world.

The direct challenges for science and modern medicine include explaining how spiritual interventions can result in physical healing. That is especially significant when the healing is accomplished over long distances and with no direct contact between the healer and the patient. A more generic issue derives from situations of spirit possession, such as I witnessed with Victoria at the Umbanda ceremony in Curitiba. It would be hard to prove that spirits take over physical bodies during these rituals, but prima facie evidence does support a detectable shift in both physiology and consciousness. Some ceremonies did include ingestion of mind-altering chemicals with DMT being a known active ingredient. But those chemicals do not explain some of the results, such as precognition and clairvoyance.

CHAPTER 21
VOODOO. YES, VOODOO

If you are a typical American, everything you know about voodoo, as popularized in movies and television programs, is simply wrong. Very misunderstood, voodoo, sometimes called vodun, has about 30 million followers in the world today.

My fascination with voodoo began decades ago, mostly for the wrong reasons. When studying anthropology at Beloit College, I wrote my very first term paper; it was on voodoo. I pointed out that most of the books were based on demented concepts by 19th century adventurists who dramatized their contact with voodoo while sitting in bars or on ships. Hearing the throbbing Haitian rada drums, engulfed in the humid night air, they conjured up grotesque images of what perverted activities must be going on. Tales of zombies and human sacrifice, supported by lurid details, captured the imagination of readers in the developed world.

Voodoo did not arise in Haiti, as many believe, but was imported from the Dahomey Empire of West Africa.[145] Men and women who had been captured from different tribes and forced into slavery contributed to variations from their animist religions. Those cultural variations became integrated and new ceremonies developed over time. Tribes large and small were preyed upon by other tribes, who made arrangements with the Portuguese slave traders. That area today is known as the countries of Benin, Togo, Ghana, and Burkina Faso. They are some of the poorest countries in the world and not exactly hospitable for Western tourists.

As we had ventured into other remote areas, Victoria and I found the allure of seeing the foundations of voodoo nearly irresistible, though it's not for the fainthearted. It is important to understand that in parts of Western Africa voodoo is not just a religion but, even today, *a way of life*. Practitioners incorporate voodoo into every aspect of their daily lives. For them, nothing happens by accident, and everything in the universe is integrated and codependent. For a religion that many people consider to be primitive, voodoo's fundamental concepts are actually in line with some of our most advanced thinking. How its followers go about their practice, however, would be aversive to most Westerners.

Traveling to Togo, Benin, and Ghana, we observed firsthand and recorded things that are physically impossible according to modern scientific theories. First, just getting there can be a challenge. It was late evening when we arrived in Lomé, the capital of Togo, and the airport was shutting down for the night. The ride we had booked to take us to the hotel was nowhere to be found. As in many countries in West Africa, few people speak English. The area was once known as French Equatorial Africa for a reason.

Overcoming that hurdle, the next day we met our guide Noah Katcha, son of Seventh Day Adventist ministers who was nonetheless well-versed in the principles of voodoo. Quickly, he explained that people from other religions, including Christians and Muslims, often engage in similar practices. This suggests that the choice of religion is as much based on culture as ideology. In West African countries, the southern areas tend to embrace Christianity, while the northern ones are predominantly Islamic. That came about as the Christian missionaries arrived on ships and landed on the southern beaches and then only ventured a short distance inland. Islam dominated most of the Sahel and thus the northern areas of these countries. But the animist-oriented voodoo religion blurs all lines.

Amulets and talismans are ubiquitous, and the fetish markets in Lomé are overflowing with them. There is a vast array of animal parts, especially horns, though not the ivory kind. There are Hippo skulls available, along with dolls, small animal skins, and carved wooden, clay, and metal statues. Throughout the open-air markets, the odor of decaying animal parts weighs heavily and attracts an abundance of flies.

Traveling in a marginally functional bus, we drove north over roads that were in urgent need of repair. Though designated as a highway, the driver had to share the road with wandering people and herded animals. The trees of nearly every home we passed were wrapped with white ribbons, signifying that the occupants practiced voodoo and invoked the spirits for protection. The poverty levels we saw throughout the trip were extreme; it was as bad as anywhere we have traveled, and that is saying a lot. Our searches have been for ancient cultures. We do not engage in what some call "poverty tourism" that exploits local peoples.

The event of most significance, a fire dance, took place in a tiny village east of Sokode. Our timing was perfect as these rituals are conducted only at the beginning and end of the rainy season. It was about 8:00 p.m. when our bus pulled into what passed for a town square. Here everything was dirt, roads, parking areas, and old buildings. Electricity was sparse; a few isolated bulbs dimly lit the portions of the village. As always when Caucasian travelers arrive, children rush forward with a unique combination of fascination and begging for whatever they can get. What is palpable is their exuberance and boundless energy. White people are rare in these parts, and children are fascinated by skin, especially with any hair on your arms. Often the kindergarten-age children want to hold your hand. Runny noses and sores with visible scabs were the norm. Willfully we complied, but with an awareness of the very high rate of infectious diseases that ravage these territories. Most of us carried antiseptic wipes and used them liberally. Surrounded in droves, it was not uncommon to have six or more children attached to us in some manner.

What we witnessed that evening was one of the most extraordinary displays of fire handling imaginable. Scientifically, these events defied the laws of thermodynamics. Culturally, they are imperative and keep traditions alive. As we approached the area designated for the ceremony, the drumming increased in intensity. Across the dirt street a fire was blazing, and children were jumping up and down, emulating the dancing of the adults. Even children who can barely walk get into the intoxicating and complex rhythms of the voodoo drummers.

An elderly man was clearly in charge. There was no conversation. He just began by taking burning sticks and applying them to various parts of his body. Slowly, he placed the roaring flames above and below his arm. While aware of our presence, he seemed impervious to the physical effects of the fire, which was hot enough to cause some of our party to shy away. As I filmed with both my Sony Handycam video and a Nikon still camera, the heat was penetrating. The gentleman sat on the ground, applied the fire to the bottom of his feet, and then laid the raging pole on his arm and left it there for about half a minute.

In one sequence I captured on video, he took the flaming stick and placed it firmly on his tongue, holding it there for several seconds. Upon reviewing the video, I noticed that even though the flames were high enough to obscure his face, his long chin whiskers remained intact and were not singed. That is simply impossible, yet I recorded it as it happened. Several other adult men joined the ritual. At times participants stood in the fire, and one even sat down in it. Another striking demonstration involved a man who grabbed a glowing pole and bit off a burning piece. Standing still, the coal burnt brightly as he inhaled and exhaled. Timing the video later, I calculated that he had the burning ember visibly in his mouth for more than a minute. He never so much as flinched, before finally chewing the coal and swallowing it directly in front of us.

Voodoo priest demonstrating seeming immunity from fire.
Not even his whiskers were singed from the flames.

For verification that no tricks were employed, I took my video and showed it to Jeff McBride who is a magician's magician. Jeff trains magicians after they have been performing for years. He is also a consultant to many of the big-name performers such as David Copperfield and Criss Angel. Jeff was amazed by what he saw and agreed this was not a hoax of any kind. We discussed exactly what I had observed as I filmed. He then showed me some of the magician's stagecraft for handling fire. It didn't remotely approach what we had seen.

A few skeptics have suggested that the voodoo practitioners used some form of chemical protection. That's absurd! First, the chemical these skeptics hypothesize does not exist. Second, these people are so poor there is no way they would have the means to access any expensive chemical materials.

But there was more to the ritual that intrigued me. After the man had eaten the coals, two young boys came forward carrying smaller flaming wooden poles. They appeared to be about 10 years of age and were just beginning their training. As they crouched in front of us, the priest took a position behind them. With his elbows, he gently tapped each boy on the head. It was explained to us that the priest was "passing the power" to protect them from

238

being burned.

True to fashion, the boys began to handle the fire just as the adults had. They placed the flames above and below their arms and held it in place for several seconds. To be clear, this is not a matter of withstanding pain. There was no pain or burning of any tissue at any time during the ceremony. In time, these boys will become fully initiated into the tribal traditions.

How this tribe came to engage in fire dancing is a fascinating story that is both tragic and horrifying. The explanation explicitly incorporates the spirit world, albeit differently than the other stories I have written about. During the slave trading days, intertribal warfare was common and extremely brutal. They allege that once after a fierce battle most of the surviving members of their tribe were rounded up by the enemy. They were then herded into small huts and the exits barred, before being deliberately set on fire, immolating everyone. Only a very few escaped the carnage by hiding in the forest, watching it all in total shock and anguish. Those who did survive made an agreement with the fire spirits. The tribe members agreed that if they would honor the fire spirits, in return they would forever be immune to the effects of the flame.

While that explanation is hard to reconcile with Western beliefs, the empirical evidence suggests that something protected them. Further, there is no scientific theory that covers the apparent violation of the "laws of thermodynamics" that I documented.[146] That is particularly true for the priest's facial hair, which burns at a much lower temperature than flesh yet remained unsinged.[147]

We saw voodoo in action throughout the rural areas. Every mud dwelling had symbols and talisman displayed by the door for protection. Small altars were also prevalent, as were the white strips of cloth on at least one tree to signify their belief.

Dreams are an important part of the tradition.[148] In a small mud village we met Tsohori, a high priest whose job is to dream and advise the community about future events. He literally used dreams to determine if he should leave his hut on any given day.

There were many types of ceremonies, all with roots in their local spirits. One morning we observed an Egun mask performance.[149] Egun roughly translates as "to the ancestors," and it is the departed that the ceremony is dedicated to. Before we could see them, we heard the drums as the heavily costumed performers emerged from the forest. They wore the ornate costumes commonly seen on travel brochures for Benin. We were told that, "according to the local tradition, people perform the rituals not only to represent, but also to embody, the spirits of the ancestors." Taking turns, the spirit performers twirled wildly about the dirt clearing, carefully herded by other initiates using sticks. We were to believe that this was a secret society, and the identity of those who bore each costume was unknown to the village. The belief was that if one of them touched a person, if not an initiate they would be knocked unconscious. It was clear that the local audience was quite obliging. While colorful and energetic, science itself was not threatened in that ritual.

Mask worn by seated spirit dancer in Benin.

Later, in a village very close to the Nigerian border, we had an opportunity to observe a Gelede mask ceremony. The Gelede is cult devoted to the Earth mother divinity Oudua.[150] While extravagant and colorful, the mask and full-body costume were quite distinct from the others we had encountered. Part of the mid-afternoon ceremony was devoted to distributing minor household goods to the audience; basic items, such as plates and eating utensils, would appear from under the costume. These would be thrown into the audience, causing minor scrambles for the prizes. While the storyline was that these were mystical events, there was nothing that could not be easily explained.

Blood sacrifices are an integral part of some voodoo ceremonies. We chose to participate in one. Depending on what is desired, participants commonly provide chickens, goats, or other animals.[151] The larger the request, or the more important your objective, the greater the sacrifice should be. This occurred in an area located close to a main two-lane paved highway, the only one in the area. In general, the action is retroactive. If the designated outcome was obtained, the applicant then was obligated to provide the appropriate sacrifice. Each request was made by writing on a wooden peg. The peg then was blessed, and the participant then hammered it into the relatively soft ground.

I drove my peg request into the ground near the base of an ancient tree that was wrapped in white cloth. The dirt was surprisingly soft, and the spike sank quite easily. Victoria decided that since return to this sacred spot was unlikely, she would pay it forward. Needing a chicken, she paid a local kid with a motorcycle to buy one for her. After about 20 minutes, he returned with a distraught white chicken strapped to the seat.

What followed was not a pretty sight. Obviously, the African view of animal rights varies dramatically from our own. The voodoo priest took the chicken, waved it about, and invoked the spirits to grant Victoria's unspoken wish. With a machete, he deftly, but not fatally, sliced the throat of the bird. He then spilled the blood from the struggling animal, pulled out its feathers, and threw them at the tree. As the body was dropped carelessly to the ground, it flopped about grotesquely for several seconds before finally succumbing. For the record: despite the sacrifice, we are still waiting for the wish to be fulfilled.

As luck would have it, we arrived in Lac, Togo, on voodoo's New Year's Day. Converging at the main celebration were hundreds of priests and thousands of people. The mood was festive and the trappings much like a rural carnival found anywhere in the world. Vendors abounded, selling every manner of voodoo paraphernalia, some of it updated in crude plastic form. The most significant aspect for me was the breadth of support voodoo had in that society. It was easily on par with Western celebrations marking an annual transition.

That day we witnessed another voodoo ceremony, where things occurred that are difficult to explain. As we entered a small village, several women danced vigorously. It was amusing to see very young girls, maybe all of three years old, attempt to emulate the movements of these adults. Suddenly one woman fell into a deep trance and cavorted even more wildly. She came extremely close to me as I filmed and I could tell that she was not faking it. At times, she would collapse on the ground, then revive to pay homage to one Loa statue or another.

The clincher came when a man took gunpowder, placed it in both of her hands, and ignited it. Without flinching, she continued on. I had an opportunity to see her hands in close proximity. No injury was apparent, not even a burned spot where the flames had flared minutes before. The same man had been igniting the gunpowder around the area, either on the dirt or on a concrete step. In each case the burn marks were obvious, but not on the woman's palm.

There is a positive side to voodoo as well. In the rural areas, which is most of the country, traditional medical care is extremely rare. From a practical standpoint, the people must rely on whatever help they can find. In almost every village and even in small cities, one can find white flags flying, signifying that "the doctor is in." Their techniques vary but mostly use folk medicine and herbal remedies. One famous voodoo doctor, or bocor, we visited used dreams to find the proper treatment. The patient would come and explain the aliment. They would be advised to return in a couple of days. During that time, the bocor would have a dream that would prescribe a treatment.

Sometimes the recommended treatments work, possibly for the wrong reasons, and they are widely used. The aliment may not even be a typical physical malady. The members of many West African societies accept that curses can be applied for any number of reasons. And any number of bad things might happen to a cursed person, up to and including death.

Faith is an important factor. During the recent Ebola outbreak in West Africa, I contacted Noah, our Christian friend, and inquired about what was happening there. He informed me that Ebola would not come to Togo and Benin as they were protected from it by voodoo. He was correct. Ebola did not break out in those countries. I leave it to the reader to determine whether or not it was voodoo, or something else, that no cases of Ebola were reported there, thought it did strike the countries all around it.

The bottom line is that at voodoo services we saw things that can't happen, but did. The experiences with fire bear solid testimony that the participants would have been severely burned under normal circumstances. There are no known scientific theories that can explain how bare flesh can be so extensively exposed to open flame with no adverse consequences.

CHAPTER 22
REINDEER SHAMANS OF MONGOLIA

Remote travel has been one of our prime interests. Wherever we go, Victoria has been able to ferret out indigenous shamans. In Northern Mongolia and throughout Siberia live nomadic tribes that have domesticated reindeer in a manner unlike anywhere else in the world. The weather in these areas can be harsh and isolates the nomads for most months of the year. Thus, almost totally devoid of Western medical assistance, these people rely on their shamans for advice in a wide range of activities including health. What we experienced in the presence of these powerful healers was both stunning and defied simple explanation by traditional science.[152]

Mongolia is the least densely populated country in the world. Landlocked, it is located furthest from the sea of any country on Earth. Three times the size of France, it has only about three million inhabitants, half of which live in the capitol, Ulan Bator, which is sometimes written as one word, Ulaanbaatar. We crossed the Pacific Ocean on a direct flight from Las Vegas to Incheon, Korea. Then, a couple of hours later we flew on to Ulan Bator, landing at Genghis Khan International Airport. Met by our guide, we drove to the Genghis Khan Hotel. Worth noting is that Genghis Khan is still revered as Mongolia's most famous leader with many things named after him. A prodigious progenitor, it is estimated that he has about 35 million direct descendants today.

Our guide, Melody, whose real name is nearly unpronounceable for Westerners, was a young graduate student with excellent command of the English language. We learned that many Mongolian graduate students spend a few years as guides and interpreters to both raise money and gain experience in interacting with the English-speaking world. In a decidedly male-dominated society, this form of work provides a degree of independence not usually afforded to young women. Later during the trip, we would observe how even well-educated professionals were expected to play gender-appropriate, subservient roles. That included being the lone cook and doing other chores deemed feminine in nature. Interestingly, she would have an unexpected encounter of her own that tested the limits of her conventional education.

Barely conscious after more than a day in transit, we found the hosts had created a vigorous agenda for us. It began immediately with a city tour and visit to the neoclassical capitol building called the Government Palace. It was replete with multiple large statues of the venerable leader, Genghis Khan. Palatial, indeed! Dinner was followed by attendance at the National Orchestra with a throat singing performance, for which they are renowned. Frankly, that is an acquired taste in music, and one I have yet to fully appreciate.

The vision of the ultra-modern buildings of Ulan Bator took us by surprise. The sight of architecturally unique, glass-adorned high rises stood in stark contrast to our expectations and the more primitive housing we would encounter throughout the remainder of the country. Blessed with abundant natural resources, the country, or rather some parts of it, have benefited from an economic boom. That financial boom has focused on the capitol, which has attracted many foreign investors and created a mix of dilapidated housing and burgeoning office construction, all resting on an antiquated infrastructure. Remember, Mongolia was part of the former Soviet Union, and their block style apartment buildings still dominate much of the landscape in the few urban venues. Soviet-era investment in roads was minimal at best and catching up is well behind schedule when compared with other countries such as those in Southeast Asia or their southern neighbor, China.

As many people from the rural population have moved into Ulan Bator, so have some shamans. Therefore, before leaving for the remote hinterland, we visited one. Shaman Udval came from a lineage of female shamans. Unlike what we experienced outside of the capital, her practice was located in a nondescript four-story concrete building that bore no markings to announce the businesses residing within. Down the poorly lit hallway and on the left was a door with a simple sign bearing her name; it did not identify her business. Inside was an anachronistic mix of shaman's robes and drums with an old computer resting on a simple metal desk.

Shaman Udval graciously answered our questions, including her path to becoming accepted by the community. Born in an outlying area, she had migrated to Ulan Bator a few years earlier. Even in the capital many people still rely on shamans, even though some Western conveniences are available. There is a fundamental belief in a spirit world there, one that interacts with what we know as consensus reality. That was a feature in common with most of the other shamans we have encountered. For her, the main spirits belonged to the sky, mountains, rivers, and other earth elements. Praying to them, she could obtain information that was prescient for her clients and assist in their daily lives. It served an integral purpose for all.

A ceremony was performed right there in her small office. Donning her ornate befeathered robes, Shaman Udval seemed transformed as she picked up her drum and began to beat it. At first there was a slow rhythmic content, but soon her chanting became more excited as she seemed to fall into a trance. Given the language barrier, we could not follow the content directly, and much came too fast for any direct translation. Then, with Melody translating, she engaged in a conversation with Victoria answering questions related to her life and that of her son, Vladimir.

Almost as abruptly as it began, the ceremony ended. Shaman Udval asked if we had any other questions. Learning that we were about to travel to the very remote mountainous areas, she had an admonition for us. She stated that the shamans where we were headed possessed special powers. At all costs, we should avoid looking them directly in the eye, as they had the ability to cast spells and bring the unsuspecting person under their control. Later, we would have an experience that suggested that this might not be as crazy as it sounds. As I write this chapter, I am sailing the distant Pacific south of the Australian continent and headed for Tasmania. Even now, Shaman Udval's comments resonate.

The following morning, with Melody leading, we boarded a twin-engine Mongolian Air turboprop for the two-hour flight to the north-central city of Murom. Upon landing, we met our driver and the local guide, Chembo. We enjoyed lunch at a local restaurant, and then, after gathering a few last-minute supplies, left the vestiges of civilization behind. This was not to be an easy trip, as we travelled to the northernmost area of Mongolia which is within sight of Russian Siberia. In fact, the heavily wooded mountainous area is so remote that no one actually knows where the border is. The indigenous nomads find such contrivances as borders to be inconsequential to their daily lives. En route, we would meet several of the famed reindeer shamans.

Driving out of Murom on a paved road for about an hour, our driver suddenly turned left across an open field. We did not see another gravel road for more than 10 days. For most of those days, it was much like driving through the Rocky Mountains without roads. Navigating by the sun, we followed rivers and valleys, camping along the way. We slept on ground mats in small collapsible tents suspended from flexible tubular aluminum poles. We would invert the very light tents each morning and shake loose any dirt, a point that would gain significance on the seventh night of camping.

On our second night of camping we stayed near the ger of Shaman Bold, an isolated yak herder. We pitched our tents while Chembo made contact with

Bold. While they knew each other, it was important that Bold be willing to accept foreigners into his ger and conduct a ceremony for us.

In these remote areas, these semi-permanent gers (also known in other areas as yurts) exist as primary residences. Constructed of heavy canvass that covers a wooden frame, they form a relatively sturdy building. The focal point of all gers is the round metal stove that burns continuously with ubiquitous reindeer milk, the staple of their diet. An entire family lives in the ger with beds and other items of furniture firmly lining the walls. Most of the gers we visited had rugs, or large mats, covering the floor. The government does assist the tribal people to a modest degree. They have provided solar panels that have a capacity to provide limited power for a couple of hours in the evening. It was not uncommon to find a small television set, though we never saw one actually working.

Just before sunset, we were called to Bold's ger to join the family. We learned to walk carefully, as the yaks roam freely and their droppings are everywhere. For the locals, that is a good thing, as they gather the dung, dry it, and burn it as fuel all winter. Just as we had learned in Tibet years before, burning dung produces an unmistakable odor and can have deleterious effects on the occupant's health. Although the outside temperature was declining quickly, the inside of the ger was very warm, in fact hotter than we keep most American homes in the winter.

Chembo made the obligatory introductions, and I was allowed to ask Bold questions about how he became a shaman. While there has been a recent boom in "certified shaman training" in some Western countries, the process is very different for indigenous people and it's usually arduous. Several of the shamans we met experienced periods that we would call psychotic breaks. Their friends, family, and community often assumed they were crazy and thus ostracized them. These were emotionally painful experiences; sometimes they would end up wandering about the countryside. With luck, they would encounter a shaman who recognized their situation and agrees to take them as an apprentice and train them. That process can take months, or even years, before they strike out on their own. For each shaman who manages to do so, there are many more troubled individuals who do not make it through the process.

Shaman Bold told of his path and reaffirmed his belief in a spirit world, one that he could contact when in trance. Like Udval, Bold too had a heavy feathered robe that, when worn, seemed to transform him. Graciously, we were ushered to a bed on the left side of the ger. A few local folks entered the ger and sat respectively on the opposite side with Bold's family. The only light inside now came from the fire, but it was sufficient to see what was happening. After a few moments of introspective prayer, Bold began drumming, chanting, and dancing. In this ger was a small area that had a large piece of wood covering the floor. That was the place that he occupied as the ceremony intensified. Melody did what she could to translate the activities as the drumming and chanting intensified.

As Bold danced, seemingly oblivious to our presence, we suddenly heard a distinct sound of a hard object hitting the floor and rolling about. It landed near us, and I picked up a hard, plastic-looking ball about the size of a large marble. Slightly uneven and amber in color, it seemed out of place. When he came out of his trance state, Bold claimed he had no idea what the object was, but that I was to keep it for at least three years. What was most significant to me was the reaction of the local people who had seen these ceremonies many times before. They seemed amazed at the incident and were very interested in examining the object. They noted it was unlike anything they had seen before. Their reactions suggested to me that dropping objects was not part of Shaman Bold's standard routine.

Given the robes he was wearing, it would not have been impossible for him to have intentionally dropped the item. But based on the feedback and apparent surprise of the local people, I do not believe that to be the case. Another factor would come into play more than a year later while I was visiting Hal Puthoff's laboratory in Austin, Texas. Until then we did not know what the object was made of. Hal's staff members were able to confirm that it was a tektite, an object formed by ejecta from a meteorite hitting the Earth. These are relatively rare items and thus relatively expensive. Bold, and the people of that area of Mongolia, are very poor. It is extremely improbable that they would have access to tektites, let alone decide to discard one for me to find. It is my opinion, and that of other experts I've consulted, that the object is an example of a real apport.

About 50 kilometers from the Russian border, we stopped at a remote military outpost that monitors all travelers in the region. While the nomads traverse the area freely, the same is not true for others. The commander carefully checked our passports and papers that allowed us to be in the region before permitting passage. Then, when the Toyota Land Cruiser could go no farther, we mounted horses for a four-day trek over the mountains that towered above us to about 11,000 feet.

Mongolian horses are smaller than their cousins in other parts of the world. The saddles, which were provided by local herders, were far below acceptable standards. On several occasions, the flimsy cords connecting the stirrup unexpectedly broke as I attempted to mount my horse, dropping me to the ground. Their fix was to tie the remaining strings together, but that shortened the length and produced considerable discomfort in my legs. However, there was no other option but to go forward. Long before this point in our journey we had left any vestige of support behind.

For hours at a time we followed barely recognizable trails passing small glaciers and the streamlets created by the melting ice. Although it was August, it would be only a few weeks before the winter snows resumed and these streamlets would again freeze. Despite the altitude, the ground was often soggy and some areas were treacherous bogs. The first afternoon we entered an area where the footing was extremely difficult, even for our sure-footed animals. Without warning my horse suddenly lost its footing, dropped to the ground and began to roll. To avoid being crushed, I was intentionally thrown from the saddle and I opted to roll as far from the horse as possible. A more experienced equestrian might have been able to arrest the horse's fall, but that was well beyond my skill level. In addition, the horn on the Mongolian saddles are more like an inverted U-bolt than the posts we are used to in the West. A painful lesson ensued as my thumb got caught in it, restricting my efforts to evade the weight of the rolling horse. While sustaining substantial bruising, I managed to avoid serious injury. My thumb was ripped but not broken. We then learned just how lucky I was: the guides informed us that there was only one hospital in the entire country that was authorized to treat foreigners and that was located hundreds of miles away in Ulan Bator. The only viable means of evacuation from this area would have been to call on a phenomenally expensive helicopter. We always carry traveler's insurance but are well aware that aeromedical evacuations from remote areas can break the bank.

As we travelled on we luckily passed two European pilgrims who had visited the tribe we were to meet. They informed us that because the weather had been warmer than usual, the reindeer had moved to higher ground to keep cool, and the herders had followed them to a different valley than where we were headed. Reindeer require very cool temperatures and often lie down on the glaciers during the day.

After two days riding, enduring a chilly thunderstorm at about the 9,000-foot level, we finally descended into the valley where nomads tended the herds of these docile beasts. Upon arrival, we saw about eight teepee-like tents that were dispersed several hundred feet apart. While not as sturdy as gers, they provide more mobility, which is necessary as the herds move. There was no obvious communal center and no adults showed any interest in our party. A few children did come around to watch as we established our own camp near a rapidly flowing stream. Inquisitive reindeer came and poked about, demonstrating more interest in us than did the occupants of the village.

Victoria and author with nomad reindeer herd in Northern Mongolia near the Siberian border while visiting the local shaman.

During our entire stay, I did not see any interaction between the members of the village except when our guides contacted them. They did not seem to mind as we wandered about the area. Politely, they invited us into their tents when we came within sight. Given their isolated status, I expected to see a higher degree of social interaction. It would not be long before these people once again would be completely cut off from the rest of the world until late in the next spring. I did find one tent designated as a classroom, but the education provided was minimal; the teacher was a local woman with little formal education herself.

A fire burned in every tent and milk was cooking. Here, the tribe relied on reindeer milk, which is considerably thicker than yak or cow milk. Since the reindeer herds have been declining, the local people no longer butcher them for meat to supplement their very restrictive diet. They did have a small amount of rice, which is brought in on horseback, like all supplies. It is hard for us to imagine how tribes, which live days from any trading post, must prepare for total isolation for most of the year.

Passing another tent, I heard a woman inside speaking fluent English. Intrigued, I poked my head in to find a young woman talking to an outsider in colloquial American. When I inquired about this strange happenstance, she informed me that she had gone to high school in Boulder, Colorado. Her parents had moved from Ulan Bator to Colorado when she was a teenager. Somewhat disenchanted with life in the U.S., she returned to her home country and subsequently moved to this desolate area near the Siberian border.

Melody acted somewhat strangely when Tsetseg (a pseudonym) appeared. Later we learned why; it had to do with Udval's admonition at our first ceremony back in the capital. As it turned out, Melody had gone to school with Tsetseg. She had heard stories that Tsetseg had moved to America and then returned to Mongolia. As a city girl, Melody could not believe that Tsetseg would voluntarily marry and move to this remote area. The answer, she assumed, was that one of the reindeer shaman had cast a spell on Tsetseg and brought her to this camp. Clearly, Melody thought, it was impossible that a woman exposed to urban and Western civilization would choose this extremely austere lifestyle.

Melody confronted Tsetseg, saying "I know you." Avoiding her, Tsetseg claimed they had never met, but that was not the case. The prospect was somewhat frightening for Melody, as she had heard stories about what happened to this woman now standing before her. Now she had proof that the tales were real. Following this incident, Melody never allowed herself to be alone with any members of the tribe or to eat any food they had prepared. As Udval had also warned, drugs might be used to reduce your resistance. She was especially careful not to look them directly in the eye, as that is how, she believed, they could capture and enslave any unsuspecting person. Though well educated in Western traditions, Melody still accepted the traditional beliefs and the power they possessed.

Before leaving, we witnessed another ceremony, this one held by the tribal shaman, a woman known as Saintseese. This was very similar to our previous experience, interesting but unremarkable. Spirits were invoked and hot reindeer milk dispersed in the air to sustain them. A message of general good health and happiness was received.

Returning to our Land Cruiser, we continued driving in search of other shamans. That is when another mystifying event occurred. It was the eighth day of camping and we had chosen a spot along the Shishged River. We spent the evening talking with a local tribesman who explained the inequities they endured from the central government. There are considerable natural resources in these areas and the government was making deals with various industries for mining rights. Not consulted in the process were the indigenous tribes. As nomads, they required the freedom to roam. As time passed since the end of the Soviet era, capitalism and greed trumped their need for land. That is a story heard from many indigenous people who are devoid of power in national governments.

The night seemed uneventful, until the following morning. After waking, we discovered a shiny 50 pence Australian coin lying neatly between our two sleeping mats. Remember, each morning we would hold these light tents upside down and shake them. That process had been repeated at least seven times on this trip. Every morning, we would expel the dirt collected from the night before. It seems nearly impossible this coin might have remained stuck in some corner of the tent, only to become dislodged that night and fall directly between us.

How a 50 pence Australian coin ended up in a tent in Northern Mongolia remains a mystery. Like the object that fell from Shaman Bold, the most prosaic answer— as strange as it sounds—is that it materialized.

We visited two additional shamans and each performed a ceremony for us. One of them, Shaman Tunjee, we had seen previously as he features prominently in the American movie *The Horse Boy*, the story of an American couple who took their autistic son to Mongolia in hopes that the reindeer shamans could heal him.[153]

We can attest to the authenticity and power of these shamans. As noted previously, Victoria is very sensitive to her environmental surroundings and the influence of spiritual healers. We found that merely being in the presence of the shamans resulted in visible effects. In several of my videos taken with them, Victoria is seen swaying under the influence of some unexplained power. Importantly, this movement is not volitional or being done to please the shaman. I acknowledge that there are possible psychological explanations for her reaction, but they appear unlikely.

During our visits with the reindeer shamans two incidents stand out that are direct challenges for science. They are the materialization of the tektite during the ceremony with Shaman Bold. From a probability standpoint, it is reasonable to eliminate the possibility that Bold had somehow acquired the tektite and intentionally dropped it for us to find. Again, the reaction of the locals who have attended many ceremonies with him strongly indicates materialization of foreign objects is not part of his routine.

The second challenge is the materialization of the Australian coin inside our sealed tent. Given the vigorous shaking and emptying of the tents each morning it is safe to say the coin had not remained deposited by some previous visitor and stuck in a corner only to appear late in our trip. We also discount the probability that one of our native Mongolian guides slipped it into our tent during that night. Any spontaneous materialization of an object with no known source of origin defies all current scientific theories. But in Mongolia it happened.

PART IV

REFLECTIONS

CHAPTER 23
THE FLAME

Some people are drawn like moths to a flame when it comes to psychic phenomena. Therefore, there is good reason to be cautious when engaging in the study or application of such topics. During my foray into various phenomena, I have personally witnessed several highly competent people simply "go off the deep end." By that, I refer to individuals who were very skilled and respected in their professional fields, yet after intense exposure to various phenomena began engaging in inexplicable, and often bizarre, behavior.

For obvious reasons, I choose not to name most of the offenders.[154] Some readers might be able to guess who I'm referring to, but I will leave it up to them to make the connection. What is far more important is to know that personal threats do exist. There are three domains that may be at risk: *economic*, *mental*, and *spiritual*. The first, *economic*, refers to the financial costs of engaging in phenomena. Association with phenomena may inhibit employment in other fields. Second, your *mental* well-being may be at stake if you do not proceed carefully. Finally, there well may be *spiritual* risks. Such risks are more speculative, rarely provable, but may be just as real. To be forewarned is to be forearmed.

Self-proclaimed skeptics and debunkers will argue that anyone who voluntarily ventures into studies of psychic and other phenomena might be considered delusional. But I would suggest that it is the skeptics, those who refuse to even examine data, who are engaging in self-denial. Many of us are well-grounded and guided by solid evidence and personal observations. A Gallop Poll found that about three-quarters of all Americans believe in paranormal experiences.[155] Many have had personal experiences that they cannot explain.

For neophytes, know that the danger is real, but that alone should not deter your quest. From my experience, the best way to maintain a solid mental balance is to ensure that you stay engaged in multiple activities, the majority of which are founded on real-world activities or objective reality. Personally, I work mostly on matters of national and international security. Anyone who follows my writing knows that the majority of my articles, which appear in publications such as the *Huffington Post*, have nothing to do with phenomena.[156] As the Moody Blues pointed out, it's "A Question of Balance."

Smart People/Crazy Choices

Unfortunately, Western societies today are rife with conspiracy theories. Many people do not trust the mainstream media for accurate information, and a plethora of fake news sites have inundated the internet. By fake news, I mean stories that are totally contrived; they don't simply involve someone disagreeing with the facts. Fear and conspiracy theories do sell. They have permeated the topic of psychic phenomena as well. It is often hard to determine if the progenitor actually believes what they are putting forth, or just doing it for their own economic or ego-driven interests. Confidence games always have been an integral part of psychic phenomena; they often target the most vulnerable victims.

Examples of demonstrably false information related to phenomena abound. Take for instance the claim that a large space capsule was hidden behind the Hale-Bopp comet and was going to disperse pathogens that would destroy mankind. That was a prominent remote viewer's prediction. Or, consider the claims that the U.S. Government has reverse-engineered a UFO and has had the capability of interplanetary travel for decades. Again, this is from a leading UFO conspiracy speaker. Then there are those supporting the 9/11 conspiracies, concluding that it was a missile, not an airplane, that hit the Pentagon. That was alleged by a former senior military intelligence officer. Privately, one researcher told me that he believed operatives of the Israeli intelligence agency, Mossad, had more than once broken into his home using their capability of invisibility. This was done, he claimed, to warn him about his foray into alternative energy systems. His proof of the home invasions? He thought his car keys had been moved.

Several of these people have made a number of public proclamations on television, radio, or in other media that have been proven to be absolutely and irrefutably wrong. What is most disconcerting is that their fan base of true believers does not seem to care. They continue to support the repeatedly falsified claims, often financially by donating substantial amounts of money. These incongruities have broad implications when they apply to the actions of general population. That was conclusively demonstrated in the 2016 national election that heralded the post-truth era.

Anyone attending UFO conferences knows that there are no lower limits to how crazy an idea is; there will always be those who support it. What should be most worrisome is that these ideas tend to draw the largest crowds. Unfortunately, these phenomena often attract people who have serious mental issues to begin with. A significant problem is that rampant confabulations often mask very real phenomena. They also serve to drive otherwise open-minded scientists away from engaging in and seriously studying the real issues.

The theme of *Targeted Individuals*, or TIs as they are often called, is a classic example, and one that I am all too familiar with. These are people who believe that they have been targeted, usually by the government, and are the subjects of mind control experiments. For reasons inexplicable, they believe that there is a selection process during which they were chosen. They often claim it began when they were young children, and they have been constantly monitored ever since. While many indicate that it is a human source who is tracking or controlling them, some people think they are part of an interstellar conspiracy, and that the origin of their dilemma is extraterrestrial.

While over time my views on anomalous abductions have changed, I now think there often is a component driven by psychosis. Others I believe are reporting information as accurately as they can perceive it. However, when it comes to nefarious governmental agents or agencies conducting illegal and undocumented operations, that falls beyond the pale, as far as I'm concerned.

One such conspiracy theory involves what are called MILABS, or Military Abductions. I have been falsely accused of participating in, or even running, such operations. At one conference, a middle-age woman approached me stating she had seen me aboard a UFO while she was being examined. Other stories have me leading a nuclear attack against aliens ensconced in an underground base near Dolce, New Mexico. That base, they asserted, was part of a program in which the U.S. Government was trading alien technology for human body parts.

One of the main proponents of the MILAB conspiracy theory was actually a doctorate-level astrophysicist working at a European organization equivalent to NASA. When I responded to the absurd allegations by detailing the manpower requirements to conduct such prolific operations, he became very upset. Reality has not dissuaded his supporters.

My personal favorite was the internet story that announced my death in 2011. In that confabulation, I was chased from an underground bunker near Ft. Huachuca, Arizona, by a group of U.S. Marines. Once on the run, they tracked me down in the desert off of I-15 near Baker, California, and fatally shot me. That became problematic the following night, as I was interviewed by my friend, George Knapp, on *Coast to Coast A.M.* That did not deter the creator of this fantasy, a defrocked California therapist. His next missive stated simply that I was an imposter whose name was Will Quinn. The "morbidly obese" real John Alexander, and his wife, he asserted, had been replaced physically several years before.[157]

He went on to explain that the photos of me on my website were of Quinn after he had plastic surgery. Having watched my weight rather carefully and maintained exceptional physical conditioning, I did not appreciate the "morbidly obese" comment. The fantasy is obvious to the many people who have known me on a consistent basis over the years. It is worth noting that this person holds a doctoral degree and for a time was a licensed therapist whose job was to treat mentally unstable people. As a warning, it should be noted that "intelligence" and "crazy" are not mutually exclusive.

One person I will identify who engaged in inexplicably strange behavior with me is Jesse Ventura, the former governor of Minnesota. Born James George Janos, he officially changed his name for his professional wrestling career. He really was in the U.S. Navy and did complete the extremely grueling Basic Underwater Demolition/SEALs (BUDS) course under his birth name. He then served with an Underwater Demolition Team (UDT 21) but never entered combat.[158]

A tiny portion of my personal encounter with Jesse Ventura can be found in his television program, *Conspiracy Theory*. The episode was called "Skinwalker Ranch,"[159] though that was not the topic for which the interview with me was requested. His producer, someone I had previously met on another series, asked if Ventura could ask me about civilians in space. Since I knew both Burt Rutan and Bob Bigelow, the request made sense. In fact, I was greatly honored when Burt invited me to the launch of Mike Melvill into space on SpaceShipOne, the first totally civilian enterprise to do so.[160] Standing next to me at that event was Captain James T. Kirk of the USS Enterprise, aka William Shatner.

After about two hours of chat and taping the interview for Jesse Ventura, I was getting up to take off the microphone when some assistant from the sidelines yelled out, "What about Skinwalker Ranch?" The questions Ventura was to ask me had been sent in a prior email. They all were about how private citizens were getting into the business of space travel. This, it turned out, was an ambush, not an obscure question. None of my discussion about space issues aired. They did, however, air my response to this question, which was "I thought we agreed not to talk about that." That was designed to make me look like I was hiding something.

What is germane to this chapter is what followed. Ventura asked me, in a manner I took to be serious, if I knew that Bob had aliens working at Bigelow Aerospace here in Las Vegas. It seemed clear to me he was not talking about people from south of the U.S. border. I took him to mean space aliens! Seriously. They also used my response to that question, which was, "You need to check your bullshit filter." Of course, they bleeped the BS.

When I saw the program for the first time, I was surprised to see Alex Jones of *Infowars* warn Ventura about me. *Infowars* is a hyper-conspiracy oriented production, with an audience that will believe almost anything. What is really scary is the that President Trump sometimes uses Jones as a reference for his opinions. For the record, using Oliver Stone's son, Sean, that program also ambushed Bob Bigelow when he was speaking at a conference.

Ventura's series went on to do an entire program about Targeted Individuals in an episode titled "Brain Wars." It was strikingly clear that the producers took advantage of some seriously disturbed people. In my view, these people should have been receiving psychiatric assistance and not have been exploited for entertainment value.

The TI issue has followed me in several venues. There is an erroneous assumption that non-lethal weapons include work on mind control. That is false, yet it is a persistent rumor. While speaking at bi-annual non-lethal weapons conferences in Ettlingen, Germany, which is just south of Karlsruhe, I was picketed by protestors claiming to have been injured by our experiments. Demonstrating a substantial level of concern and dedication, these alleged TIs had traveled to the conference from several countries. While generally peaceful, the Bundespolizei deemed that interventions were necessary.

That was not new, as it had happened at the first Non-Lethal Weapons (NLW) conference I developed and chaired at Johns Hopkins Applied Physics Laboratory in Laurel, Maryland. There, in 1993, I was asked by the complainant to hold a moment of silence for the 50,000 people we had allegedly killed in NLW experiments. Of course, there were no 50,000 victims. In fact, there were no fatalities, but that did not stop the protests. The stories got even more bizarre. One time I was accused of breaking into a former military intelligence officer's home and executing her pet mouse by putting it in her blender. It matters not that the tales are unfounded. They persist.

The number of people in America with mental health issues is appalling. Studies suggest that nearly half of the U.S. population will suffer from mental illness in their lifetime.[161] Consider that somewhere between 2.3 and 4.4 percent of the American population exhibits paranoid characteristics.[162] By the most conservative estimates, that translates to six million people with substantial mental issues regarding mistrust and suspicion of others in the U.S. alone. Therefore, we should be concerned but not surprised at the confabulations put forward by conspiracy theorists.

It is important to note that in the examples I have provided here, all the fabricated stories were disseminated by people with very respectable credentials. Likewise, the leaders of the NLW protest demonstrations were people who would be considered competent under most circumstances. All of the folks discussed in this section were well-educated and previously had held responsible positions either in government or the civilian sector.

Where did the money go?

There are also dangers for individuals who become enamored with psychic phenomena and begin following nefarious self-proclaimed "prophets" who are basically running age-old con games. There are charlatans who prey on the most vulnerable. People in grief are an easy and opportunistic target. So are patients with terminal illnesses for whom traditional medicine has no further benefits to offer.

One conundrum is that there are mediums who have the ability to intercede in post-mortem communication but don't always get it correct. This is a means of information exchange that is not well understood. There are times in which the mediums appear to get accurate information, but that is not always the case. Just because the reading is not accurate, does not mean the medium is a fraud or being intentionally devious. The flip side is that there are con artists who are intentionally defrauding victims. Discerning the difference is a trying task. The best approach is to check with other people who have engaged that medium and get firsthand reports from them. You cannot rely on published comments on the medium's website or social media.

You should also check your own emotions. There is a reason that con artists target grieving individuals. Too frequently, those targeted are unable to make an honest appraisal of the information. The will to believe and obtain information from a departed loved-one can cloud judgement. One red flag is when large sums of money are involved. There are a host of known tricks they ply on their unsuspecting marks. Some of them are very sophisticated. If you hear that your money or personal property is cursed and you should hand it over for blessing, run, don't walk to the nearest exit.

Healthy skepticism is advisable. Too frequently, the professional skeptics and debunkers use any error in content as proof of fraud. That is not the case, but one we will have to live with. The skeptics are correct, however, on the subject of cold reading. A cold reading is a technique practiced by unscrupulous crooks, and the information it produces can be perceived as accurate. But it entails providing information that is so general that it can apply to anyone or almost any situation. It also incorporates feedback from the individual via verbal or visual clues. Using advanced techniques, such as those taught in Neuro-Linguistic Programming (NLP), the clues can be very subtle, and physically uncontrollable. They are well-known in the gambling world and referred to as a "tell," a change in demeanor or behavior that unconsciously signals the player's intent. Many clients of mediums also unintentionally pass along such information.

There are also hot readings in which information about the victim is already known to the reader. Today, *hot readings* are far easier to conduct than a couple of decades ago. There is an amazing amount of personal information about you available on the internet. There are websites dedicated to acquiring your data, including relationships, and selling it to anyone who will pay the asking price. With just your name, the "reader" can obtain a lot of information about you. With an accomplice, that can be done in real-time. While you are sitting with the reader, an aide can be running background checks and passing the information obtained through a concealed ear piece.

In the end, common sense is probably your best barometer and greatest defense. Each individual has intuition, albeit to varying degrees. The more you use it and become aware of your capabilities, the better it will serve you. Two rules should be followed. One, if it feels wrong, don't do it. Two, when you have experienced a great loss, do not make critical decisions for a considerable period of time. If post-mortem communication is your wish, definitely wait. The one who has passed will still be there, and you will be in a better position to evaluate and appreciate the contact.

Those rules should also apply to those experiencing a health crisis. The problems are just as emotional and complex as those of a person experiencing grief from the loss of a loved one. Here again a conundrum emerges: what is worth trying and what is just false hope provided by the promise of a cure that will not materialize. Compounding the issue is that with, or without, intervention, miracles sometimes happen. The case of Anita Moorjani (see chapter on near-death experiences) is one such example.[163] The case of Eben Alexander is one who defied the odds for survival.[164]

Medical research on the effectiveness of new drugs often relies on the use of a placebo. As most people now know, a chemical placebo is a compound that is believed to be inert and thus should have no effect on the patient's treatment. But some patients also get well with placebos. How this can work is still not well-understood.

Philosopher Michael Grosso cites a 1947 case study in which a patient who had been given a terminal diagnosis was provided an experimental drug.[165] Though suffering from lymphosarcoma, he responded well and his tumors disappeared. Once the drug was declared useless by the AMA, his tumors returned. Given a second drug, the patient again appeared to recover. When that drug was also reported to be useless, the patient relapsed and died. It was the patient's faith in the trial drugs that apparently have kept him alive. When he lost faith, he lost his life.

Doctors' attitudes toward placebos are changing. A report from Harvard Medical School indicates that placebos may actually alter brain chemistry.[166] It seems the effects were more than just a matter of the patient's expectations. The article also suggests that the act of caring made a difference in recovery. Finally, they stated the obvious: that medical professionals are a long way from understanding how placebos work.

A placebo can be more than just a sugar pill. Placebos can include medical procedures, or even counselling sessions. The ethics of using surgery as a placebo, which sometimes works, have been discussed.[167] There is also one study indicating that sham surgery worked as well as real surgery. The patient's perception of the cost of the drug might also play a role. If it was perceived to be expensive, the drug was deemed more effective.[168] All of the factors studied regarding placebos suggest that it is the patient's trust and belief that makes the biggest difference.

That leads to the difficult problem of determining the effectiveness of any treatment. On one side are the expensive scams in which people pay for treatments that, based on chemical or biological input, should have no positive outcome. On the other side of the equation is the power of expectation and faith. The skeptics rail against all sham treatments. They often claim that exposing fraud is a major benefit they provide to society. They would save us from ourselves. They tend to see humanity as ignorant savages in need of external intervention that delivers their version of truth. The problem with that approach is that, sometimes, alternative therapies work, and miracles do happen.

If these scams can be likened to the attraction of a flickering flame, be aware that there are bonfires burning as well. Not all operations are small. Scientology is the mother of all games, and has drawn in thousands of participants at exorbitant financial and personal cost. There are numerous credible books, articles, television programs,[169] and even movies,[170] extolling the dangers associated with that organization. Therefore, I will not provide a lot of details but simply reference some of these materials. Among the most vocal ex-Scientologists are Leah Remini[171] and Mike Rinder who made the A&E television network series *Scientology and the Aftermath*. Both were in the organization for decades, and Rinder, formerly part of the inner circle, admits that he actively engaged in unscrupulous acts against people who attempted to expose the organization. Their efforts are supported by a host of other former Scientologists, including Ron Miscavige, the father of the "Pope" of Scientology, David Miscavige.[172] The problem is international and has been addressed by foreign journalists such as Steve Cannane from Australia[173] and John Sweeney of the BBC.[174] Unlike a simple con man who takes your money and runs, it is alleged that those who run afoul of Scientology may be subjected to enormous psychological pressure and social degradation from the organization. As indicated by Hollywood director Paul Haggis, a former Scientologist, bullying and innuendo are approved tactics.[175]

There are three reasons for mentioning Scientology in this book. First, as I've pointed out, it's a warning sign when adherents ask for big money. According to most of Scientology's defectors, they each spent tens, if not hundreds of thousands, of dollars to participate. Understand that Scientology, a global enterprise, is worth more than a billion dollars.[176] The second reason for including the topic is that some of the key people I've mentioned prominently were former high-level members in Scientology. Among them were Ingo Swann and Hal Puthoff. Hal told me that although he had taken some training as an auditor, he was asked to leave since he was affiliated with the U.S. Government and therefore could not be trusted. By that time, he realized the cult nature of Scientology. He has also found that even though his involvement ended over three decades ago, his long-passed association still comes back to haunt him. Ingo was officially declared a Suppressive Person (SP), which is a formal announcement that he became an enemy of the church. And third, Scientology's antagonistic position toward all psychiatry. Considering the confluence between many phenomena and mental health issues, a rejection of psychology and psychiatry is extremely dangerous to people experiencing strange events.

It should be remembered that people have a right to be stupid. Stupidity is almost impossible to defend against, even if you see a friend making such a mistake. My favorite quote by Albert Einstein is: "There are two things that are infinite, the universe and human stupidity, and I'm not sure about the former." While misconstrued as a quote by P.T. Barnum, the notion that "there is a sucker born every minute" is the theme by which charlatans have gotten away with so much for so long.

Spiritual Concerns

Many people believe that the spirit world functions in parallel with the physical world. I have addressed some of the evidence supporting the reality of that concept, including near-death experiences, post-mortem communications, and shamans who transit between these worlds. Within religious practices there are prescriptions for what can and cannot be done regarding interactions with discarnate entities. Several sects warn against all such interaction, while others express concern but establish limits. For the most part, our secular society disregards sanctions and safeguards, but it does so at its own peril

Exorcism is routinely practiced in many parts of the world. The venerable Roman Catholic Church has priests who are trained specifically to conduct exorcisms. Very demanding requirements must be met before an exorcism is approved. There is, rightfully, great concern about determining whether the victim simply has psychological problems or whether demonic possession is involved. The number of authorized exorcisms is said to be increasing, though publicity about them is kept to a minimum.

Of course, most Western scientists would reject the notions of demons and possession without giving them further thought. If demons don't exist, then the rest of the hullabaloo must be nonsense. This does not fit with the facts. But then, in Western countries, few scientists have encountered spirits or demons. One possible reason was proffered by a Catholic priest I once heard address the problem. When asked why more demons were not visible in the U.S., he replied that based on our behavior, the Devil was already winning and did not need to attract more attention. That is a pejorative statement and assumes belief that an entity called the Devil actually exists. It also imposes a personal judgment about the character of our society. That is not my intent, but having personally experienced encounters with nonhuman entities with malevolent intent, I find the concept worth considering.

Decades ago I met Father John Nicola, who had been a technical director on the spine-chilling 1973 movie *The Exorcist*.[177] The story he told about the real events were mind blowing, and certainly raise serious issues of caution for individuals who wish to dabble with the black arts or think such activities might be fun and games.

According to Father Nicola, the events in the movie were a composite from several cases, but they were all true with one glaring exception. Anyone who saw the movie remembers Linda Blair with her head turning a full 360 degrees. That was a Hollywood invention. The head actually reversed on the priest who fell down the stairs, but it happened nearly a century prior. The real victim was a boy with the pseudonym Robbie Mannheim, but it was changed in the movie to a girl, Reagan, for dramatic effect.[178] Furthermore, the exorcism, which took place in the Alexian Brothers Hospital in St. Louis, Missouri, lasted weeks, not the short time depicted in the film. One reason the exorcism was conducted in a hospital was that the patient was suffering the equivalent of multiple grand mal seizures every day, and at the age of 14, they were not sure his heart could withstand the physical violence being inflicted on him.

Most scientists would discount the case, as they would deem demons mere figments of one's imagination. What poses a challenge for them is the levitation, the violent shaking of the bed, and the objects that were thrown about the room via psychokinetic energy. The victim also displayed superhuman strength, far beyond the capability and limitations of his physique. In addition, at times words were seen to be carved from the inside of his skin.

Father Nicola was not one of the exorcists directly involved in Mannheim case, but he did study the procedure. As I recall, when he was studying to become a Jesuit, he asked for permission to explore exorcism. The request was granted under one condition: if any unusual or demonic incidents occurred, he would be expelled. Everything went as scheduled up until the last few days prior to his ordination. Unexplained events did happen and he dutifully reported them. True to their agreement, he was not allowed to join the Jesuits.

According to Father Nicola, there is substantial personal danger to the exorcist, as the demon may leave the victim and possess the exorcist. He indicated that this happened in about one-fifth of the cases. To prepare for serious exorcisms, a second team must be prepared to step in when a transposition from victim to exorcist occurs.

The point of this explanation is not to rehash a relatively well-known case. Rather, it is to acknowledge the potential dangers to those who travel down these paths without guidance or adequate protection. In the Mannheim case, the victim's aunt introduced him to a Ouija board. At first there was minor activity masquerading as fun. But in time the events turned truly diabolical. The danger appears to be in inviting discarnate forces to enter this domain.

For a more recent case, I recommend William Friedkin's article, "The Devil and Father Amorth: Witnessing 'the Vatican Exorcist' at Work," in the October 2016 issue of *Vanity Fair*.[179] The Vatican holds an annual course to train exorcists. They take the issue very seriously, and each session is reported to be filled with about 170 attendees. According to Breitbart, "The course consists in a series of meetings aimed at giving priests, doctors, psychologists, teachers, and pastoral workers the instruments they need to recognize and deal with cases of demonic possession and distinguish them from disturbances of a psychological or medical nature."[180]

Similar warnings are given to people who engage in psychic healing. Most healers are careful to cleanse themselves when doing such work. By "cleansing," I mean they mentally and spiritually protect themselves so that the affliction does not transfer to the healer. It is much like preventative measures that are taken when treating contagious diseases, just on a different level. Many practitioners use prayer before and after assisting a patient.

Being well grounded is an important aspect of spiritual healing. If the healer is scattered or distracted, the probability of a successful outcome diminishes. While most scientists and skeptics will take umbrage with the concept, most people who engage in spiritual healing accept the notion that there are both positive and negative forms of psychic energy. Therefore, they use protective measures to keep out negative forces. Some of the procedures include an emphasis on positive thoughts. Just as faith is important to the patient, it should be of equal concern to the healer.

There are various physical forms of protection as well. The use of smoke, or smudging, is common in several native societies. Almost all of the shamans we have dealt with all over the world incorporate smoke into their services. They believe that the smoke will dispel negative forces and help create a safe environment in which they can function.

The range of protective devices is quite broad. Healing crystals are very popular in many cultures. When visiting John of God in Brazil, we found crystals everywhere. In voodoo ceremonies, symbols have great significance. In Hawaii, I saw kahunas place salt around a building or across doors and windows to block evil spirits from entering. Some healers employ specific sounds and smells.

One can argue about the lack of any scientific theory to support these personal security measures. Practitioners, including alternative healers, priest, and shamans who function in the spiritual domain, operate from belief systems and worldviews that are fundamentally different from the materialistic science of Western societies. Throughout this book, I have provided examples that support concepts of the reality of unacknowledged energy systems, unseen entities, and spirit worlds. Therefore, my admonition stands: if you choose to participate in any of the practices that engage discarnate entities or alternative healing energy systems, understand the risks and take adequate protective measures. Some of the powers you may encounter are far greater than you can imagine.

It's worth saying again

This chapter has elucidated three areas of concern for people venturing into engagement with phenomena for the first time. Caution, but not aversion, is advised. The first segment demonstrated that some very competent people have become captive to aspects of phenomena and been burned. Loss of credibility is an undesirable outcome and should be avoided if possible.

The second segment dealt with the danger to vulnerable people when they become enamored with unscrupulous charlatans who will take advantage of them. Such victims are most vulnerable in periods of grief or when experiencing life-threatening illnesses.

The final segment addressed issues related to involvement with discarnate entities or the spirit world. While highly speculative from a perspective of consensus reality, previous chapters have demonstrated our confidence that they do exist and can interact with humans as we go about our daily life.

In all of these situations, awareness and precautions are recommended. Rely on your own intuition, but with a firm understanding of your current emotional state. If it feels wrong, don't do it. You should maintain balance, which is best accomplished by engaging in multiple activities, including those with real-world applications. It is easier to go down the rabbit hole, than it is to get back out. I've provided some examples of folks who have lost their way.

In all special operations training, be that Rangers, SEALs, or Special Forces, members are assigned to a buddy, someone you do everything with and learn to trust them with your life. That is sound advice for those involved in phenomena as well. Therefore, a final suggestion is to utilize a confidant that you trust implicitly. Preferably, they should not be embroiled in the same emotional issues you are experiencing. Sanity checks are essential. If you choose wisely, a phenomena-buddy can provide an invaluable service. In the end, it is a question of balance.

CHAPTER 24
FINAL THOUGHTS

"I'd rather have questions that can't be answered than answers that can't be questioned." That comment by Richard Feynman articulates what this book seeks to convey. Unfortunately, most skeptics view it the other way around. I have presented a series of personal experiences, many of which raise questions that can't be answered, at least not with current conventional theories.

Theories

To be accepted, theories must take into account all of the data. Too frequently, scientists and skeptics alike only select the information and events that fit their preconceived concepts. Observations that fall outside predicted norms, or outliers, are disregarded. The general assumption is that the error was with the observation or reporting, not the theory. Numerous outliers have been presented, and no doubt many of you have had your own experiences that defy explanation. It is the duty of scientists to take the complete body of data, then devise theories that accommodate all of it, not just the facts they find convenient.

In studying with Richard Bandler, co-founder of NLP, I learned that there are two different approaches to exploration and understanding observations. The most common occurs when the data is found to fit in a predetermined "box." That is very comfortable for most people and reassures them that the "box" is there and that their thinking is correct. But that kind of safe thinking does little to add to the universal body of knowledge. The other approach is to search for data that do not fit any preconceived concept, and attempt to determine why. Much of what has been presented here are observations that don't fit the existing conventional paradigms. As a reader of this book, you too are likely one of those people who prefers to explore and question the very principles of consensus reality.

Personal Risk

When assailing the parameters established by the bastions of the science gods, it does not matter how conscientious or meticulous you are, what you have previously accomplished, or even the quality of your evidence. Stray outside those accepted boundaries and there will be consequences. But there can also be rewards. It's a real shame that all too often that recognition comes posthumously.

It all comes down to the power of belief systems. The technologically developed world has elevated science to an exalted level, one that eclipses all others. With the dominance of science unquestioned and unquestionable, advances that nudge the envelope are encouraged. But any concept that disrupts the accepted materialistic paradigm is deemed heresy and banished from the kingdom. So too have proponents of heretical ideas been expatriated, no matter what their prior contributions in traditional science and medicine might have been. One of the worst examples of such viciousness displayed by the establishment was the investigation of Dr. John Mack by the Harvard Medical School. John was a renown psychiatrist and Pulitzer Prize winner. Based on his controversial publications, Harvard initiated a panel to determine, "whether Dr. Mack was conducting his research in accordance with Harvard's standards of scholarly investigation and whether he was exploiting his subjects or exposing them to harm." This was the first time such a procedure was initiated against a tenured professor at Harvard.[181] John, a personal friend of mine, was not suspected of ethics violations or professional misconduct. His sin was to conduct research on people who claimed to have had alien encounters and publish the results of his study.

Others venturing into fields deemed inappropriate have likewise been denigrated. Dr. Robert Jahn, former dean of the School of Engineering at Princeton, personifies the problem. Despite his stellar résumé, and decades of conventional contributions, *The New York Times* chose to write negatively about the closing of the PEAR Lab: "Over almost three decades, a small laboratory at Princeton University managed to embarrass university administrators, outrage Nobel laureates..."[182]

The Federal Drug Administration (FDA) went even further in the case of Wilhelm Reich. Initially they banned interstate transportation of his devices and then later brought criminal charges against him for contempt of court. He was sentenced to the U.S. Penitentiary in Lewisburg, Pennsylvania, where he died in 1957. Reich was very controversial. Originally from Austria-Hungary, Reich was a psychiatrist who worked under Sigmund Freud. He developed the concept of orgone energy, which drew written criticism and led to the FDA intervention.

Following World War II there was considerable concern about how Hitler's officers had organized book burnings before the war to suppress concepts he didn't like. In the post-war era, the notion that ideas could be suppressed was generally considered unconscionable, and certainly undemocratic. Therefore, it was surprising that in 1956 American courts actually ordered the destruction of Reich's files and the burning of his books. In fact, over six tons of his books were burned that year. That is certainly one of the most blatant acts of censorship in U. S. history.

Rejection of new or alternative ideas is not a new problem. Nearly 400 years before the common era (BCE), the revered teacher Socrates was tried and convicted for corrupting Athenian youth and for questioning the gods of the state of Athens. For his transgressions, Socrates was sentenced to death by drinking hemlock. Then consider the reaction of the Catholic Church when in the 17th Century Galileo Galilei presented the evidence for heliocentrism. This was regarded as an attack on Pope Urban VIII. Galileo was tried by the Inquisition, found "vehemently suspect of heresy," and was forced to recant. He then spent the rest of his life under house arrest. Galileo's accusers refused to look through his telescopes to confirm his observations. Truly, authoritarians never take kindly to unconventional discoveries.

Funding of Research

Historically, most of the funding for psychic research has come from a few wealthy dilettantes, many of whom tend to latch onto bright shiny things. For a wide variety of reasons, they become infatuated with certain aspects of one phenomenon or another. A few donors to UFO research have seen UFOs and wondered about their origin. Some donors to parapsychological research lost loved ones and desired to communicate with them. Still others experienced events they cannot explain and chose to support research into how and why those events happened.

Such motivating factors often play pivotal roles in determining what is, and is not, funded. Given the paucity of available funding, researchers are loath to share information about their benefactors. While this caution is reasonable, it does inhibit the coordination of research efforts.

Financially, the fundamental research problem is that these phenomena are, at their core, at least as complex as cancer or AIDS. Yet, the total funding for research on phenomena is minuscule by comparison. The 2017 budget for the National Institute of Health (NIH) is more than 33 billion dollars.[183] Of that, well over five billion dollars goes to the National Cancer Institute alone. And those numbers do not include the massive funding of associated medical research in the private sector. In 2015, the estimated global total spent that year on cancer research was 107 billion dollars.[184] I raise this issue only to point out what it might cost if psi research was taken as seriously as cancer research.

For another expense comparison, consider that biggest scientific instrument ever created, the Large Hadron Collider at CERN Switzerland. The device, with limited capability, cost over six billion dollars to build, plus a billion dollars per year to operate. An international project, the costs are shared, but to what end? It is estimated that the price tag was over 13 billion dollars to find the Higgs Boson, a tiny particle that lives a small fraction of a second.[185] Certainly, particle physics is worthy of study, but the real benefit is only for a handful of theoretical physicists. Then, after spotting and confirming the Higgs Boson, once thought to be the God Particle, scientists found out there existed pentaquarks, which are even smaller. And the chase goes on.

The reason so much money is splurged on these physical science projects is because of the materialistic belief systems that suggests there must be some fundamental particle that leads to the building block of everything. What has really been learned is that quantum fields exist. While there are a few theories about what they are, nobody really knows for sure. Again, quoting Richard Feynman, "If you think you understand quantum mechanics, you don't understand quantum mechanics."

There are no hard data on funding of research into phenomena, but I would estimate that globally it is less than ten million dollars per year. Consider, for example, the continuation of consciousness beyond bodily death. That topic should be of immediate concern to everyone. Termination of physical life is a situation that 100 percent of the population will confront. Yet, funding for the serious study of this topic is near non-existent. Assuming that cancer and post-mortem survival phenomena are nearly equally complex issues, research on survival is funded at a level less than 0.01 percent of cancer.

The dominance of our materialistic belief system is the determining factor in the allocation of money. If, as an atheistic worldview deems, consciousness cannot continue beyond physical death, there is no need to waste money on such research. Then too, organized religion has also played a dampening role. From their perspective, it is better to have a mystery so that priests maintain their position as arbiters of this information. That confers power unto them and allows manipulation of their constituents. It is one reason why religious officials often denigrate any means of direct experience between a person and a supreme or supernatural power. In short, when only an institution can provide the answers, those answers can be used as a control mechanism.

Interrelationships and Proposals

Like everyone else, I am biased. I have repeatedly acknowledged that it is my belief that consciousness is the cross-cutting factor that connects a myriad of unexplained events, including nonlocal consciousness, extrasensory perception, psychokinesis, remote viewing, near-death experiences, spontaneous healing, post-mortem communications, UFOs, and a few cryptozoological encounters. That is an exemplary list, not an exhaustive one.

In *UFOs: Myths, Conspiracies and Realities,* I proposed two concepts that bear repeating in an abbreviated form. The first involves the controlling nature of these phenomena. The term I created for this was Precognitive Sentient Phenomena (PSP). This concept was based on our experiences at what became known as Skinwalker Ranch. It meant that the controlling source had a precognitive aspect. The PSP knew how people would respond before they encountered the event. It was sentient, in that it is extremely intelligent. Like mythological characters such as Pan, Kokopelli, and Loki, the PSP seems to be a controlling force that permeates these incidents. Sometimes known as the "Trickster," this PSP appears to dominate the situation, determining what will be observed and under what operant conditions. The PSP always seems to be at least one step ahead, and no matter how carefully or cunningly the researchers plan, the ultimate outcome remains elusive. We have observed that many phenomena continually morph, thus perplexing attempts to identify causal relationships, or attempts to isolate dependent or independent variables for study.

Take for example UFO sightings, which have changed over time, staying just ahead of human capabilities but not beyond imagination. Airships of the 1800's morphed into spacecraft as the speed and maneuverability of these objects increased. Interactions between humans and sentient nonhuman beings have been reported for millennia, but a relatively new characteristic of these interactions involves human participants being beamed aboard spacecraft. When video, audio, or other recording devices are employed, the frequency of these incidents often diminishes, or occur just outside the range of that instrument. At Skinwalker Ranch, some physical events occurred but failed to appear on cameras pointed directly at those events.

Put together, the existence of a PSP complicates any attempt by traditional scientists to gain a basic understanding of what we are experiencing. That may seem counterintuitive, as throughout this book I have pleaded for the need to investigate these events. The problem, I believe, is that everyone wants clear and concise answers to simplistic questions. However, I think we have yet to reach the point of asking the proper questions. There is a process that I believe can help, which leads me to the second concept, what is called the Step Back.

The Step Back concept infers that we should stop the existing stovepipe approach to problem solving in which each phenomenon is researched in isolation. Rather, it is time to bring together competent scientists who have been engaged in research of the various phenomena for years or even decades. The first function of Step Back would be to describe in detail what has been observed without assessing values or naming each event. Massive amounts of data would be produced that must be displayed in a manner that allows the next phase.

This second step would also conduct macro-pattern analysis in an attempt to determine the patterns that transcend individual events. Already, some patterns have begun to be recognized, such as the similarities between near-death experiences and alien abduction reports. It has been noted that UFO reports often come in waves at specific locations, thus demonstrating temporal and/or geographic relationships. Historians have also found commonalities between veridical observations of events and folklore. As an example, stories of interactions between humans and sentient beings, including abductions, are found in nearly all cultures throughout recorded time.

While it is far too early to proclaim what the common factors are, it is vital that this comprehensive identification process begins. Only after substantial effort has been accomplished will we be ready for the next phase of analysis: to isolate the underlying issues and formulate the right questions. For years the public has been speculating about the surface issues. *Where do UFOs come from? Can we communicate with the dead? Where does Sasquatch live?* But those very questions are based on assumptions about the validity of the phenomena for which there is serious doubt.

There is no question that modern science has produced a vast number of practical applications, many of which have improved our lives. The problem arises at the theoretical level when there are outliers that fail to conform to the thesis. From a practical perspective, as long as things work, and on a continuous basis, that is good enough from an engineering perspective. That is, when you throw a switch, the light comes on or the engine starts. The problem comes when we extrapolate from the practical partial capability to an entire universal whole. Unfortunately, the slaves to the science gods have done this and created the laws of physics, which are understood to be inviable.

There is, however, a difference between useful guidelines that function most of the time, versus immutable laws that should encompass all of the observations. Again, to be validated, theories must accommodate all the data, not just that which conveniently fits the model. When it comes to the phenomena discussed in this book, science remains challenged and seriously in default.

Throughout the preceding chapters, you have read about many events that appear to contradict some of the established laws of science. The skeptic likely will suggest it is the observations that are inaccurate. Their assumption is that if the event is prohibited by established science, the error must therefore be in the measurement or human observer, which, in fairness, has been proven to be the case in some instances. As Hal Puthoff, and other scientists have learned, honest mistakes can be made when the limits of measurement are not definitively understood.[186] Even intelligent people can be deceived or can misinterpret data. But, there have been too many white crows to accept the adage, "It can't be, therefore it isn't."

The evidence gathered in this book to support the claim that the established laws of science are inaccurate or incomplete include:

Metal objects bent with no physical force applied (macro-scale PKMB), contravening the concept of conservation of energy

Human exposure to flame without sustaining injury, violating known thermodynamics

A table and bed levitating sans physical force, defying gravity

Objects of many compositions levitating, or being repulsed, seeming to defy gravity

Metal objects partially changing composition and softening while other parts remain in the original configuration

Existence of unidentified aerial phenomena that defy all known flight capabilities

Obtaining accurate information about future events (precognition)

Obtaining accurate information concerning current events albeit from a nonlocal or remote perspective (OOBE)

Spontaneous healing, unaccounted for by traditional medical practices

Apparent retrocausation in altering the outcome of prior medical events

Documented healing of laboratory test animals using thought and/or unknown human energy

Strong evidence supportive of telepathic interspecies communications

Monitored remote connections between white cells, plants, and humans that have no basis in traditional scientific theory

Perturbation of the weather employing an unrecognized energy system

Contrary to the Western materialistic paradigm, strong evidence was presented to support the existence of other dimensions, and acceptance of one or more spirit worlds. The evidence included:

Communication with discarnate entities
Physical interaction with discarnate entities
Human possession by discarnate entities
Validation of near-death experiences, including situations in which
      survival should have been an impossibility
Numerous events with physical impact at Skinwalker Ranch that
      strongly suggested interactions with unseen entities
Spontaneous healing at a distance via discarnate medical practitioners
Transference of extraordinary capabilities from one person to another

The reality of any one of those incidents is significant. More important, when viewed in aggregate, the evidence in favor of multiple phenomena physically interacting with humans in consensus reality is overwhelming. Furthermore, some of these events appear to defy the known laws of science. In general, scientists just ignore these events. They assume they are not valid and understand that there is personal danger to their livelihood in engaging in researching them.

Roles: Science and Yours

I have been rather harsh on science and scientists in this book. Least I leave the reader with the wrong impression, I should state that I strongly support science when done properly. There is a saying that *scientists will follow wherever the data lead*. That is exactly what scientists *should* be doing. Science must be willing to make and respect all observations. It is strong enough to withstand jolts from anomalous data. What some of us rail against are the dogmatic proclamations, often made by esteemed scientists, that are contraindicated by veridical events.

In 1980, while attending the U.S. Army Command and General Staff College, a classmate who was previously assigned as an astronaut, told me that "We already know 99 percent of everything there is to know (about science), now we are just tidying up the details." While demonstrably false, the comment illustrates the stunning arrogance with which some people approach science. And they often manifest an equal level of assuredness about the Laws of Science.

Most scientists are skeptical to negative in dealing with the phenomena explored in this book, usually without ever having examined the data. Worth noting is that scientists in the physical disciplines are far more likely to reject these phenomena than those in the behavioral or social sciences. This a priori rejection of the reality of phenomena is at odds with the veridical personal experiences that vast numbers report. This denial of what people know to be true will influence their acceptance of, and cause doubt about, scientific opinion in other fields. That is to the detriment of society, which has an urgent need for scientific expertise, particularly in the current unstable international environment.

Unfortunately, politics has become embroiled with science. To further political and economic agendas, all of science has been called into question. The issue of climate change provides the most egregious current example. Despite near universal agreement by scientists that climate change is real—and that humans are an integral cause—the refrain of "not-settled" is proffered to the media by many conservative politicians. The greatest concern regarding climate change is that the impact of being wrong is catastrophic. For these politicians, short-term local interests are deemed more important than planetary survival.

Like climate change, the phenomena discussed here also have dramatic and overarching implications for all of humanity. Many before me have noted that the universe appears to be completely interconnected. All the research done on nonlocal consciousness infers that to be true. The complexity of that concept is nearly impossible to understand or even contemplate. But the implications for the world of consensus reality, that is the world we live in, cannot be understated. Philosophers through the ages have noted them, yet when viewed through the prism of separateness, these fundamental truths become obscured.

There is a role for both scientists and everyone else to play. Those of you who have firsthand experiences with these phenomena can share those observations with others. You'll be surprised at the number of affirmations you'll hear: *Oh, that happened to me, too!* Exposure will encourage others to speak out. Only then might we comprehend the true extent of phenomena and how they point to a far greater understanding of our existence here on Earth. Likewise, scientists should be encouraged to seriously investigate these events. And they should be able to do so without risk to their reputation or livelihood.

From our interactions as individuals through to international relationships, we have an overwhelming tendency to define those interests in terms of disjuncture. People usually view their skin as the limit of themselves as individuals, and organizations, and especially nations, talk of their interests, usually to the exclusion of those of others. We live in a world of disparate consumption of resources, ones that are finitely constrained. On the one hand competition drives innovation and advancement, yet when stretched beyond reasonable limits, competition leads to conflict and, in extreme cases, war.

An understanding and acceptance of universal consciousness could lead to the next stage of our evolution, but the paradox created by living in a physical world appears to subsume us all. Master Po, on the television program *Kung Fu,* wisely stated: "Evil cannot be overcome in this lifetime, it can only be resisted in oneself." So too must we resist the innate tendency to emphasize our separateness and instead incorporate our interconnectedness. That is not an all-or-nothing proposition, and any effort to encourage such behavior is beneficial in the long run.

The choice is yours. With, or without your consent, you play a role in the drama unfolding before us. Entering into the fray consciously has advantages seen and unseen. The implications of the events we have all witnessed are awe-inspiring. *Yes, you are your brother's keeper, for you are a spiritual being having a human experience.*

ENDNOTES

1   Peter A. Sturrock, A Tale of Two Sciences: Memoirs of a Dissident Scientist, Exoscience, 2009

2   Peter A. Sturrock, The UFO Enigma: A New Review of the Physical Evidence, Aspect, 2000

3   Williams' book was published in 2011 as The Dynamic Theory: A New View of Space-Time-Matter, He died of Mesothelioma in 2014

4   Murry Gel-Mann, The Quark and the Jaguar: Adventures in the Simple and the Complex, St. Martin's Press, 1994

5   It should be known that Robert Bigelow is a major funder of UNLV. In the mainstream science world, he also donated the Robert L. Bigelow Physics Building and the Rod Lee Bigelow Health Science Building.

6   Johndale Solem's concept later became mainstream thinking as numerous previously undetected objects came whizzing close by the Earth

7   In earlier writings, I and others used the name Gorman as a pseudonym for the Shermans. He has since been publicly identified. We still believe the information he provided us was truthful and as accurate as could be expected given the difficult circumstances that existed.

8   Colm Kelleher and George Knapp, Hunt for the Skinwalker: Science Confronts the Unexplained at a Remote Ranch in Utah, Paraview Pocket Books, 2005

9   See UFOs: Myths, Conspiracies, and Realities, page 227. This is where the term was first formally introduced.

10   Philip J. Corso, The Day After Roswell, Simon and Schuster, 1997

11   Popularity of UFOs or Flying Saucers did not begin until the Ken Arnold sighting in June 1947.

12   John C. Lilly, Lilly on Dolphins: Humans of the Sea, Anchor Press. 1975. ISBN 0-385-01037-0.

13   https://www.scientificamerican.com/article/dolphin-die-off-tied-to-virus-related-to-human-measles/

14   http://www.dolphins-world.com/atlantic-spotted-dolphin/

15   http://darrenjew.com/

16   http://www.usatoday.com/story/news/world/2015/03/11/whale-kills-tourist/70184294/

17   http://www.independent.co.uk/news/great-white-shark-thrashes-into-cage-with-diver-inside-attack-watch-video-a7364391.html

18   https://www.theguardian.com/world/2004/nov/23/1

19   Anita Moorjani, *Dying to be Me, My Journey from Cancer, to Near Death, to True Healing*, Hay House, Inc., 2012

20   https://www.washingtonpost.com/national/health-science/us-life-expectancy-declines-for-the-first-time-since-1993/2016/12/07/7dcdc7b4-bc93-11e6-91ee-1adddfe36cbe_story.html

21   http://www.nationmaster.com/country-info/stats/Health/Physicians/Per-1,000-people

22   http://theconversation.com/biopiracy-when-indigenous-knowledge-is-patented-for-profit-55589

23   Bill Bengston's website: http://www.bengstonresearch.com/

24   For those who are too young to remember, Parkland Memorial Hospital is where President Kennedy was taken after he was assassinated on November 22, 1963.

25   Larry Dossey M.D., *One Mind: How Our Individual Mind Is Part of A Greater Consciousness And Why it Matters*, Hay House, Inc., 2016

26   Stephan A. Schwartz alerted me to this important article. The citation is Lenard Leibovici, "Effects of remote, retroactive intercessory prayer on outcomes in patients with bloodstream infection: randomised controlled trial", *BMJ*, 2001;323;1450-1451

27   Brian Olshansky, Larry Dossey, *BMJ*, 2003;327:1465

28   https://www.academia.edu/12847939/Australian_Experiment_shows_Retrocausality

29   Alpha brainwave states are still being explored for similar exploitation https://www.psychologytoday.com/blog/the-athletes-way/201504/alpha-brain-waves-boost-creativity-and-reduce-depression

30   Open heart surgery in China, https://www.ncbi.nlm.nih.gov/pubmed/21570137

31   https://www.ncbi.nlm.nih.gov/pmc/articles/PMC3778453/

32   For more details see my book, *The Warrior's Edge*, William Morrow and Company, 1990

33   NLP is also covered in *The Warrior's Edge*

34 http://www.cnn.com/2016/06/24/us/tony-robbins-hot-coal-walkers-burned/

35 USGS, https://water.usgs.gov/edu/dowsing.html

36 Uri Geller, http://www.urigeller.com/uri-gellers-hidden-agenda-prospecting/

37 One of the popular explanation by skeptics for the movement of dowsing instruments, be they L-rods, pendants, or whatever, is that the person is consciously or unconsciously causing the motion by small muscles in the hand. The use of bottles meant unequivocally that was not the case.

38 Tim Cridland, his website is, http://www.astoundingshow.com/

39 David Blaine, the segment can be seen at, http://www.davidblaine.com/magic

40 The U.S. Air Force study of technology that addressed weather modification: "The Ultimate Weapon of Mass Destruction: 'Owning the Weather' for Military Use," http://www.globalresearch.ca/the-ultimate-weapon-of-mass-destruction-owning-the-weather-for-military-use-2/5306386

41 James DeMeo, Ph.D. his website is: http://www.orgonelab.org/

42 http://channel.nationalgeographic.com/the-truth-behind/galleries/the-truth-behind-the-crystal-skulls-pictures/at/barry-lui-crystal-skull-42166/

43 http://www.emmytvlegends.org/interviews/people/alan-neuman

44 For more detail about MIG Alley, see the "World's First Jet Dog Fights: MIG Alley: Korean War," https://www.youtube.com/watch?v=MZJsMLcCRV8

45 The Tet Offensive initiated by the VC and NVA was a game changer. Although a military defeat for them, it was the beginning of the end of the support of the American people for the war.

46 Each CBU-75 bomb held 1800, 1 lb. bomblets, many of which failed to detonate. The VC would collect the unexploded ordnance and convert them into booby-traps.

47 Koichi Tohei's history can be found at http://shinshintoitsuaikido.org/english/about/koichi.html

48 Professor Morihei Ueshiba's history can be found at http://www.torontoaikikai.com/m_ueshiba.htm

49 Mami Kido, Professor, Tohoku Gakuin University, Japan, "Measurements of Remote Qi-Gong Effects"

50 Captain Rocky Versace would be awarded the Medal of Honor posthumously for his resistance. It was reported he was singing God Bless America as he was led to his execution.

51 In 1989, Colonel Nick Roe was assassinated in Quezon City while serving a military attaché in the Philippines.

52   Bert Stubblebine played a key role in our research projects. He died on February 6, 2017, as I was writing this book.

53   The film is available at http://www.urigeller.com/oscar-winning-vikram-jayantis-the-secret-life-of-uri-geller-bbc-documentary-uncut/

54   John Hasted, *The Metal Benders*, Routledge, 5 March 1981

55   Robert Jahn and Brenda Dunne, *Margins of Reality, The Role of Consciousness in the Physical World*, Harcourt, Brace, Jovanovich, 1987

56   Robert A. Monroe, *Journeys Out of the Body*, Doubleday & Company, 1971

57   Charles Tart, *Altered States of Consciousness*, John Wiley & Sons, 1969

58   Some charts reflect slightly different bands for alpha and theta brain wave frequencies.

59   Joe McMoneagle, *Mind Trek*, Hampton Roads, 1993

60   Eben Alexander, *Proof of Heaven*, Simon and Schuster, 2012

61   John C. Lilly, *The Center of the Cyclone*, HarperCollins, 1973

62   For a complete history of the military remote viewing program, I recommend Dr. Paul Smith's book *Reading the Enemy's Mind*. Paul was the unit historian and had the best record.

63   Dale Graff, *Tracks in the Psychic Wilderness: An Exploration of Remote Viewing, ESP, Precognitive Dreaming, and Synchronicity*, Element Books, 1998

64   Commander L.R. Rick Bremseth, "Unconventional Human Intelligence Support: Transcendent and Asymmetric Warfare Implications of Remote Viewing," U.S. Marine Corps War College, 28 April, 2001.

65   Michael Mumford, et al, "An evaluation of Remote Viewing: Research and Applications," American Institutes for Research, 29 Sept, 1995

66   The RV description is taken with permission from *Margins of Reality: The Role of Consciousness in the Physical World*, by Robert Jahn and Brenda Dunne. I also used this example in *The Warrior's Edge*.

67   Scott Jones has been a personal friend for decades. These incidents came from many personal conversations with him.

68   Stephan Schwartz, *The Alexandria Project*, Delacorte Press, 1983

69   Sheila Ostander and Lynn Schroeder, *Psychic Discoveries Behind the Iron Curtain*, Prentice-Hall, 1970

70   John B. Alexander, "The New Mental Battlefield," *Military Review*, December, 1980. A copy is available on my website, www.johnbalexander.com

71   Ed May, et al, *ESP Wars: East and West: An Account of the Military Use of Psychic Espionage as Narrated by the Key Russian and American Players*, Crossroads Press, 2016

72   Cleve Backster, *Primary Perception: Biocommunication with Plants, Living Foods, and Human Cells*, White Rose Millennium Press, 2003

73   http://www.polygraph.org/assets/docs/APA-Journal.Articles/2013/backster_techniques.pdf

74   This is based on private conversations with Hal Puthoff.

75   Ted participated in metal bending parties and was the one who introduced me to Anne Gehman.

76   Peter Thompkins and Chris Bird, *The Secret Life of Plants*, Harper, 1973

77   http://www.dtic.mil/dtic/tr/fulltext/u2/a202888.pdf

78   https://www.nap.edu/catalog/1025/enhancing-human-performance-issues-theories-and-techniques

79   Lawrence previously worked at DARPA and had sponsored a study of the SRI project resulting in a negative report.

80   A copy of my article is available on my website at www.johnbalexander.com

81   George Hathaway, *Mindbending: The Hutchison Files: 1981 to 1995*, Integrity Research Institute Publishers

82   Elisabeth Kübler-Ross, *On Death and Dying: What the Dying Have to Teach Doctors, Nurses, Clergy and Their Own Families*, The Macmillan Company, 1969

83   Kenneth Ring, *Life at Death: A Scientific Investigation of the Near-Death Experience*, Wm. Morrow & Company, 1980

84   Kenneth Ring, *Heading Toward Omega: In Search of the Meaning of the Near-Death Experience*, Wm. Morrow & Company, 1984

85   Raymond Moody, *Life After Life*, Bantam Doubleday Dell, 1975

86   IANDS website, http://iands.org/home.html, it contains massive amounts of information on the topic of NDEs.

87   Mary C. Neal, *To Heaven and Back: A Doctor's Extraordinary Account of Her Death, Heaven, Angels, and Life Again: A True Story*, Random House LLC, May 2012

88   Anita Moorjani, *Dying to Be Me: My Journey from Cancer, to Near Death, to True Healing*, Hay House, 2014

89   Eben Alexander, *Proof of Heaven: A Neurosurgeon's Journey into the Afterlife*, Simon and Schuster, 2012

90   Eben Alexander, *Map of Heaven: How Science, Religion, and Ordinary People Are Proving the Afterlife*, Simon and Schuster, 2014

91   Michael Sabom, *Light and Death*, Zondervan, 1998

92   Parti, Dr. Rajiv with Paul Perry, *Dying to Wake Up: A Doctor's Voyage into the Afterlife and the Wisdom He Brought Back*, Hay House, 2016

93   Melvin Morse, *Closer to the Light: Learning From the Near-Death Experiences of Children*, Villard, 1990

94   Raymond Moody, *Glimpses of Eternity: Sharing A Loved One's Passage From This Life to the Next*, Guidepost, 2010

95   Raymond Moody, *Reunions: Visionary Encounters With Departed Loved Ones*, Villard, 1993

96   Scrying is a method of divining the future by staring at a reflective surface (like mirror, crystal ball, or even smooth water).

97   James Randi, *The Faith Healers*, Prometheus Books, 1989

98   James Avila, "Selling Salvation," *20/20 ABC News*, 11 May, 2007 available at: http://abcnews.go.com/2020/story?id=3164858&page=

99   "No One Dies at Lily Dale," *HBO*, July 8, 2010, http://www.hbo.com/documentaries/no-one-dies-in-lily-dale

100 Suzanne Giesemann, see http://www.suzannegiesemann.com/

101 Suzanne Giesemann, *The Priest and the Medium*, Hay House, 2009

102 The Arthur Findley College, The World's Foremost College for the Advancement of Spiritualism and Psychic Sciences, website: http://www.arthurfindlaycollege.org/

103 Gary Schwartz, *The Afterlife Experiments: Breakthrough Scientific Evidence of Life After Death*, Pocket Books, 2002

104 Thomas Sugrue, *There is a River: The Story of Edgar Cayce*, A.R.E. Press, 1942

105 Adele Tinning, *God's Way of Life: Given Through Adele Gerard Tinning: Part 1*, God's Way of Life Foundation, 1975

106 Shirley, MacLaine, *It's All in the Playing*, Bantam, 1987

107 AC Rocha, et al, "Investigating the fit and accuracy of alleged mediumistic writing: a case study of Chico Xavier's letters," *Explore* (NY). 2014 Sep-Oct;10(5):300-8. doi: 10.1016/j.explore.2014.06.002., available at: https://www.ncbi.nlm.nih.gov/pubmed/25103071

108   An excellent film of Chico Xavier's life can be found at https://www.youtube.com/watch?v=ITDAwqbJ1WQ

109   Fr. Angelo Rizzo, *Fr. Angelo Rizzo Speaks: I Believe; Using Mind Power; We Are All Healers*, Healing Arts Press, 1980

110   Catholic Culture, https://www.catholicculture.org/culture/library/dictionary/index.cfm?id=36520

111   Kathrine Kuhlman, *I Believe in Miracles*, Bridge-Logos Publishing, update 1992

112   There are many videos available. Just search for Benny Hinn under videos.

113   Columbus College is now Columbus State University

114   For more information check http://www.mysteriousplanchette.com/History/history1.html

115   Details about the real story behind *The Men Who Stare at Goats* can be found on my website at http://www.johnbalexander.com/articles

116   My friend Bert Stubblebine died on February 6, 2017, as I was writing this book. The running into the wall episode depicted in the movie is nonsense. However, he was hyper-allergic to bee stings. As such, he was treated at Walter Reed Army Medical Center and received lots of shots. His mental preparation was to acknowledge that the atoms in the needle were mostly empty space. The same was true for his tissue. Therefore, he visualized the atoms of the needle slipping between the atoms of his body. Therefore, he should not feel it. That was purely a mental exercise.

117   More information about the Large Hadron Collider can be found on their website: https://home.cern/topics/large-hadron-collider

118   Leon Lederman, *The God Particle: If the Universe Is the Answer, What Is the Question?*, Bantam Press, 1993

119   http://www.ayahuasca.com/science/what-foods-and-drugs-need-to-be-avoided/

120   James Cameron, *Avatar*, Produced by, Lightstorm Entertainment, Dune Entertainment, Ingenious Film Partners. The film made over $2.8B. More information is available at http://www.avatarmovie.com/index.html

121   Richard Strassman, *DMT: The Spirit Molecule: A Doctor's Revolutionary Research into the Biology of Near-Death and Mystical Experiences*, Park Street Press, 2000

122   http://reset.me/story/ayahuasca-promising-treatment-post-traumatic-stress-disorder/

123   His web site is: http://elpurguero.com/

124   http://www.cnn.com/2014/10/22/health/ayahuasca-medicine-six-things/

125   Pablo Amaringo and Eduardo Lune, *Ayahuasca Visions: The Religious Iconography of a Peruvian Shaman*, North Atlantic Books, April, 1999

126   http://www.johnbalexander.com/yahoo_site_admin/assets/docs/Shamanism_Conference_2014_Web.248153435.pdf

127   Terence McKenna, *The Archaic Revival: Speculations on Psychedelic Mushrooms, the Amazon, Virtual Reality, UFOs, Evolution, Shamanism, the Rebirth of the Goddess, and the End of History*, Harper San Francisco, 1992

128   http://www2.fiu.edu/~mizrachs/daime.htm

129   https://breakingmuscle.com/learn/being-in-the-zone-the-flow-state-in-athletic-endeavors

130   https://wwwnc.cdc.gov/eid/article/5/2/99-0204_article

131   This is taken from my best recollection of that conversation at which Victoria was present.

132   http://www.extremescience.com/biggest-snake.htm

133   David Gann, http://www.newyorker.com/magazine/2005/09/19/the-lost-city-of-z

134   Simon Romero, https://www.nytimes.com/2016/12/14/world/americas/brazil-amazon-megaliths-stonehenge.html

135   http://www.survivalinternational.org/articles/3106-uncontacted-tribes-the-threats

136   http://www.survivalinternational.org/about/funai

137   Awaju Poty: http://awajupoty.blogspot.com/p/tese.html

138   The Policia Militar, or Military police, are nothing like American MPs. Rather, it is a national police force that has jurisdiction over the civilian sector.

139   http://oglobo.globo.com/sociedade/conte-algo-que-nao-sei/john-alexander-militar-armas-nao-letais-nao-devem-ser-usadas-como-castigo-19192107

140   Alexander Moreira-Almeida, https://www.academia.edu/1619158/Allan_Kardec_and_the_Development_of_a_Research_Program_in_Psychic_Experiences

141   http://johnofgod.com/

142 While I have mentioned this case in presentations, never before have I identified the recipient. This is included in this book with Whitley Strieber's consent.

143 Wayne Dyer, http://www.drwaynedyer.com/blog/meeting-spiritual-healer/

144 Heather Cumming, *John of God: The Brazilian Healer Who's Touched the Lives of Millions*, Atria Books/Beyond Words, 2007

145 http://www.africanholocaust.net/news_ah/vodoo.htm

146 http://latimesblogs.latimes.com/world_now/2012/02/what-happens-after-someone-sets-themself-on-fire.html

147 http://projects.nfstc.org/trace/docs/Trace%20Presentations%20CD-2/Pangerl.pdf

148 http://www.ezilikonnen.com/vodou/vodou-and-dreams/

149 https://sites.google.com/site/theyorubareligiousconcepts/egungun-the-ancestors

150 https://africa.uima.uiowa.edu/topic-essays/show/13

151 In the past there were human sacrifices, but they reportedly ended over a century ago.

152 Details of this adventure with many photos is available at http://www.johnbalexander.com/yahoo_site_admin/assets/docs/Mongolia_2013_Final.251153329.pdf

153 Information on The Horse Boy can be found at http://www.pbs.org/independentlens/horse-boy/film.html

154 My former boss, MG Bert Stubblebine, died as I was writing this book. Unfortunately, he is an example of this problem. While he appropriately pushed the envelope while on Active Duty, in retirement he adopted causes that were demonstrably false. That included becoming a "Truther" regarding the attacks on 9/11.

155 http://www.gallup.com/poll/16915/three-four-americans-believe-paranormal.aspx

156 As an example, http://www.huffingtonpost.com/john-b-alexander-phd/the-day-american-democrac_b_10073652.html

157 http://www.theoutpostforum.com/tof/showthread.php?311-Breaking-Dr-Boylan-s-Report-of-Co-Alexander-s-Demise-is-Premature

158 http://www.military.com/veteran-jobs/career-advice/military-transition/famous-veteran-jesse-ventura.html

159   http://www.dailymotion.com/video/x18usv8_conspiracy-theory-with-jesse-ventura-skinwalker_shortfilms

160   http://www.space.com/16769-spaceshipone-first-private-spacecraft.html

161   http://www.thekimfoundation.org/html/about_mental_ill/statistics.html

162   http://psychcentral.com/disorders/paranoid-personality-disorder-symptoms/

163   Anita Moorjani, *Dying to be Me*

164   Eben Alexander *Proof of Heaven*

165   Michael Grosso, https://consciousnessunbound.blogspot.com/2017/01/where-impossible-becomes-possible.html

166   http://www.health.harvard.edu/mind-and-mood/putting-the-placebo-effect-to-work

167   http://jamanetwork.com/journals/jama/article-abstract/331345

168   http://articles.mercola.com/sites/articles/archive/2015/03/05/placebo-effect-healing-recovery.aspx

169   See HBO's program: *Going Clear*. It was their highest rated documentary.

170   *The Master* (2012) was a thinly veiled depiction of the founder, L. Ron Hubbard.

171   See Leah Remini book: *Troublemaker: Surviving Hollywood and Scientology*

172   See Ron Miscavige book: *Ruthless: Scientology, My Son David Miscavige, and Me*

173   See Steve Cannane's book: *Fair Game: The incredible untold story of Scientology in Australia*

174   http://www.dailymotion.com/video/x12cdw1_bbc-panorama-the-secrets-of-scientology-with-john-sweeney_people

175   http://www.inquisitr.com/1310907/paul-haggis-scientology-defectors-are-terrified-of-the-churchs-bullying/

176   In their 2011 IRS 990T form, Scientology reported a wealth of just over 1.2 billion dollars.

177   The movie was based on a 1971 novel *The Exorcist* by William Peter Blatty, but many of the events were real.

178   The name Robbie Mannheim was created by an historian, Thomas B. Allen, to protect the family identity when he wrote about the case.

179   William Friedkin, http://www.vanityfair.com/hollywood/2016/10/father-amorth-the-vatican-exorcist

180   Thomas D. Williams, Ph.D., http://www.breitbart.com/national-security/2015/04/16/vatican-exorcism-course-draws-170-students-to-study-demonic-activity/, 16 April 2015

181   http://www.nytimes.com/1995/05/04/us/harvard-investigates-a-professor-who-wrote-of-space-aliens.html

182   http://www.nytimes.com/2007/02/10/science/10princeton.html

183   https://officeofbudget.od.nih.gov/pdfs/FY17/Overview-Executive%20Summary.pdf

184   http://www.cnbc.com/2016/06/02/the-worlds-2015-cancer-drug-bill-107-billion-dollars.html

185   https://www.forbes.com/forbes/welcome/?toURL=https://www.forbes.com/sites/alexknapp/2012/07/05/how-much-does-it-cost-to-find-a-higgs-boson/&refURL=https://www.google.com/&referrer=https://www.google.com/

186   Hal's laboratory, EarthTech International, tests devices that make extraordinary claims about output of energy. As happened with a system that I referred to him, the inventor did not account for all of the energy input, and thus made egregious errors in estimating output.

ACKNOWLEDGEMENTS

This journey has been long and acclivitous. Any attempt to personally thank all the people who have contributed to our experiences and growth would surely fail to render appropriate recognition to each and every one of them. As a reader, you have seen the vast array of scientists, psychics, and spiritual explorers, I encountered and interacted with over several decades. Some of them I sought out. Several repeatedly crossed my path in various ways. Still others were serendipitous exploits as if dictated by some cosmic higher power. As the path unfolded, events unplanned, at least not consciously, constantly arose. They too played significant roles. To all who contributed, in any way, shape, or form, please accept my sincere thanks. That includes everyone mentioned in the text, as well as those providing supporting material.

A sobering note is the recognition of how many of those mentioned in this book have already transitioned to another level of spiritual evolution. Though I cannot articulate with any degree of specificity in what exact manner they continue, it is my belief that they do, as the path is eternal and our consciousness integrally intertwined.

Special thanks must go to Victoria, a fearless psychic adventurer who has taken us down trails that most people rightfully would fear to travel. Without her zeal and curiosity, many of these adventures would not have happened.

Finally, thanks to my friends Joe and Cindy Buchman for their help with the book, and to Patrick Huyghe, the editor and publisher of *Reality Denied*, for allowing this effort to come to fruition.

Appendix
Metal Bending Party Format

The chapter "Bend, Bend, Bend" described the experiences we had with the metal bending (PKMB) parties as created by Jack Houck. They can be reproduced, though the results will vary. This is the process I learned from Jack, and I've repeated it many times. Some elements of this process many seem trivial, but each one was designed for a specific purpose. This is what worked for me, but you may choose to adapt this format to your own situation.

My experience suggests that groups of 20-50 people work best. That size is not absolute. Twenty is recommended to generate enough enthusiasm, especially if there are ardent skeptics in the group. The upper number of 50 is simply based on my ability to keep track of the crowd. With more than 50 people, subgroups tend to form, many of them demanding attention. It just gets hard to keep track of what is going on in the room.

Who attends really doesn't matter and is often beyond the leader's control. When possible, include children, especially those who are old enough to sit still for a short time and participate with the group. Children are generally unencumbered by a belief that PK can't happen.

We found that a circular formation worked best as everyone can see all of the other participants. That configuration means the party leader must keep moving and rotating to include personal contact with everyone. The leader's energy level is important, as is a playful environment. Note that we try to engage as many senses as possible including sight, sound, and touch.

If you ask people to bring silverware, many will show up with a single fork or spoon. Even if you suggest they bring more, many won't. Be sure you have a sufficient supply of items on hand. When doing these parties regularly, Jack and I would need to replenish our supplies at yard sales and secondhand stores. Remember: you are looking for junk, not good silverware. But you also do not want paper thin items, as they bend too easily.

After getting the group into the desired configuration, begin by dumping a box of silverware on the floor so that it creates a loud sound. The purpose is to engage the auditory senses of the participants. This is to be experiential, not just a cognitive exercise.

The leader should then explain the process. They should show the audience items that have been bent at previous PK parties. They may tell stories about macro-PK events that have happened before, or even stories about Uri Geller and his exploits. The purpose of this part of the program is to establish the belief system and expectation that PK is real and can happen. It is good to tell them about those who came for the first time and had dramatic experiences.

In addition to cutlery, the leader should bring material to create dowsing pendulums. All you need is string and something that can act as a weight. Washers are a cheap alternative and will work just fine. Some participants may choose to use their necklaces or other pendants. That too is fine, as it is the effect, not the instrument that is important.

The leader then explains the dowsing process. Using the pendulum participants are taught to calibrate their individual responses. Holding the string of the pendulum, the participant should ask it to show you how it will respond to yes or no questions. As an example, a yes response is often swinging back and forth away from the person's body. No, on the other hand, may be crossways, swinging from left to right. Some people may find the motion to be circular with clockwise for one answer and counterclockwise for the opposite. The purpose of this exercise is to get participants involved in basic psychic work in a failsafe way.

Once the dowsing instrument is calibrated for each individual, have them take the piece of silverware they plan to use first and place it on the floor in front of them. Have the pendulum touch the item and ask, "Will you bend for me tonight?" The purpose is to set an intention to cause bending. Note, the question states a specific time. You may use today, or this afternoon, or whatever fits that event. The point is to get agreement that the bending will happen in the next few minutes, not sometime in the distant future.

The leader should be aware of the counter arguments to the efficacy of dowsing. We know that small muscle motor functions can cause the pendulum to respond; responses can even be evoked subconsciously. But for the PK-party process, it doesn't matter. If it arises, just tell the participant to TTP, Trust the Process. Do not allow an intellectual debate to divert the group.

After everyone has selected at least one item for the first experiment, the leader should describe the mental process involved. My approach is to ask the participants to hold their fork or spoon, and then close their eyes. I then instruct them to mentally imagine a huge ball of energy floating above their heads. This is the most intense energy they have ever encountered, mentally they are then to condense that energy into a tighter and tighter ball. Next, they mentally bring that ball of energy into their body and direct it through their arm and into the fork or spoon they wish to bend.

The next step is critical as it provides the intention for what is to happen. The leader instructs the group to shout in unison loudly: BEND, BEND, BEND. Anyone who has attended a PK-party will recognize that phrase. Then have people open their eyes and stroke their spoon or fork; remind them to breath, as there is a tendency to tense up the first time this is attempted.

At this point distraction is good. The participants can talk among themselves. Remind them this is a party and not to take things too seriously. Ask each person to feel their item and be aware of any physical changes that may be taking place. By touching the item, they may note that it feels warm, soft, or like plastic. There are any number of words people have used to describe the state change of the utensil. In the beginning, during what Jack called the "kindergarten level," the use of some physical force is encouraged. Many participants will find that suddenly their fork or spoon become malleable and with little effort they can roll up the handle or twist it.

As this happens, encourage people to yell out and show others what they did. This will provide encouragement for the entire group. My experience has been that in larger groups, bending starts like popcorn. First one area will be involved, followed by another, and another. Cheering leading becomes the key job of the facilitator.

When working as the leader, I prefer not attempt any bending myself. I usually hold a spoon, but I don't work on it. The process is to engage others in bending. If the leader bends an item, participants will begin to rationalize how it was accomplished. The important issue is for them to have the experience. Rationalization is more difficult if they must explain what they did themselves.

While the group is actively bending objects, the leader is a cheerleader. Many people experience some bending but seem embarrassed to announce it or show others. By moving through the group, a leader can spot those reluctant to come forward with their bent spoon or fork. This encouragement is important as it contributes to the emotional component of the environment.

In my opinion, a psychic field effect takes place. While I cannot support that comment scientifically, my observation of many metal bending sessions suggests it is real. Therefore, building on success seems to improve the results, especially in the early stages of the PK-party.

Once someone has bent an item, encourage them to try to do more. It is not uncommon for an individual to bend eight or ten objects. As they become familiar with the process, they often become artistic with the objects, especially forks. They will bend the tines as if they were flowers. Also, encourage the participants to deform the bowl of spoons. Structurally that is more difficult than simply bending the neck of either a fork or spoon. Note that our experience with bending knives has not been very good. They do bend on occasion, but people must also be careful not to cut themselves.

Usually about an hour into the party, it is time to move to the graduate session. This takes planning on the part of the leader or organizer. You need a lot of forks. If at all possible, those forks should be matched pairs. That means that the forks fit snuggly together with tines at the same position. When testing the forks, it is important to put forks together, one on top of the other. Then trade places with the top and bottom fork. This is important so that if minor spontaneous bending occurs, it will be visibly detectable.

The next step is to have each participant take a pair of matched forks and hold them at the base, preferably with the thumb and forefinger of each hand. It is important to stress that from this point on, there is to be no other touching of the fork or any physical force applied. The initial mental exercise, visualizing energy, putting it into the forks, and shouting BEND three times is repeated by the group. This is what Jack called the "Graduate level." Any bending that happens using this strict protocol can be attributed to PK. Participants can repeat the energy input as often as the like.

Remember, the reports of forks or spoons spontaneously folding over are quite rare. It is more likely that you will see bending of the tines, and it is possible that no spontaneous bending happens. It usually does, but non-results are also possible at this level.

Feel free to experiment with the process. One alternative that attracted attention was to attempt to germinate seeds. Geller has demonstrated this on a few occasions. Some people running PK parties have done it also. Acquire some seeds; Mung Bean seems to work well. Have the participants hold them in the closed palm of their hands. This time the instructions should be to GROW or SPROUT.

Anyone can participate in a PK party, which is the beauty of the protocol. Most participants will usually be naïve subjects, meaning they have never engaged in PKMB before. Both Jack and I found two groups that were very difficult to work with: scientists/engineers and parapsychologists. Once I made the mistake of having a PK party in a laboratory. The director had attended several sessions previously and wanted his staff to have the experience. It was as if they did not want psi events to occur on their hallowed ground and were very reluctant to participate. Believing that psi happens is integral to the process. That is why children seem to do better than adults.

INDEX

www.ingramcontent.com/pod-product-compliance
Lightning Source LLC
Chambersburg PA
CBHW050224270326
41914CB00003BA/563